Early praise for *Programming Elixir*

Dave Thomas has done it again. *Programming Elixir* is what every programming book aspires to be. It goes beyond the basics of simply teaching syntax and mechanical examples. It teaches you how to *think* Elixir.

➤ **Bruce Tate**
CTO, icanmakeitbetter.com. Author.

In *Programming Elixir*, Dave has done an excellent job of presenting functional programming in a way that is fun, practical, and full of inspirational insights into how we can rethink our very approach to designing programs. As you progress through the book, you will often find yourself smiling after discovering a certain aspect of Elixir that lets you do things in a new, more elegant way that will almost seem too natural and intuitive to have been neglected by the programming community at large for so long.

The book provides a detailed overview of Elixir and its tooling, aimed at making the development process smooth and productive. Dave explains the core parts of the Erlang runtime system, such as distribution, concurrency, and fault tolerance, that imbue Elixir with the power to write scalable and resilient applications.

➤ **Alexei Sholik**

The era of sequential programming is over—today's high-performance, scalable, and fault-tolerant software is concurrent. Elixir is a key player in this new world, bringing the power of Erlang and OTP to a wider audience. Read this book for a head start on the next big thing in software development.

➤ **Paul Butcher**
Author of *Seven Concurrency Models in Seven Weeks*

Just like the *Pickaxe* book for Ruby, this book is the de facto standard for Elixir. Dave, in his impeccable style, provides a thorough coverage of the Elixir language, including data structures, macros, OTP, and even Dialyzer. This book is a joy to read, as it walks the reader through learning Elixir and the thought processes involved in writing functional programs. If you want to accelerate your mastery of the Elixir language, *Programming Elixir* is your best investment.

➤ **Jim Freeze**
    Organizer of the world's first Elixir Conference

This will undoubtedly become the *Pickaxe for Elixir*. ... Thomas excitedly guides the reader through the awesomeness of Elixir. Worth picking up for anyone interested in Elixir.

➤ **Dan Kozlowski**

Programming Elixir is another smash hit from Dave Thomas. Prior to *Programming Elixir* I tried my hand at several functional programming languages only to trip all over myself. You can feel Dave's enthusiasm and joy of using the language in each and every chapter. He will have you thinking about solving problems in ways you never thought of before. This book has drastically changed the way I think about programming in any language for the better.

➤ **Richard Bishop**

I've really enjoyed this book. It's not just some whirlwind tour of syntax or features; I found it to be a very thoughtful introduction to both Elixir and functional programming in general.

➤ **Cody Russell**

Programming Elixir 1.2

Functional |> Concurrent |> Pragmatic |> Fun

Dave Thomas

The Pragmatic Bookshelf

Dallas, Texas • Raleigh, North Carolina

EATON

Many of the designations used by manufacturers and sellers to distinguish their products are claimed as trademarks. Where those designations appear in this book, and The Pragmatic Programmers, LLC was aware of a trademark claim, the designations have been printed in initial capital letters or in all capitals. The Pragmatic Starter Kit, The Pragmatic Programmer, Pragmatic Programming, Pragmatic Bookshelf, PragProg and the linking *g* device are trademarks of The Pragmatic Programmers, LLC.

Every precaution was taken in the preparation of this book. However, the publisher assumes no responsibility for errors or omissions, or for damages that may result from the use of information (including program listings) contained herein.

Our Pragmatic courses, workshops, and other products can help you and your team create better software and have more fun. For more information, as well as the latest Pragmatic titles, please visit us at *https://pragprog.com*.

For international rights, please contact *rights@pragprog.com*.

Printed in the United States of America.
ISBN-13: 978-1-68050-166-7
Printed on acid-free paper.
Book version: P1.0—March, 2016

Contents

Part I — Conventional Programming

Part II — Concurrent Programming

Part III — More-Advanced Elixir

Foreword

I have always been fascinated with how changes in hardware affect how we write software.

A couple of decades ago, memory was a very limited resource. It made sense back then for our software to take hold of some piece of memory and mutate it as necessary. However, allocating this memory and cleaning up after we no longer needed it was a very error-prone task. Some memory was never freed; sometimes memory was allocated over another structure, leading to faults. At the time, garbage collection was a known technique, but we needed faster CPUs in order to use it in our daily software and free ourselves from manual memory management. That has happened—most of our languages are now garbage-collected.

Today, a similar phenomenon is happening. Our CPUs are not getting any faster. Instead, our computers get more and more cores. This means new software needs to use as many cores as it can if it is to maximize its use of the machine. This conflicts directly with how we currently write software.

In fact, mutating our memory state actually slows down our software when many cores are involved. If you have four cores trying to access and manipulate the same piece of memory, they can trip over each other. This potentially corrupts memory unless some kind of synchronization is applied.

I quickly learned that applying this synchronization is manual, error prone, and tiresome, and it hurts performance. I suddenly realized that's not how I wanted to spend time writing software in the next years of my career, and I set out to study new languages and technologies.

It was on this quest that I fell in love with the Erlang virtual machine and ecosystem.

In the Erlang VM, all code runs in tiny concurrent processes, each with its own state. Processes talk to each other via messages. And since all communication happens by message-passing, exchanging messages between different machines on the same network is handled transparently by the VM, making it a perfect environment for building distributed software!

However, I felt there was still a gap in the Erlang ecosystem. I missed first-class support for some of the features I find necessary in my daily work, things such as metaprogramming, polymorphism, and first-class tooling. From this need, Elixir was born.

Elixir is a pragmatic approach to functional programming. It values its functional foundations and it focuses on developer productivity. Concurrency is the backbone of Elixir software. As garbage collection once freed developers from the shackles of memory management, Elixir is here to free you from antiquated concurrency mechanisms and bring you joy when writing concurrent code.

A functional programming language lets us think in terms of functions that transform data. This transformation never mutates data. Instead, each application of a function potentially creates a new, fresh version of the data. This greatly reduces the need for data-synchronization mechanisms.

Elixir also empowers developers by providing macros. Elixir code is nothing more than data, and therefore can be manipulated via macros like any other value in the language.

Finally, object-oriented programmers will find many of the mechanisms they consider essential to writing good software, such as polymorphism, in Elixir.

All this is powered by the Erlang VM, a 20-year-old virtual machine built from scratch to support robust, concurrent, and distributed software. Elixir and the Erlang VM are going to change how you write software and make you ready to tackle the upcoming years in programming.

José Valim
Creator of Elixir
Tenczynek, Poland, October 2014

A Vain Attempt at a Justification

I'm a language nut. I love trying languages out, and I love thinking about their design and implementation. (I know; it's sad.)

I came across Ruby in 1998 because I was an avid reader of comp.lang.misc (ask your parents). I downloaded it, compiled it, and fell in love. As with any time you fall in love, it's difficult to explain why. It just worked the way I work, and it had enough depth to keep me interested.

Fast-forward 15 years. All that time I'd been looking for something new that gave me the same feeling.

I came across Elixir a while back, but for some reason never got sucked in. But a few months before starting this book, I was chatting with Corey Haines. I was bemoaning the fact that I wanted a way to show people functional programming concepts without the academic trappings those books seem to attract. He told me to look again at Elixir. I did, and I felt the same way I felt when I first saw Ruby.

So now I'm dangerous. I want other people to see just how great this is. I want to evangelize. So my first step is to write a book.

But I don't want to write another 900-page Pickaxe book. I want this book to be short and exciting. So I'm not going into all the detail, listing all the syntax, all the library functions, all the OTP options, or....

Instead, I want to give you an idea of the power and beauty of this programming model. I want to inspire you to get involved, and then point to the online resources that will fill in the gaps.

But mostly, I want you to have fun.

Acknowledgments

It seems to be a common thread—the languages I fall in love with are created by people who are both clever and extremely nice. José Valim, the creator of Elixir, takes both of these adjectives to a new level. I owe him a massive thank-you for giving me so much fun over the last 18 months. Along with him, the whole Elixir core team has done an amazing job of cranking out an entire ecosystem that feels way more mature than its years. Thank you, all.

A conversation with Corey Haines reignited my interest in Elixir—thank you, Corey, for good evenings, some interesting times in Bangalore, and the inspiration.

Bruce Tate is always an interesting sounding board, and his comments on early drafts of the book made a big difference. And I've been blessed with an incredible number of active and insightful beta readers who have made literally hundreds of suggestions for improvements. Thank you, all.

A big tip of the hat to Jessica Kerr, Anthony Eden, and Chad Fowler for letting me steal their tweets.

Candace Cunningham copy edited the book. Among the hundreds of grammatical errors she also found errors in some of the code. Bless her.

The crew at Potomac did their customary stellar job of indexing.

Susannah Pfalzer was a voice of sanity throughout the project (as she is in so many of our Bookshelf projects), and Janet Furlow kept us all honest.

Finally, this is the first time I've written a book with an editor who works down at the prose level. It's been a fantastic experience, as Lynn Beighley has taken what I felt was finished text and systematically shown me the error of my assumptions. The book is way better for her advice. Thank you.

Dave Thomas
dave@pragprog.com
Dallas, TX, October 2014

## CHAPTER 1

Take the Red Pill

The Elixir programming language wraps functional programming with immutable state and an actor-based approach to concurrency in a tidy, modern syntax. And it runs on the industrial-strength, high-performance, distributed Erlang VM. But what does all that mean?

It means you can stop worrying about many of the difficult things that currently consume your time. You no longer have to think too hard about protecting your data consistency in a multithreaded environment. You worry less about scaling your applications. And, most importantly, you can think about programming in a different way.

Programming Should Be About Transforming Data

If you come from an object-oriented world, then you are used to thinking in terms of classes and their instances. A class defines behavior, and objects hold state. Developers spend time coming up with intricate hierarchies of classes that try to model their problem, much as Victorian gentleman scientists created taxonomies of butterflies.

When we code with objects, we're thinking about state. Much of our time is spent calling methods in objects and passing them other objects. Based on these calls, objects update their own state, and possibly the state of other objects. In this world, the class is king—it defines what each instance can do, and it implicitly controls the state of the data its instances hold. Our goal is data-hiding.

But that's not the real world. In the real world, we don't want to model abstract hierarchies (because in reality there aren't that many true hierarchies). We want to get things done, not maintain state.

Right now, for instance, I'm taking empty computer files and transforming them into files containing text. Soon I'll transform those files into a format you can read. A web server somewhere will transform your request to download the book into an HTTP response containing the content.

I don't want to hide data. I want to transform it.

Combine Transformations with Pipelines

Unix users are used to the philosophy of small, focused command-line tools that can be combined in arbitrary ways. Each tool takes an input, transforms it, and writes the result in a format that the next tool (or a human) can use.

This philosophy is incredibly flexible and leads to fantastic reuse. The Unix utilities can be combined in ways undreamed of by their authors. And each one multiplies the potential of the others.

It's also highly reliable—each small program does one thing well, which makes it easier to test.

There's another benefit. A command pipeline can operate in parallel. If I write

```
$ grep Elixir *.pml | wc -l
```

the word-count program, wc, runs at the same time as the grep command. Because wc consumes grep's output as it is produced, the answer is ready with virtually no delay once grep finishes.

Just to give you a taste of this kind of thing, here's an Elixir function called pmap. It takes a collection and a function, and returns the list that results from applying that function to each element of the collection. But…it runs a separate process to do the conversion of each element. Don't worry about the details for now.

```
spawn/pmap1.exs
defmodule Parallel do
  def pmap(collection, func) do
    collection
    |> Enum.map(&(Task.async(fn -> func.(&1) end)))
    |> Enum.map(&Task.await/1)
  end
end
```

We could run this function to get the squares of the numbers from 1 to 1000.

```
result = Parallel.pmap 1..1000, &(&1 * &1)
```

And, yes, I just kicked off 1,000 background processes, and I used all the cores and processors on my machine.

The code may not make much sense, but by about halfway through the book, you'll be writing this kind of thing for yourself.

Functions Are Data Transformers

Elixir lets us solve the problem in the same way the Unix shell does. Rather than have command-line utilities, we have functions. And we can string them together as we please. The smaller—more focused—those functions, the more flexibility we have when combining them.

If we want, we can make these functions run in parallel—Elixir has a simple but powerful mechanism for passing messages between them. And these are not your father's boring old processes or threads—we're talking about the potential to run millions of them on a single machine and have hundreds of these machines interoperating. Bruce Tate commented on this paragraph with this thought: "Most programmers treat threads and processes as a necessary evil; Elixir developers feel they are an important simplification." As we get deeper into the book, you'll start to see what he means.

This idea of transformation lies at the heart of functional programming: a function transforms its inputs into its output. The trigonometric function *sin* is an example—give it $\frac{\pi}{4}$, and you'll get back 0.7071.... An HTML templating system is a function; it takes a template containing placeholders and a list of named values, and produces a completed HTML document.

But this power comes at a price. You're going to have to unlearn a whole lot of what you *know* about programming. Many of your instincts will be wrong. And this will be frustrating, because you're going to feel like a total n00b.

Personally, I feel that's part of the fun.

You didn't learn, say, object-oriented programming overnight. You are unlikely to become a functional programming expert by breakfast, either.

But at some point things will click. You'll start thinking about problems in a different way, and you'll find yourself writing code that does amazing things with very little effort on your part. You'll find yourself writing small chunks of code that can be used over and over, often in unexpected ways (just as wc and grep can be).

Your view of the world may even change a little as you stop thinking in terms of responsibilities and start thinking in terms of getting things done.

And just about everyone can agree that will be fun.

Installing Elixir

This book assumes you're using at least Elixir 1.2. The most up-to-date instructions for installing Elixir are available at http://elixir-lang.org/install.html. Go install it now.

Running Elixir

In this book, I show a terminal session like this:

```
$ echo Hello, World
Hello, World
```

The terminal prompt is the dollar sign, and the stuff you type follows. (On your system, the prompt will likely be different.) Output from the system is shown without highlighting.

iex—Interactive Elixir

To test that your Elixir installation was successful, let's start an interactive Elixir session. At your regular shell prompt, type iex.

```
$ iex
Erlang/OTP 18 [erts-7.1] [source] [64-bit] [smp:4:4] [async-threads:10]
            [hipe] [kernel-poll:false] [dtrace]
Interactive Elixir (x.y.z) - press Ctrl+C to exit (type h() ENTER for help)
iex(1)>
```

(The various version numbers you see will likely be different—I won't bother to show them on subsequent examples.)

Once you have an iex prompt, you can enter Elixir code and you'll see the result. If you enter an expression that continues over more than one line, iex will prompt for the additional lines with an ellipsis (...).

```
iex(1)> 3 + 4
7
iex(2)> String.reverse "madamimadam"
"madamimadam"
iex(3)> 5 *
...(3)> 6
30
iex(4)>
```

The number in the prompt increments for each complete expression executed. I'll omit the number in most of the examples that follow.

There are several ways of exiting from iex—none are tidy. The easiest two are typing Ctrl-C twice or typing Ctrl-G followed by q and Return.

IEx Helpers

iex has a number of helper functions. Type h (followed by return) to get a list:

```
iex> h
                        IEx.Helpers
Welcome to Interactive Elixir. You are currently seeing the documentation for
the module IEx.Helpers which provides many helpers to make Elixir's shell more
joyful to work with.

This message was triggered by invoking the helper h(), usually referred to as
h/0 (since it expects 0 arguments).

You can use the h function to invoke the documentation for any Elixir module or
function:

  h Enum
  h Enum.map
  h Enum.reverse/1

You can also use the i function to introspect any value you have in the shell:

  i "hello"

There are many other helpers available:

    • b/1            — prints callbacks info and docs for a given module
    • c/2            — compiles a file at the given path
    • cd/1           — changes the current directory
    • clear/0        — clears the screen
    • flush/0        — flushes all messages sent to the shell
    • h/0            — prints this help message
    • h/1            — prints help for the given module, function or macro
    • i/1            — prints information about the given data type
    • import_file/1  — evaluates the given file in the shell's context
    • l/1            — loads the given module's beam code
    • ls/0           — lists the contents of the current directory
    • ls/1           — lists the contents of the specified directory
    • pid/3          — creates a PID with the 3 integer arguments passed
    • pwd/0          — prints the current working directory
    • r/1            — recompiles and reloads the given module's source file
    • respawn/0      — respawns the current shell
    • s/1            — prints spec information
    • t/1            — prints type information
    • v/0            — retrieves the last value from the history
    • v/1            — retrieves the nth value from the history

Help for all of those functions can be consulted directly from the command line
using the h helper itself. Try:

  h(v/0)
```

To learn more about IEx as a whole, just type h(IEx).

In the list of helper functions, the number following the slash is the number of arguments the helper expects.

Probably the most useful is h itself. With an argument, it gives you help on Elixir modules or individual functions in a module. This works for any modules loaded into iex (so when we talk about projects later on, you'll see your own documentation here, too).

For example, the IO module performs common I/O functions. For help on the module, type h(IO) or h IO.

```
iex> h IO      # or...
iex> h(IO)

Functions handling IO.

Many functions in this module expects an IO device as argument. An IO device
must be a PID or an atom representing a process. For convenience, Elixir
provides :stdio and :stderr as shortcuts to Erlang's :standard_io and
:standard_error....
```

This book frequently uses the puts function in the IO module, which in its simplest form writes a string to the console. Let's get the documentation.

```
iex> h IO.puts

* def puts(device \\ group_leader(), item)

Writes the argument to the device, similarly to write
but adds a new line at the end. The argument is expected
to be a chardata.
```

Another informative helper is i, which displays information about a value:

```
iex> i 123
Term
  123
Data type
  Integer
Reference modules
  Integer

iex> i "cat"
Term
  "cat"
Data type
  BitString
Byte size
```

```
   3
Description
  This is a string: a UTF-8 encoded binary. It's printed surrounded by
  "double quotes" because all UTF-8 codepoints in it are printable.
Raw representation
  <<99, 97, 116>>
Reference modules
  String, :binary

iex> i %{ name: "Dave", likes: "Elixir" }
Term
  %{likes: "Elixir", name: "Dave"}
Data type
  Map
Reference modules
  Map

iex> i Map
Term
  Map
Data type
  Atom
Module bytecode
  /Users/dave/Play/elixir/bin/../lib/elixir/ebin/Elixir.Map.beam
Source
  /Users/dave/Play/elixir/lib/elixir/lib/map.ex
Version
  [136119987195443140315307232506105292657]
Compile time
  2015-12-29 16:33:20
Compile options
  [:debug_info]
Description
  Use h(Map) to access its documentation.
  Call Map.module_info() to access metadata.
Raw representation
  :"Elixir.Map"
Reference modules
  Module, Atom
```

iex is a surprisingly powerful tool. You can use it to compile and execute entire projects, log in to remote machines, and access already-running Elixir applications.

Customizing iex

You can customize iex by setting options. For example, I like showing the results of evaluations in bright cyan. To find out how to do that, I used this:

```
iex> h IEx.configure
def configure(options)
```

```
Configures IEx.

The supported options are: :colors, :inspect, :default_prompt, :alive_prompt
and :history_size.

Colors

A keyword list that encapsulates all color settings used by the shell. See
documentation for the IO.ANSI module for the list of supported colors and
attributes.

The value is a keyword list. List of supported keys:

• :enabled      - boolean value that allows for switching the coloring on and off
• :eval_result  - color for an expression's resulting value
• :eval_info    - … various informational messages
• :eval_error   - … error messages
• :stack_app    - … the app in stack traces
• :stack_info   - … the remaining info in stack traces
• :ls_directory - … for directory entries (ls helper)
• :ls_device    - … device entries (ls helper)

This is an aggregate option that encapsulates all color settings used by the
shell. See documentation for the IO.ANSI module for the list of supported
colors and attributes.
    . . .
```

I then created a file called .iex.exs in my home directory, containing:

IEx.configure *colors:* [*eval_result:* [*:cyan*, *:bright*]]

If your iex session looks messed up (and things such as [33m appear in the output), it's likely your console does not support ANSI escape sequences. In that case, disable colorization using

IEx.configure *colors:* [*enabled:* false]

You can put any Elixir code into .iex.exs.

Compile and Run

Once you tire of writing one-line programs in iex, you'll want to start putting code into source files. These files will typically have the extension .ex or .exs. This is a convention—files ending in .ex are intended to be compiled into bytecodes and then run, whereas those ending in .exs are more like programs in scripting languages—they are effectively interpreted at the source level. When we come to write tests for our Elixir programs, you'll see that the application files have .ex extensions, whereas the tests have .exs because we don't need to keep compiled versions of the tests lying around.

Let's write the classic first program. Go to a working directory and create a file called hello.exs.

intro/hello.exs
```
IO.puts "Hello, World!"
```

The previous example shows how most of the code listings in this book are presented. The bar before the code itself shows the path and file name that contains the code. If you're reading an ebook, you'll be able to click on this to download the source file. You can also download all the code by visiting the book's page on our site and clicking on the *Source Code* link.[1]

Source file names are written in lowercase with underscores. They will have the extension .ex for programs that you intend to compile into binary form, and .exs for scripts that you want to run without compiling. Our "Hello, World" example is essentially throw-away code, so we used the .exs extension for it.

Having created our source file, let's run it. In the same directory where you created the file, run the elixir command:

```
$ elixir hello.exs
Hello, World!
```

We can also compile and run it inside iex using the c helper:

```
$ iex
iex> c "hello.exs"
Hello, World!
[]
iex>
```

The c helper compiled and executed the source file. (The [] that follows the output is the return value of the c function—if the source file had contained any modules, their names would have been listed here.

The c helper compiled the source file as freestanding code. You can also load a file as if you'd typed each line into iex using import_file. In this case, local variables set in the file are available in the iex session.

---

1. http://pragprog.com/titles/elixir12

As some folks fret over such things, the Elixir convention is to use two-column indentation and spaces (not tabs).

Suggestions for Reading the Book

This book is not a top-to-bottom reference guide to Elixir. Instead, it is intended to give you enough information to know what questions to ask and when to ask them. So approach what follows with a spirit of adventure. Try the code as you read, and don't stop there. Ask yourself questions and then try to answer them, either by coding or searching the Web.

Participate in the book's discussion forums and consider joining the Elixir mailing list.[2,3]

You're joining the Elixir community while it is still young. Things are exciting and dynamic, and there are plenty of opportunities to contribute.

Exercises

You'll find exercises sprinkled throughout the book. If you're reading an ebook, then each exercise will link directly to a topic in our online forums. There you'll find an initial answer, along with discussions of alternatives from readers of the book.

If you're reading this book on paper, visit the forums to see the list of exercise topics.[4]

Think Different(ly)

This is a book about thinking differently; about accepting that some of the things folks say about programming may not be the full story:

- Object orientation is not the only way to design code.
- Functional programming need not be complex or mathematical.
- The foundations of programming are not assignments, if statements, and loops.
- Concurrency does not need locks, semaphores, monitors, and the like.
- Processes are not necessarily expensive resources.
- Metaprogramming is not just something tacked onto a language.
- Even if it is work, programming should be fun.

---

2. http://forums.pragprog.com/forums/elixir12
3. https://groups.google.com/forum/?fromgroups#!forum/elixir-lang-talk
4. http://forums.pragprog.com/forums/322

Of course, I'm not saying Elixir is a magic potion (well, technically it is, but you know what I mean). There isn't the *one true way* to write code. But Elixir is different enough from the mainstream that learning it will give you more perspective and it will open your mind to new ways of thinking about programming.

So let's start.

And remember to make it fun.

Part I

Conventional Programming

Elixir is great for writing highly parallel, reliable applications.

But to be a great language for parallel programming, a language first has to be great for conventional, sequential programming. In this part of the book we'll cover how to write Elixir code, and we'll explore the idioms and conventions that make Elixir so powerful.

In this chapter, you'll see:
- pattern matching binds values to variables
- matching handles structured data
- _ (underscore) lets you ignore a match

## CHAPTER 2

Pattern Matching

We started the previous chapter by saying Elixir engenders a different way of thinking about programming.

To illustrate this and to lay the foundation for a lot of Elixir programming, let's start reprogramming your brain by looking at something that's one of the cornerstones of all programming languages—assignment.

Assignment:
I Do Not Think It Means What You Think It Means.

Let's use the interactive Elixir shell, iex, to look at a really simple piece of code. (Remember, you start iex at the command prompt using the iex command. You enter Elixir code at its iex> prompt, and it displays the resulting values.)

```
iex> a = 1
1
iex> a + 3
4
```

Most programmers would look at this code and say, "OK, we assign one to a variable a, then on the next line we add 3 to a, giving us 4."

But when it comes to Elixir, they'd be wrong. In Elixir, the equals sign is not an assignment. Instead it's like an assertion. It succeeds if Elixir can find a way of making the left-hand side equal the right-hand side. Elixir calls = a *match operator*.

In this case, the left-hand side is a variable and the right-hand side is an integer literal, so Elixir can make the match true by binding the variable a to value 1. You could argue it *is* just an assignment. But let's take it up a notch.

```
iex> a = 1
1
iex> 1 = a
1
iex> 2 = a
** (MatchError) no match of right hand side value: 1
```

Look at the second line of code, 1 = a. It's another match, and it passes. The variable a already has the value 1 (it was set in the first line), so what's on the left of the equals sign is the same as what's on the right, and the match succeeds.

But the third line, 2 = a, raises an error. You might have expected it to assign 2 to a, as that would make the match succeed, but Elixir will only change the value of a variable on the left side of an equals sign—on the right a variable is replaced with its value. This failing line of code is the same as 2 = 1, which causes the error.

More Complex Matches

First, a little background syntax. Elixir lists can be created using square brackets containing a comma-separated set of values. Here are some lists:

```
[ "Humperdinck", "Buttercup", "Fezzik" ]
[ "milk", "butter", [ "iocane", 12 ] ]
```

Back to the match operator.

```
iex> list = [ 1, 2, 3 ]
[1, 2, 3]
```

To make the match true, Elixir bound the variable list to the list [1, 2, 3].

But let's try something else:

```
iex> list = [1, 2, 3]
[1, 2, 3]
iex> [a, b, c ] = list
[1, 2, 3]
iex> a
1
iex> b
2
iex> c
3
```

Elixir looks for a way to make the value of the left side the same as on the right. The left side is a list containing three variables, and the right is a list of three values, so the two sides could be made the same by setting the variables to the corresponding values.

Elixir calls this process *pattern matching*. A pattern (the left side) is matched if the values (the right side) have the same structure and if each term in the pattern can be matched to the corresponding term in the values. A literal value in the pattern matches that exact value, and a variable in the pattern matches by taking on the corresponding value.

Let's look at a few more examples.

```
iex> list = [1, 2, [ 3, 4, 5 ] ]
[1, 2, [3, 4, 5]]
iex> [a, b, c ] = list
[1, 2, [3, 4, 5]]
iex> a
1
iex> b
2
iex> c
[3, 4, 5]
```

The value on the right side corresponding the term c on the left side is the sublist [3,4,5]; that is the value given to c to make the match true.

Let's try a pattern containing some values and variables.

```
iex> list = [1, 2, 3]
[1, 2, 3]
iex> [a, 2, b ] = list
[1, 2, 3]
iex> a
1
iex> b
3
```

The literal 2 in the pattern matched the corresponding term on the right, so the match succeeds by setting the values of a and b to 1 and 3. But...

```
iex> list = [1, 2, 3]
[1, 2, 3]
iex> [a, 1, b ] = list
** (MatchError) no match of right hand side value: [1, 2, 3]
```

Here the 1 (the second term in the list) cannot be matched against the corresponding element on the right side, so no variables are set and the match fails. This gives us a way of matching a list that meets certain criteria—in this case a length of 3, with 1 as its second element.

Your Turn

➤ *Exercise: PatternMatching-1*

Which of the following will match?

- a = [1, 2, 3]
- a = 4
- 4 = a
- [a, b] = [1, 2, 3]
- a = [[1, 2, 3]]
- [a] = [[1, 2, 3]]
- [[a]] = [[1, 2, 3]]

Ignoring a Value with _ (Underscore)

If we didn't need to capture a value during the match, we could use the special variable _ (an underscore). This acts like a variable but immediately discards any value given to it—in a pattern match, it is like a wildcard saying, "I'll accept any value here." The following example matches any three-element list that has a 1 as its first element.

```
iex> [1, _, _] = [1, 2, 3]
[1, 2, 3]
iex> [1, _, _] = [1, "cat", "dog"]
[1, "cat", "dog"]
```

Variables Bind Once (per Match)

Once a variable has been bound to a value in the matching process, it keeps that value for the remainder of the match.

```
iex> [a, a] = [1, 1]
[1, 1]
iex> a
1
iex> [a, a] = [1, 2]
** (MatchError) no match of right hand side value: [1, 2]
```

The first expression in this example succeeds because a is initially matched with the first 1 on the right side. The value in a is then used in the second term to match the second 1 on the right side.

In the next expression, the second a on the left side tries to match a 1 in the second element of the right. It doesn't, and so the match fails.

However, a variable can be bound to a new value in a subsequent match, and its current value does not participate in the new match.

```
iex> a = 1
1
iex> [1, a, 3] = [1, 2, 3]
[1, 2, 3]
iex> a
2
```

What if you instead want to force Elixir to use the existing value of the variable in the pattern? Prefix it with ^ (a caret). In Elixir, we call this the *pin operator*.

```
iex> a = 1
1
iex> a = 2
2
iex> ^a = 1
** (MatchError) no match of right hand side value: 1
```

This also works if the variable is a component of a pattern:

```
iex> a = 1
1
iex> [^a, 2, 3 ] = [ 1, 2, 3 ]      # use existing value of a
[1, 2, 3]
iex> a = 2
2
iex> [ ^a, 2 ] = [ 1, 2 ]
** (MatchError) no match of right hand side value: [1, 2]
```

There's one more important part of pattern matching, which we'll look at when we start digging deeper into lists on page 69.

Your Turn

➤ *Exercise: PatternMatching-2*
Which of the following will match?

- [a, b, a] = [1, 2, 3]
- [a, b, a] = [1, 1, 2]
- [a, b, a] = [1, 2, 1]

➤ *Exercise: PatternMatching-3*
The variable a contains the value 2. Which of the following will match?

- [a, b, a] = [1, 2, 3]
- [a, b, a] = [1, 1, 2]
- a = 1
- ^a = 2

- ^a = 1
- ^a = 2 - a

Another Way of Looking at the Equals Sign

Elixir's pattern matching is similar to Erlang's (the main difference being that Elixir allows a match to assign to a variable that was assigned in a prior match, whereas in Erlang a variable can be assigned only once).

Joe Armstrong, Erlang's creator, compares the equals sign in Erlang to that used in algebra. When you write the equation $x = a + 1$, you are not assigning the value of $a + 1$ to x. Instead you're simply asserting that the expressions x and $a + 1$ have the same value. If you know the value of x, you can work out the value of a, and vice versa.

His point is that you had to unlearn the algebraic meaning of = when you first came across assignment in imperative programming languages. Now's the time to un-unlearn it.

That's why I talk about pattern matching as the first chapter in this part of the book. It is a core part of Elixir—we'll also use it in conditions, function calls, and function invocation.

But really, I wanted to get you thinking differently about programming languages and to show you that some of your existing assumptions won't work in Elixir.

And speaking of existing assumptions...the next chapter kills another sacred cow. Your current programming language is probably designed to make it easy to change data. After all, that's what programs do, right? Not Elixir. Let's talk about a language in which *all* data is immutable.

Change and decay in all around I see…

➤ *Henry Francis Lyte, "Abide with Me"*

## CHAPTER 3

Immutability

If you listen to functional-programming aficionados, you'll hear people making a big deal about immutability—the fact that in a functional program, data cannot be altered once created.

And, indeed, Elixir enforces immutable data.

But why?

You Already Have (Some) Immutable Data

Forget about Elixir for a moment. Think about your current programming language of choice. Let's imagine you'd written this:

```
count = 99
do_something_with(count)
print(count)
```

You'd expect it to output 99. In fact, you'd be very surprised if it didn't. At your very core, you believe that 99 will always have the value 99.

Now, you could obviously bind a new value to your *variable*, but that doesn't change the fact that the value 99 is still 99.

Imagine programming in a world where you couldn't rely on that—where some other code, possibly running in parallel with your own, could change the value of 99. In that world, the call to do_something_with might kick off code that runs in the background, passing it the value 99 as an argument. And that could change the contents of the parameter it receives. Suddenly, 99 could be 100.

You'd be (rightly) upset. And, what's worse, you'd never really be able to guarantee your code produced the correct results.

Still thinking about your current language, consider this:

```
array = [ 1, 2, 3 ]
do_something_with(array)
print(array)
```

Again, you'd hope the print call would output [1,2,3]. But in most languages, do_something_with will receive the array as a reference. If it decides to change the second element or delete the contents entirely, the output won't be what you expect. Now it's harder to look at your code and reason about what it does.

Take this a step further—run multiple threads, all with access to the array. Who knows what state the array will be in if they all start changing it?

All this is because most compound data structures in most programming languages are mutable—you can change all or part of their content. And if pieces of your code do this in parallel, you're in a world of hurt.

By coincidence, Jessica Kerr (@jessitron) tweeted the following on the day I updated this section.

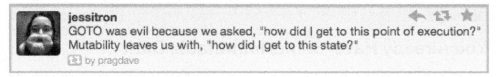

> **jessitron**
> GOTO was evil because we asked, "how did I get to this point of execution?"
> Mutability leaves us with, "how did I get to this state?"
> by pragdave

It's spot-on.

Immutable Data Is Known Data

Elixir sidesteps these problems. In Elixir, all values are immutable. The most complex nested list, the database record—these things behave just like the simplest integer. Their values are all immutable.

In Elixir, once a variable references a list such as [1,2,3], you know it will always reference those same values (until you rebind the variable). And this makes concurrency a lot less frightening.

But what if you *need* to add 100 to each element in [1,2,3]? Elixir does it by producing a copy of the original, containing the new values. The original remains unchanged, and your operation will not affect any other code holding a reference to that original.

This fits in nicely with the idea that programming is about transforming data. When we update [1,2,3], we don't hack it in place. Instead we transform it into something new.

Performance Implications of Immutability

It would be easy to assume that this approach to programming is inefficient. After all, you have to create a new copy of data whenever you update it, and that's going to leave lots of old values around to be garbage-collected. Let's look at these in turn.

Copying Data

Although common sense might dictate that all this copying of data is inefficient, the reverse is true. Because Elixir knows that existing data is immutable, it can reuse it, in part or as a whole, when building new structures.

Consider this code. (It uses a new operator, [head | tail], which builds a new list with head as its first element and tail as the rest. We'll spend a whole chapter on this when we talk about lists and recursion. For now, just trust.)

```
iex> list1 = [ 3, 2, 1 ]
[3, 2, 1]
iex> list2 = [ 4 | list1 ]
[4, 3, 2, 1]
```

In most languages, list2 would be built by creating a new list containing a 4, a 3, a 2, and a 1. The three values in list1 would be copied into the tail of list2. And that would be necessary because list1 would be mutable.

But Elixir knows list1 will never change, so it simply constructs a new list with a head of 4 and a tail of list1.

Garbage Collection

The other performance issue with a transformational language is that you quite often end up leaving old values unused when you create new values from them. This leaves a bunch of things using up memory on the heap, so garbage collection has to reclaim them.

Most modern languages have a garbage collector, and developers have grown to be suspicious of them—they can impact performance quite badly.

But the cool thing about Elixir is that you write your code using lots and lots of processes, and each process has its own heap. The data in your application is divvied up between these processes, so each individual heap is much, much smaller than would have been the case if all the data had been in a single heap. As a result, garbage collection runs faster. And when a process terminates before its heap becomes full, all its data is discarded—no garbage collection is required.

Coding with Immutable Data

Once you accept the concept, coding with immutable data is surprisingly easy. You just have to remember that any function that transforms data will return a new copy of it. Thus, we never capitalize a string. Instead, we return a capitalized copy of a string.

```
iex> name = "elixir"
"elixir"
iex> cap_name = String.capitalize name
"Elixir"
iex> name
"elixir"
```

If you're coming from an object-oriented language, you may dislike the idea that we write String.capitalize name and not name.capitalize(). But in OO languages, objects mostly have mutable state. When you make a call such as name.capitalize() you have no immediate indication whether you are changing the internal representation of the name, returning a capitalized copy, or both. There's plenty of scope for ambiguity.

In a functional language, we *always* transform data. We never modify it in place. The syntax reminds us of this every time we use it.

That's enough theory. It's time to start learning the language. In the next chapter we'll quickly go over the basic data types and some syntax, and in the following chapters we'll look at functions and modules.

CHAPTER 4

Elixir Basics

In this chapter we'll look at the types that are baked into Elixir, along with a few other things you need to know to get started. This chapter is deliberately terse—you're a programmer and you know what an integer is, so I'm not going to insult you. Instead, I try to cover the Elixir-specific stuff you need to know.

Built-in Types

Elixir's built-in types are

- Value types:
  - Arbitrary-sized integers
  - Floating-point numbers
  - Atoms
  - Ranges
  - Regular expressions

- System types:
  - PIDs and ports
  - References

- Collection types:

  - Tuples
  - Lists
  - Maps
  - Binaries

Functions are a type too. They have their own chapter, following this one.

You might be surprised that this list doesn't include things such as strings and structures. Elixir has them, but they are built using the basic types from this list. However, they are important. Strings have their own chapter, and we have a couple of chapters on lists and maps (and other dictionary-like types). The maps chapter also describes the Elixir structure facilities.

Finally, there's some debate about whether regular expressions and ranges are value types. Technically they aren't—under the hood they are just structures. But right now it's convenient to treat them as distinct types.

Value Types

The value types in Elixir represent numbers, names, ranges, and regular expressions.

Integers

Integer literals can be written as decimal (1234), hexadecimal (0xcafe), octal (0o765), and binary (0b1010).

Decimal numbers may contain underscores—these are often used to separate groups of three digits when writing large numbers, so one million could be written 1_000_000.

There is no fixed limit on the size of integers—their internal representation grows to fit their magnitude.

```
factorial(10000) # => 28462596809170545189...and so on for 35640 more digits...
```

(You'll see how to write a function such as factorial in Modules and Named Functions, on page 51.)

Floating-Point Numbers

Floating-point numbers are written using a decimal point. There must be at least one digit before and after the decimal point. An optional trailing exponent may be given. These are all valid floating-point literals:

```
1.0    0.2456    0.314159e1 314159.0e-5
```

Floats are IEEE 754 double precision, giving them about 16 digits of accuracy and a maximum exponent of around 10^{308}.

Atoms

Atoms are constants that represent something's name. We write them using a leading colon (:), which can be followed by an atom word or an Elixir operator. An atom word is a sequence of letters, digits, underscores, and at signs (@). It may end with an exclamation point or a question mark. You can also create atoms containing arbitrary characters by enclosing the characters following the colon in double quotes. These are all atoms:

`:fred  :is_binary?  :var@2  :<>  :===  :"func/3"  :"long john silver"`

An atom's name is its value. Two atoms with the same name will always compare as being equal, even if they were created by different applications on two computers separated by an ocean.

We'll be using atoms a lot to tag values.

Ranges

Ranges are represented as *start..end*, where *start* and *end* are integers.

Regular Expressions

Elixir has regular-expression literals, written as ~r{regexp} or ~r{regexp}opts. Here I show the delimiters for regular-expression literals as { and }, but they are considerably more flexible. You can choose any nonalphanumeric characters as delimiters, as described in the discussion of sigils on page 116. Some people use ~r/.../ for nostalgic reasons, but this is less convenient than the bracketed forms, as any forward slashes inside the pattern must be escaped.

Elixir regular expression support is provided by PCRE,[1] which basically provides a Perl 5–compatible syntax for patterns.

You can specify one or more single-character options following a regexp literal. These modify the literal's match behavior or add functionality.

Opt	Meaning
f	Force the pattern to start to match on the first line of a multiline string.
g	Support named groups.
i	Make matches case insensitive.
m	If the string to be matched contains multiple lines, ^ and $ match the start and end of these lines. \A and \z continue to match the beginning or end of the string.
r	Normally modifiers like * and + are greedy, matching as much as possible. The r modifier makes them *reluctant*, matching as little as possible.
s	Allow . to match any newline characters.
u	Enable unicode-specific patterns like \p.
x	Enable extended mode—ignore whitespace and comments (# to end of line).

---

1.   http://www.pcre.org/

You manipulate regular expressions with the `Regex` module.

```
iex> Regex.run ~r{[aeiou]}, "caterpillar"
["a"]
iex> Regex.scan ~r{[aeiou]}, "caterpillar"
[["a"], ["e"], ["i"], ["a"]]
iex> Regex.split ~r{[aeiou]}, "caterpillar"
["c", "t", "rp", "ll", "r"]
iex> Regex.replace ~r{[aeiou]}, "caterpillar", "*"
"c*t*rp*ll*r"
```

System Types

These types reflect resources in the underlying Erlang VM.

PIDs and Ports

A PID is a reference to a local or remote process, and a port is a reference to a resource (typically external to the application) that you'll be reading or writing.

The PID of the current process is available by calling `self`. A new PID is created when you spawn a new process. We'll talk about this in Part II.

References

The function `make_ref` creates a globally unique reference; no other reference will be equal to it. We don't use references in this book.

Collection Types

The types we've seen so far are common in other programming languages. Now we're getting into types that are more exotic, so we'll go into more detail here.

Elixir collections can hold values of any type (including other collections).

Tuples

A tuple is an ordered collection of values. As with all Elixir data structures, once created a tuple cannot be modified.

You write a tuple between braces, separating the elements with commas.

```
{ 1, 2 }      { :ok, 42, "next" }   { :error, :enoent }
```

A typical Elixir tuple has two to four elements—any more and you'll probably want to look at maps, on page 83, or structs, on page 88.

You can use tuples in pattern matching:

```
iex> {status, count, action} = {:ok, 42, "next"}
{:ok, 42, "next"}
iex> status
:ok
iex> count
42
iex> action
"next"
```

It is common for functions to return a tuple where the first element is the atom :ok if there were no errors. For example (assuming you have a file called Rakefile in your current directory):

```
iex> {status, file} = File.open("Rakefile")
{:ok, #PID<0.39.0>}
```

Because the file was successfully opened, the tuple contains an :ok status and a PID, which is how we access the contents.

A common idiom is to write matches that assume success:

```
iex> { :ok, file } = File.open("Rakefile")
{:ok, #PID<0.39.0>}
iex> { :ok, file } = File.open("non-existent-file")
** (MatchError) no match of right hand side value: {:error, :enoent}
```

The second open failed, and returned a tuple where the first element was :error. This caused the match to fail, and the error message shows that the second element contains the reason—enoent is Unix-speak for "file does not exist."

Lists

We've already seen Elixir's list literal syntax, [1,2,3]. This might lead you to think lists are like arrays in other languages, but they are not (in fact, tuples are the closest Elixir gets to a conventional array). Instead, a list is effectively a linked data structure. A list may either be empty or consist of a head and a tail. The head contains a value and the tail is itself a list. (If you've used the language Lisp, then this will all seem very familiar.)

As we'll discuss in Chapter 7, *Lists and Recursion*, on page 69, this recursive definition of a list is the core of much Elixir programming.

Because of their implementation, lists are easy to traverse linearly, but they are expensive to access in random order (to get to the nth element, you have to scan through n–1 previous elements). It is always cheap to get the head of a list and to extract the tail of a list.

Lists have one other performance characteristic. Remember that we said all Elixir data structures are immutable? That means once a list has been made, it will never be changed. So, if we want to remove the head from a list, leaving just the tail, we never have to copy the list. Instead we can return a pointer to the tail. This is the basis of all the list-traversal tricks we'll cover in Chapter 7, *Lists and Recursion*, on page 69.

Elixir has some operators that work specifically on lists:

```
iex> [ 1, 2, 3 ] ++ [ 4, 5, 6 ]        # concatenation
[1, 2, 3, 4, 5, 6]
iex> [1, 2, 3, 4] -- [2, 4]            # difference
[1, 3]
iex> 1 in [1,2,3,4]                     # membership
true
iex> "wombat" in [1, 2, 3, 4]
false
```

Keyword Lists

Because we often need simple lists of key/value pairs, Elixir gives us a shortcut. If we write

```
[ name: "Dave", city: "Dallas", likes: "Programming" ]
```

Elixir converts it into a list of two-value tuples:

```
[ {:name, "Dave"}, {:city, "Dallas"}, {:likes, "Programming"} ]
```

Elixir allows us to leave off the square brackets if a keyword list is the last argument in a function call. Thus,

```
DB.save record, [ {:use_transaction, true}, {:logging, "HIGH"} ]
```

can be written more cleanly as

```
DB.save record, use_transaction: true, logging: "HIGH"
```

We can also leave off the brackets if a keyword list appears as the last item in any context where a list of values is expected.

```
iex> [1, fred: 1, dave: 2]
[1, {:fred, 1}, {:dave, 2}]
iex> {1, fred: 1, dave: 2}
{1, [fred: 1, dave: 2]}
```

Maps

A map is a collection of key/value pairs. A map literal looks like this:

```
%{ key => value, key => value }
```

Here are some maps:

```
iex> states = %{ "AL" => "Alabama", "WI" => "Wisconsin" }
%{"AL" => "Alabama", "WI" => "Wisconsin"}

iex> responses = %{ { :error, :enoent } => :fatal, { :error, :busy } => :retry }
%{{:error, :busy} => :retry, {:error, :enoent} => :fatal}

iex> colors = %{ :red => 0xff0000, :green => 0x00ff00, :blue => 0x0000ff }
%{blue: 255, green: 65280, red: 16711680}
```

In the first case the keys are strings, in the second they're tuples, and in the third they're atoms. Although typically all the keys in a map are the same type, that isn't required.

```
iex> %{ "one" => 1, :two => 2, {1,1,1} => 3 }
%{:two => 2, {1, 1, 1} => 3, "one" => 1}
```

If the key is an atom, you can use the same shortcut that you use with keyword lists:

```
iex> colors = %{ red: 0xff0000, green: 0x00ff00, blue: 0x0000ff }
%{blue: 255, green: 65280, red: 16711680}
```

You can also use expressions for the keys in map literals:

```
iex> name = "José Valim"
"José Valim"
iex> %{ String.downcase(name) => name }
%{"josé valim" => "José Valim"}
```

Why do we have both maps and keyword lists? Maps allow only one entry for a particular key, whereas keyword lists allow the key to be repeated. Maps are efficient (particularly as they grow), and they can be used in Elixir's pattern matching, which we discuss in later chapters.

In general, use keyword lists for things such as command-line parameters and for passing around options, and use maps when you want an associative array.

Accessing a Map

You extract values from a map using the key. The square-bracket syntax works with all maps:

```
iex> states = %{ "AL" => "Alabama", "WI" => "Wisconsin" }
%{"AL" => "Alabama", "WI" => "Wisconsin"}
iex> states["AL"]
"Alabama"
iex> states["TX"]
nil

iex> response_types = %{ { :error, :enoent } => :fatal,
...>                      { :error, :busy } => :retry }
%{{:error, :busy} => :retry, {:error, :enoent} => :fatal}
iex> response_types[{:error,:busy}]
:retry
```

If the keys are atoms, you can also use a dot notation:

```
iex> colors = %{ red: 0xff0000, green: 0x00ff00, blue: 0x0000ff }
%{blue: 255, green: 65280, red: 16711680}
iex> colors[:red]
16711680
iex> colors.green
65280
```

You'll get a KeyError if there's no matching key when you use the dot notation.

Binaries

Sometimes you need to access data as a sequence of bits and bytes. For example, the headers in JPEG and MP3 files contain fields where a single byte may encode two or three separate values.

Elixir supports this with the binary data type. Binary literals are enclosed between << and >>.

The basic syntax packs successive integers into bytes:

```
iex> bin = << 1, 2 >>
<<1, 2>>
iex> byte_size bin
2
```

You can add modifiers to control the type and size of each individual field. Here's a single byte that contains three fields of widths 2, 4, and 2 bits. (The example uses some built-in libraries to show the result's binary value.)

```
iex> bin = <<3 :: size(2), 5 :: size(4), 1 :: size(2)>>
<<213>>
iex> :io.format("~-8.2b~n", :binary.bin_to_list(bin))
11010101
:ok
iex> byte_size bin
1
```

Binaries are both important and arcane. They're important because Elixir uses them to represent UTF strings. They're arcane because, at least initially, you're unlikely to use them directly.

Names, Source Files, Conventions, Operators, and So On

Elixir identifiers consist of upper- and lowercase ASCII characters, digits, and underscores. They may end with a question or an exclamation mark.

Module, record, protocol, and behaviour names start with an uppercase letter and are bumpycase (like this: BumpyCase). All other identifiers start with a lowercase letter or an underscore, and by convention use underscores between words. If the first character is an underscore, Elixir doesn't report a warning if the variable is unused in a pattern match or function parameter list.

Source files are written in UTF-8, but identifiers may use only ASCII.

By convention, source files use two-character indentation for nesting—and they use spaces, not tabs, to achieve this.

Comments start with a hash sign (#) and run to the end of the line.

The community is compiling a coding style guide. As I write this, it is at https://github.com/niftyn8/elixir_style_guide, but I'm told it may move in the future.

Truth

Elixir has three special values related to Boolean operations: true, false, and nil. nil is treated as false in Boolean contexts.

(A bit of trivia: all three of these values are aliases for atoms of the same name, so true is the same as the atom :true.)

In most contexts, any value other than false or nil is treated as true. We sometimes refer to this as *truthy* as opposed to true).

Operators

Elixir has a very rich set of operators. Here's a subset we'll use in this book.

Comparison operators
```
a === b    # strict equality   (so 1 === 1.0 is false)
a !== b    # strict inequality (so 1 !== 1.0 is true)
a ==  b    # value equality    (so 1 ==  1.0 is true)
a !=  b    # value inequality  (so 1 !=  1.0 is false)
a  >  b    # normal comparison
a >= b     #  :
a  <  b    #  :
a <= b     #  :
```

The ordering comparisons in Elixir are less strict than in many languages, as you can compare values of different types. If the types are the same or are compatible (for example 3 > 2 or 3.0 < 5), the comparison uses natural ordering. Otherwise comparison is based on type according to this rule:

number < atom < reference < function < port < pid < tuple < map < list < binary

Boolean operators

(These operators expect true or false as their first argument.)

```
a or  b    # true if a is true, otherwise b
a and b    # false if a is false, otherwise b
not a      # false if a is true, true otherwise
```

Relaxed Boolean operators

These operators take arguments of any type. Any value apart from nil or false is interpreted as true.

```
a || b  # a if a is truthy, otherwise b
a && b  # b if a is truthy, otherwise a
!a      # false if a is truthy, otherwise true
```

Arithmetic operators

+ - * / div rem

Integer division yields a floating-point result. Use div(a,b) to get an integer.

rem is the *remainder operator*. It is called as a function (rem(11, 3) => 2). It differs from normal modulo operations in that the result will have the same sign as the function's first argument.

Join operators

```
binary1 <> binary2    # concatenates two binaries (later we'll
                      # see that binaries include strings)
list1   ++ list2      # concatenates two lists
list1   -- list2      # returns elements in list1 not in list2
```

The in operator

```
a in enum             # tests if a is included in enum (for example,
                      # a list or a range)
```

Variable Scope

Elixir is lexically scoped. The basic unit of scoping is the function body. Variables defined in a function (including its parameters) are local to that function. In addition, modules define a scope for local variables, but these are only accessible at the top level of that module, and not in functions defined in the module.

Several Elixir structures also define their own scope. We'll look at one of these, for, in *Comprehensions*, on page 109. The other is with.

The with Expression

The with expression serves double duty. First, it allows you to define a local scope for variables: if you need a couple of temporary variables when calculating something, and don't want those variables to leak out into the wider scope, use with.

For example, the /etc/passwd file contains lines such as:

```
_installassistant:*:25:25:Install Assistant:/var/empty:/usr/bin/false
_lp:*:26:26:Printing Services:/var/spool/cups:/usr/bin/false
_postfix:*:27:27:Postfix Mail Server:/var/spool/postfix:/usr/bin/false
```

The two numbers are the user and group ids for the given user name. This code finds the values for the _lp user.

```
basic-types/with-scope.exs
content = "Now is the time"

lp  = with {:ok, file}    = File.open("/etc/passwd"),
           content        = IO.read(file, :all),
           :ok            = File.close(file),
           [_, uid, gid] = Regex.run(~r/_lp:.*?:(\d+):(\d+)/, content)
      do
           "Group: #{gid}, User: #{uid}"
      end

IO.puts lp               #=> Group: 26, User: 26
IO.puts content          #=> Now is the time
```

The with expression lets us work with what are effectively temporary variables as we open the file, read its content, close it, and search for the line we want. The value of the with is the value of its do parameter.

The inner variable content is local to the with, and does not affect the variable in the outer scope.

with and Pattern Matching

In the previous example, the head of the with expression contained basic pattern matches using =. If any of these had failed, a MatchError exception would be raised. But perhaps we'd want to handle this case in a more elegant way. That's where the <- operator comes in. If you use <- instead of = in a with expression, it performs a match, but if it fails it returns the value that can't be matched. Rather than raising an exception it exits the with early, returning the value that couldn't be matched:

```
iex> with [a|_] <- [1,2,3], do: a
1
iex> with [a|_] <- nil,    do: a
nil
```

We can use this to let the with in the previous example return nil if the user can't be found, rather than raising an exception.

basic-types/with-match.exs
```
result = with {:ok, file} = File.open("/etc/passwd"),
              content     = IO.read(file, :all),
              :ok         = File.close(file),
              [_, uid, gid] <- Regex.run(~r/xxx:.*?:(\d+):(\d+)/, content)
         do
              "Group: #{gid}, User: #{uid}"
         end

IO.puts inspect(result)        #=> nil
```

When we try to match the user xxx, Regex.run returns nil. This causes the match to fail, and the nil becomes the value of the with.

A Minor Gotcha

Underneath the covers, with is treated by Elixir as if it were a call to a function or macro. This means that you cannot write this:

```
mean = with                            # WRONG!
        count = Enum.count(values),
        sum   = Enum.sum(values)
      do
        sum/count
      end
```

Instead, you can put the first parameter on the same line as the with:

```
mean = with count = Enum.count(values),
            sum   = Enum.sum(values)
      do
        sum/count
      end
```

or use parentheses:

```
mean = with(
        count = Enum.count(values),
        sum   = Enum.sum(values)
      do
        sum/count
```

end)

As with all other uses of do, you can also use the shortcut:

```
mean = with count = Enum.count(values),
            sum   = Enum.sum(values),
       do:  sum/count
```

End of the Basics

We've now covered the low-level ingredients of an Elixir program. In the next two chapters we'll discuss how to create anonymous functions, modules, and named functions.

CHAPTER 5

Anonymous Functions

Elixir is a functional language, so it is no surprise that functions are a basic type.

An anonymous function is created using the fn keyword.

```
fn
  parameter-list -> body
  parameter-list -> body ...
end
```

Think of fn...end as being a bit like the quotes that surround a string literal, except here we're returning a function as a value, not a string. We can pass that function value to other functions. We can also invoke it, passing in arguments.

At its simplest, a function has a parameter list and a body, separated by ->.

For example, the following defines a function, binding it to the variable sum, and then calls it.

```
iex> sum = fn (a, b) -> a + b end
#Function<12.17052888 in :erl_eval.expr/5>
iex> sum.(1, 2)
3
```

The first line of code creates a function that takes two parameters (named a and b). The implementation of the function follows the -> arrow (in our case it simply adds the two parameters), and the whole thing is terminated with the keyword end. We store the function in the variable sum.

On the second line of code, we invoke the function using the syntax sum.(1,2). The dot indicates the function call, and the arguments are passed between parentheses. (You'll have noticed we don't use a dot for named function calls—this is a difference between named and anonymous functions.)

If your function takes no arguments, you still need the parentheses to call it:

```
iex> greet = fn -> IO.puts "Hello" end
#Function<12.17052888 in :erl_eval.expr/5>
iex> greet.()
Hello
:ok
```

You can, however, omit the parentheses in a function definition.

```
iex> f1 = fn a, b -> a * b end
#Function<12.17052888 in :erl_eval.expr/5>
iex> f1.(5,6)
30
iex> f2 = fn -> 99 end
#Function<12.17052888 in :erl_eval.expr/5>
iex> f2.()
99
```

Functions and Pattern Matching

When we call sum.(2,3), it's easy to assume we simply assign 2 to the parameter a and 3 to b. But that word, *assign*, should ring some bells. Elixir doesn't have assignment. Instead it tries to match values to patterns. (We came across this when we looked at pattern matching and assignment on page 15.)

If we write

```
a = 2
```

then Elixir makes the pattern match by binding a to the value 2. And that's exactly what happens when our sum function gets called. We pass 2 and 3 as arguments, and Elixir tries to match these arguments to the parameters a and b, which it does by giving a the value 2 and b the value 3. It's the same as when we write

```
{a, b} = {1, 2}
```

This means we can perform more complex pattern matching when we call a function. For example, the following function reverses the order of elements in a two-element tuple.

```
iex> swap = fn { a, b } -> { b, a } end
#Function<12.17052888 in :erl_eval.expr/5>
iex> swap.( { 6, 8 } )
{8, 6}
```

We'll use this pattern-matching capability when we look at functions with multiple implementations in the next section.

Your Turn

➤ *Exercise: Functions-1*

Go into iex. Create and run the functions that do the following:

— list_concat.([:a, :b], [:c, :d]) #=> [:a, :b, :c, :d]
— sum.(1, 2, 3) #=> 6
— pair_tuple_to_list.({ 1234, 5678 }) #=> [1234, 5678]

One Function, Multiple Bodies

A single function definition lets you define different implementations, depending on the type and contents of the arguments passed. (You cannot select based on the number of arguments—each clause in the function definition must have the same number of parameters.)

At its simplest, we can use pattern matching to select which clause to run. In the example that follows, we know the tuple returned by File.open has :ok as its first element if the file was opened, so we write a function that displays either the first line of a successfully opened file or a simple error message if the file could not be opened.

```
Line 1  iex> handle_open = fn
     2  ...>   {:ok, file}  -> "Read data: #{IO.read(file, :line)}"
     3  ...>   {_,    error} -> "Error: #{:file.format_error(error)}"
     4  ...> end
     5  #Function<12.17052888 in :erl_eval.expr/5>
     6  iex> handle_open.(File.open("code/intro/hello.exs"))   # this file exists
     7  "Read data: IO.puts \"Hello, World!\"\n"
     8  iex> handle_open.(File.open("nonexistent"))            # this one doesn't
     9  "Error: no such file or directory"
```

Let's start by looking inside the function definition. On lines 2 and 3 we define two separate function bodies. Each takes a single tuple as a parameter. The first of them requires that the first term in the tuple is :ok. The second line uses the special variable _ (underscore) to match any other value for the first term.

Now look at line 6. We call our function, passing it the result of calling File.open on a file that exists. This means the function will receive the tuple {:ok,file}, and this matches the clause on line 2. The corresponding code calls IO.read to read the first line of this file.

We then call handle_open again, this time with the result of trying to open a file that does not exist. The tuple that is returned ({:error,:enoent}) is passed to our function, which looks for a matching clause. It fails on line 2 because the first term is not :ok, but it succeeds on the next line. The code in that clause formats the error as a nice string.

Note a couple of other things in this code. On line 3 we call :file.format_error. The :file part of this refers to the underlying Erlang File module, so we can call its format_error function. Contrast this with the call to File.open on line 6. Here the File part refers to Elixir's built-in module. This is a good example of the underlying environment leaking through into Elixir code. It is good that you can access all the existing Erlang libraries—there are hundreds of years of effort in there just waiting for you to use. But it is also tricky because you have to differentiate between Erlang functions and Elixir functions when you call them.

And finally, this example shows off Elixir's *string interpolation*. Inside a string, the contents of #{...} are evaluated and the result is substituted back in.

Working with Larger Code Examples

Our handle_open function is getting uncomfortably long to type directly into iex. One typo, and we'd have to type it all in again.

Instead, let's use our editor to type it into a file in the same directory we were in when we started iex. Let's call the file handle_open.exs.

```
first_steps/handle_open.exs
handle_open = fn
  {:ok, file}  -> "First line: #{IO.read(file, :line)}"
  {_,   error} -> "Error:  #{:file.format_error(error)}"
end
IO.puts handle_open.(File.open("Rakefile"))      # call with a file that exists
IO.puts handle_open.(File.open("nonexistent"))   # and then with one that doesn't
```

Now, inside iex, type:

```
c "handle_open.exs"
```

This compiles and runs the code in the given file.

We can do the same thing from the command line (that is, not inside iex) using this:

```
$ elixir handle_open.exs
```

We used the file extension .exs for this example. This is used for code that we want to run directly from a source file (think of the s as meaning *script*). For files we want to compile and use later, we'll employ the .ex extension.

Your Turn

➤ *Exercise: Functions-2*

Write a function that takes three arguments. If the first two are zero, return "FizzBuzz." If the first is zero, return "Fizz." If the second is zero, return "Buzz." Otherwise return the third argument. Do not use any language features that we haven't yet covered in this book.

➤ *Exercise: Functions-3*

The operator rem(a, b) returns the remainder after dividing a by b. Write a function that takes a single integer (n) and calls the function in the previous exercise, passing it rem(n,3), rem(n,5), and n. Call it seven times with the arguments 10, 11, 12, and so on. You should get "Buzz, 11, Fizz, 13, 14, FizzBuzz, 16."

(Yes, it's a FizzBuzz solution with no conditional logic.)[1]

Functions Can Return Functions

Here's some strange code:

```
iex> fun1 = fn -> fn -> "Hello" end end
#Function<12.17052888 in :erl_eval.expr/5>
iex> fun1.()
#Function<12.17052888 in :erl_eval.expr/5>
iex> fun1.().()
"Hello"
```

The strange thing is the first line. It's a little hard to read, so let's spread it out.

```
fun1 = fn ->
         fn ->
            "Hello"
         end
       end
```

The variable fun1 is bound to a function. That function takes no parameters, and its body is a second function definition. That second function also takes no parameters, and it evaluates the string "Hello".

When we call the outer function (using fun1.()), it returns the inner function. When we call that (fun1.().()) the inner function is evaluated and "Hello" is returned.

---

1. http://c2.com/cgi/wiki?FizzBuzzTest

We wouldn't normally write something such as fun1.().(). But we might call the outer function and bind the result to a separate variable. We might also use parentheses to make the inner function more obvious.

```
iex> fun1 = fn -> (fn -> "Hello" end) end
#Function<12.17052888 in :erl_eval.expr/5>
iex> other = fun1.()
#Function<12.17052888 in :erl_eval.expr/5>
iex> other.()
"Hello"
```

Functions Remember Their Original Environment

Let's take this idea of nesting functions a little further.

```
iex> greeter = fn name -> (fn -> "Hello #{name}" end) end
#Function<12.17052888 in :erl_eval.expr/5>
iex> dave_greeter = greeter.("Dave")
#Function<12.17052888 in :erl_eval.expr/5>
iex> dave_greeter.()
"Hello Dave"
```

Now the outer function has a name parameter. Like any parameter, name is available for use throughout the body of the function. In this case, we use it inside the string in the inner function.

When we call the outer function, it returns the inner function definition. At this point it has not yet substituted the name into the string. But when we call the inner function (dave_greeter.()), the substitution takes place and the greeting appears.

But something strange happens here. The inner function uses the outer function's name parameter. But by the time greeter.("Dave") returns, that outer function has finished executing and the parameter has gone out of scope. And yet when we run the inner function, it merrily uses that parameter's value.

This works because functions in Elixir automatically carry with them the bindings of variables in the scope in which they are defined. In our example, the variable name is bound in the scope of the outer function. When the inner function is defined, it inherits this scope and carries the binding of name around with it. This is a *closure*—the scope encloses the bindings of its variables, packaging them into something that can be saved and used later.

Let's play with this some more.

Parameterized Functions

In the previous example, the outer function took an argument and the inner one did not. Let's try a different example where both take arguments.

```
iex> add_n = fn n -> (fn other -> n + other end) end
#Function<12.17052888 in :erl_eval.expr/5>
iex> add_two = add_n.(2)
#Function<12.17052888 in :erl_eval.expr/5>
iex> add_five = add_n.(5)
#Function<12.17052888 in :erl_eval.expr/5>
iex> add_two.(3)
5
iex> add_five.(7)
12
```

Here the inner function adds the value of its parameter other to the value of the outer function's parameter n. Each time we call the outer function, we give it a value for n and it returns a function that adds n to its own parameter.

Your Turn

➤ *Exercise: Functions-4*

Write a function prefix that takes a string. It should return a new function that takes a second string. When that second function is called, it will return a string containing the first string, a space, and the second string.

```
iex> mrs = prefix.("Mrs")
#Function<erl_eval.6.82930912>
iex> mrs.("Smith")
"Mrs Smith"
iex> prefix.("Elixir").("Rocks")
"Elixir Rocks"
```

Passing Functions As Arguments

Functions are just values, so we can pass them to other functions.

```
iex> times_2 = fn n -> n * 2 end
#Function<12.17052888 in :erl_eval.expr/5>
iex> apply = fn (fun, value) -> fun.(value) end
#Function<12.17052888 in :erl_eval.expr/5>
iex> apply.(times_2, 6)
12
```

In this example, apply is a function that takes a second function and a value. It returns the result of invoking that second function with the value as an argument.

We use the ability to pass functions around pretty much everywhere in Elixir code. For example, the built-in Enum module has a function called map. It takes two arguments: a collection and a function. It returns a list that is the result of applying that function to each element of the collection.

```
iex> list = [1, 3, 5, 7, 9]
[1, 3, 5, 7, 9]
iex> Enum.map list, fn elem -> elem * 2 end
[2, 6, 10, 14, 18]
iex> Enum.map list, fn elem -> elem * elem end
[1, 9, 25, 49, 81]
iex> Enum.map list, fn elem -> elem > 6 end
[false, false, false, true, true]
```

Pinned Values and Function Parameters

When we originally looked at pattern matching, we saw that the pin operator (^) allowed us to use the current value of a variable in a pattern. You can use this with function parameters, too.

```
functions/pin.exs
defmodule Greeter do

  def for(name, greeting) do
    fn
      (^name) -> "#{greeting} #{name}"
      (_)      -> "I don't know you"
    end
  end

end

mr_valim = Greeter.for("José", "Oi!")

IO.puts mr_valim.("José")     # => Oi! José
IO.puts mr_valim.("dave")     # => I don't know you
```

In this example, the Greeter.for function returns a function with two heads. The first head matches when its first parameter is the value of the name passed to for.

The & Notation

The strategy of creating short helper functions is so common that Elixir provides a shortcut. Let's look at it in use before we explore what's going on.

```
iex> add_one = &(&1 + 1)       # same as add_one = fn (n) -> n + 1 end
#Function<6.17052888 in :erl_eval.expr/5>
iex> add_one.(44)
```

```
iex> square = &(&1 * &1)
#Function<6.17052888 in :erl_eval.expr/5>
iex> square.(8)
64
iex> speak = &(IO.puts(&1))
&IO.puts/1
iex> speak.("Hello")
Hello
:ok
```

The & operator converts the expression that follows into a function. Inside that expression, the placeholders &1, &2, and so on correspond to the first, second, and subsequent parameters of the function. So &(&1 + &2) will be converted to fn p1, p2 -> p1 + p2 end.

Elixir is even more clever. Look at the speak line in the previous code. Normally Elixir would have generated an anonymous function, so &(IO.puts(&1)) would become fn x -> IO.puts(x) end. But Elixir noticed that the body of the anonymous function was simply a call to a named function (the IO function puts) and that the parameters were in the correct order (that is, the first parameter to the anonymous function was the first parameter to the named function, and so on). So Elixir optimized away the anonymous function, replacing it with a direct reference to the function, IO.puts/1.

For this to work, the arguments must be in the correct order:

```
iex> rnd = &(Float.round(&1, &2))
&Float.round/2
iex> rnd = &(Float.round(&2, &1))
#Function<12.17052888 in :erl_eval.expr/5>
```

You might see references to Erlang pop up when you define functions this way. That's because Elixir runs on the Erlang VM. There's more evidence of this if you try something like &abs(&1). Here Elixir maps your use of the abs function directly into the underlying Erlang library, and returns &:erlang.abs/1.

Because [] and {} are operators in Elixir, literal lists and tuples can also be turned into functions. Here's a function that returns a tuple containing the quotient and remainder of dividing two integers:

```
iex> divrem = &{ div(&1,&2), rem(&1,&2) }
#Function<12.17052888 in :erl_eval.expr/5>
iex> divrem.(13, 5)
{2, 3}
```

There's a second form of the & function capture operator. You can give it the name and arity (number of parameters) of an existing function, and it will return an anonymous function that calls it. The arguments you pass to the anonymous function will in turn be passed to the named function. We've already seen this: when we entered &(IO.puts(&1)) into iex, it displayed the result as &IO.puts/1. In this case, puts is a function in the IO module, and it takes one argument. The Elixir way of naming this is IO.puts/1. If we place an & in front of this, we wrap it in a function. Here are some other examples:

```
iex> l = &length/1
&:erlang.length/1
iex> l.([1,3,5,7])
4

iex> len = &Enum.count/1
&Enum.count/1
iex> len.([1,2,3,4])
4

iex> m = &Kernel.min/2    # This is an alias for the Erlang function
&:erlang.min/2
iex> m.(99,88)
88
```

This works with named functions we write, as well (but we haven't covered how to write them yet).

The & shortcut gives us a wonderful way to pass functions to other functions.

```
iex> Enum.map [1,2,3,4], &(&1 + 1)
[2, 3, 4, 5]
iex> Enum.map [1,2,3,4], &(&1 * &1)
[1, 4, 9, 16]
iex> Enum.map [1,2,3,4], &(&1 < 3)
[true, true, false, false]
```

Your Turn

➤ *Exercise: Functions-5*

Use the &... notation to rewrite the following.

- Enum.map [1,2,3,4], fn x -> x + 2 end
- Enum.each [1,2,3,4], fn x -> IO.inspect x end

Functions Are the Core

At the start of the book, we said the basis of programming is transforming data. Functions are the little engines that perform that transformation. They are at the very heart of Elixir.

So far we've been looking at anonymous functions—although we can bind them to variables, the functions themselves have no name. Elixir also has named functions. In the next chapter we'll cover how to work with them.

In this chapter, you'll see:
- Modules, the basic unit of code
- Defining public and private named functions
- Guard clauses
- Module directives and attributes
- Calling functions in Erlang modules

## CHAPTER 6

Modules and Named Functions

Once a program grows beyond a couple of lines, you'll want to structure it. Elixir makes this easy. You break your code into *named functions* and organize these functions into *modules*. In fact, in Elixir named functions must be written inside modules.

Let's look at a simple example. Navigate to a working directory and create an Elixir source file called times.exs.

mm/times.exs
```
defmodule Times do
  def double(n) do
    n * 2
  end
end
```

Here we have a module named Times. It contains a single function, double. Because our function takes a single argument and because the number of arguments forms part of the way we identify Elixir functions, you'll see this function name written double/1.

Compiling a Module

Let's look at two ways to compile this file and load it into iex. First, if you're at the command line, you can do this:

```
$ iex times.exs
iex> Times.double 4
8
```

Give iex a source file's name, and it compiles and loads the file before it displays a prompt.

If you're already in iex, you can use the c helper to compile your file without returning to the command line.

```
iex> c "times.exs"
[Times]
iex> Times.double(4)
8
iex> Times.double(123)
246
```

The line c "times.exs" compiles your source file and loads it into iex. We then call the double function in the Times module a couple of times using Times.double.

What happens if we make our function fail by passing it a string rather than a number?

```
iex> Times.double("cat")
** (ArithmeticError) bad argument in arithmetic expression
    times.exs:3: Times.double/1
```

An exception (ArithmeticError) gets raised, and we see a stack backtrace. The first line tells us what went wrong (we tried to perform arithmetic on a string), and the next line tells us where. But look at what it writes for the name of our function: Times.double/1.

In Elixir a named function is identified by both its name and its number of parameters (its *arity*). Our double function takes one parameter, so Elixir knows it as double/1. If we had another version of double that took three parameters, it would be known as double/3. These two functions are totally separate as far as Elixir is concerned. But from a human perspective, you'd imagine that if two functions have the same name they are somehow related, even if they have a different number of parameters. For that reason, don't use the same name for two functions that do unrelated things.

The Function's Body Is a Block

The do...end block is one way of grouping expressions and passing them to other code. They are used in module and named function definitions, control structures...any place in Elixir where code needs to be handled as an entity.

However, do...end is not actually the underlying syntax. The actual syntax looks like this:

```
def double(n), do: n * 2
```

You can pass multiple lines to do: by grouping them with parentheses.

```
def greet(greeting, name), do: (
  IO.puts greeting
  IO.puts "How're you doing, #{name}?"
)
```

The do...end form is just a lump of syntactic sugar—during compilation it is turned into the do: form. (And the do: form itself is nothing special; it is simply a term in a keyword list.) Typically people use the do: syntax for single-line blocks, and do...end for multiline ones.

This means our times example would probably be written as

```
mm/times1.exs
defmodule Times do
  def double(n), do: n * 2
end
```

We could even write it as

```
defmodule Times, do: (def double(n), do: n*2)
```

(but please don't).

Your Turn

➤ *Exercise: ModulesAndFunctions-1*
Extend the Times module with a triple function that multiplies its parameter by three.

➤ *Exercise: ModulesAndFunctions-2*
Run the result in iex. Use both techniques to compile the file.

➤ *Exercise: ModulesAndFunctions-3*
Add a quadruple function. (Maybe it could call the double function....)

Function Calls and Pattern Matching

In the previous chapter we covered how anonymous functions use pattern matching to bind their parameter list to the passed arguments. The same is true of named functions. The difference is that we write the function multiple times, each time with its own parameter list and body. Although this looks like multiple function definitions, purists will tell you it's multiple clauses of the same definition (and they'd be right).

When you call a named function, Elixir tries to match your arguments with the parameter list of the first definition (clause). If it cannot match them, it tries the next definition of the same function (remember, this must have the same arity) and checks to see if it matches. It continues until it runs out of candidates.

Let's play with this. The factorial of *n* (written *n!*) is the product of all numbers from 1 to *n*. By convention, 0! is 1.

Another way of expressing this is to say

- factorial(0) → 1
- factorial(n) → n * factorial(n-1)

This is a specification of factorial, but it is also very close to an Elixir implementation:

```
mm/factorial1.exs
defmodule Factorial do
  def of(0), do: 1
  def of(n), do: n * of(n-1)
end
```

Here we have two definitions *of the same function*. If we call Factorial.of(2), Elixir matches the 2 against the first function's parameter, 0. This fails, so it tries the second definition, which succeeds when Elixir binds 2 to n. It then evaluates the body of this function, which calls Factorial.of(1). The same process applies, and the second definition is run. This, in turn, calls Factorial.of(0), which is matched by the first function definition. This function returns 1 and the recursion ends. Elixir now unwinds the stack, performing all the multiplications, and returns the answer. This factorial implementation works, but it could be significantly improved. We'll do that improvement when we look at tail recursion on page 182.

Let's play with this code:

```
iex> c "factorial1.exs"
[Factorial]
iex> Factorial.of(3)
6
iex> Factorial.of(7)
5040
iex> Factorial.of(10)
3628800
iex> Factorial.of(1000)
40238726007709377354370243392300398571937486421071463254379991042993851239862
90205920442084869694048004799886101971960586316668729948085589013238296699445
...
00624271243416909004153690105933983835777939410970027753472000000000000000000
0000000000000000000000000000000000000000000000000000000000000000000000000000000
0000000000000000000000000000000000000000000000000000000000000000000000000000000
0000000000000000000000000000000000000000000000000000000000000000000000000000000
```

This pattern of design and coding is very common in Elixir (and almost all functional languages). First look for the simplest possible case, one that has a definite answer. This will be the anchor. Then look for a recursive solution that will end up calling the anchor case.

Here are a couple of examples:

Sum of the first n numbers

- The sum of the first 0 numbers is 0.
- The sum of the numbers up to *n* is *n* + the sum of the numbers up to *n–1*.

Length of a list

- The length of an empty list is 0.
- The length of any other list is 1 + the length of the tail of that list.

One point worth stressing: the order of these clauses can make a difference when you translate them into code. Elixir tries functions from the top down, executing the first match. So the following code will not work:

`mm/factorial1-bad.exs`
```
defmodule BadFactorial do
  def of(n), do: n * of(n-1)
  def of(0), do: 1
end
```

The first function definition will always match and the second will never be called. But Elixir has you covered—when you try to compile this, you'll get a warning:

```
iex> c "factorial1-bad.exs"
.../factorial1-bad.ex:3: this clause cannot match because a previous clause at
                   line 2 always matches
```

One more thing: when you have multiple implementations of the same function, they should be adjacent in the source file.

Your Turn

▶ *Exercise: ModulesAndFunctions-4*
  Implement and run a function sum(n) that uses recursion to calculate the sum of the integers from 1 to *n*. You'll need to write this function inside a module in a separate file. Then load up iex, compile that file, and try your function.

▶ *Exercise: ModulesAndFunctions-5*
  Write a function gcd(x,y) that finds the greatest common divisor between two nonnegative integers. Algebraically, *gcd(x,y)* is *x* if *y* is zero; it's *gcd(y, rem(x,y))* otherwise.

Guard Clauses

We've seen that pattern matching allows Elixir to decide which function to invoke based on the arguments passed. But what if we need to distinguish based on their types or on some test involving their values? For this, you use *guard clauses*. These are predicates that are attached to a function definition using one or more when keywords. When doing pattern matching, Elixir first does the conventional parameter-based match and then evaluates any when predicates, executing the function only if at least one predicate is true.

mm/guard.exs
```
defmodule Guard do
  def what_is(x) when is_number(x) do
    IO.puts "#{x} is a number"
  end
  def what_is(x) when is_list(x) do
    IO.puts "#{inspect(x)} is a list"
  end
  def what_is(x) when is_atom(x) do
    IO.puts "#{x} is an atom"
  end
end

Guard.what_is(99)        # => 99 is a number
Guard.what_is(:cat)      # => cat is an atom
Guard.what_is([1,2,3])   # => [1,2,3] is a list
```

Recall our previous factorial example on page 54.

mm/factorial1.exs
```
defmodule Factorial do
  def of(0), do: 1
  def of(n), do: n * of(n-1)
end
```

If we were to pass it a negative number, it would loop forever—no matter how many times you decrement n, it will never be zero. So it is a good idea to add a guard clause to stop this from happening.

mm/factorial2.exs
```
defmodule Factorial do
  def of(0), do: 1
  def of(n) when n > 0 do
    n * of(n-1)
  end
end
```

If you run this code with a negative argument, none of the functions will match:

```
iex> c "factorial2.exs"
[Factorial]
iex> Factorial.of -100
** (FunctionClauseError) no function clause matching in Factorial.of/1...
```

Guard-Clause Limitations

You can write only a subset of Elixir expressions in guard clauses. The following list comes from the Getting Started guide.[1]

Comparison operators
>   ==, !=, ===, !==, >, <, <=, >=

Boolean and negation operators
>   or, and, not, !. Note that || and && are not allowed.

Arithmetic operators
>   +, -, *, /

Join operators
>   <> and ++, as long as the left side is a literal.

The in operator
>   Membership in a collection or range

Type-check functions
>   These built-in Erlang functions return true if their argument is a given type. You can find their documentation online.[2]

>   is_atom is_binary is_bitstring is_boolean is_exception is_float is_function is_integer is_list is_map is_number is_pid is_port is_record is_reference is_tuple

Other functions
>   These built-in functions return values (not true or false). Their documentation is online, on the same page as the type-check functions.

>   abs(number) bit_size(bitstring) byte_size(bitstring) div(number,number) elem(tuple, n) float(term) hd(list) length(list) node() node(pid|ref|port) rem(number,number) round(number) self() tl(list) trunc(number) tuple_size(tuple)

---

1.   http://elixir-lang.org/getting_started/5.html
2.   http://erlang.org/doc/man/erlang.html#is_atom-1

Default Parameters

When you define a named function, you can give a default value to any of its parameters by using the syntax param \\ value. When you call a function that is defined with default parameters, Elixir compares the number of arguments you are passing with the number of required parameters for the function. If you're passing fewer arguments than the number of required parameters, then there's no match. If the two numbers are equal, then the required parameters take the values of the passed arguments, and the other parameters take their default values. If the count of passed arguments is greater than the number of required parameters, Elixir uses the excess to override the default values of some or all parameters. Parameters are matched left to right.

```
mm/default_params.exs
defmodule Example do
  def func(p1, p2 \\ 2, p3 \\ 3, p4) do
    IO.inspect [p1, p2, p3, p4]
  end
end

Example.func("a", "b")            # => ["a",2,3,"b"]
Example.func("a", "b", "c")       # => ["a","b",3,"c"]
Example.func("a", "b", "c", "d")  # => ["a","b","c","d"]
```

Default arguments can behave surprisingly when Elixir does pattern matching. For example, compile the following:

```
def func(p1, p2 \\ 2, p3 \\ 3, p4) do
  IO.inspect [p1, p2, p3, p4]
end

def func(p1, p2) do
  IO.inspect [p1, p2]
end
```

and you'll get this error:

```
** (CompileError) default_params.exs:7: def func/2 conflicts with
                defaults from def func/4
```

That's because the first function definition (with the default parameters) matches any call with two, three, or four arguments.

There's one more thing with default parameters. Here's a function with multiple heads that also has a default parameter:

```
mm/default_params1.exs
defmodule DefaultParams1 do

  def func(p1, p2 \\ 123) do
    IO.inspect [p1, p2]
  end

  def func(p1, 99) do
    IO.puts "you said 99"
  end

end

IO
```

If you compile this, you'll get an error:

```
** (CompileError) default_params1.exs.exs:8: def func/2 has default
                  values and multiple clauses, define a function head
                  with the defaults
```

The intent is to reduce the confusion that can arise with defaults. Simply add a function head with no body that contains the default parameters, and use regular parameters for the rest. The defaults will apply to all calls to the function.

```
mm/default_params2.exs
defmodule Params do

  def func(p1, p2 \\ 123)

  def func(p1, p2) when is_list(p1)   do
    "You said #{p2} with a list"
  end

  def func(p1, p2) do
    "You passed in #{p1} and #{p2}"
  end

end

IO.puts Params.func(99)          # You passed in 99 and 123
IO.puts Params.func(99, "cat")   # You passed in 99 and cat
IO.puts Params.func([99])        # You said 123 with a list
IO.puts Params.func([99], "dog") # You said dog with a list
```

Your Turn

➤ *Exercise: ModulesAndFunctions-6*
I'm thinking of a number between 1 and 1000....

The most efficient way to find the number is to guess halfway between the low and high numbers of the range. If our guess is too big, then the answer lies between the bottom of the range and one less than our guess. If our guess is too small, then the answer lies between one more than our guess and the end of the range.

Your API will be guess(actual, range), where range is an Elixir range.

Your output should look similar to this:

```
iex> Chop.guess(273, 1..1000)
Is it 500
Is it 250
Is it 375
Is it 312
Is it 281
Is it 265
Is it 273
273
```

Hints:

- You may need to implement helper functions with an additional parameter (the currently guessed number).
- The div(a,b) function performs integer division.
- Guard clauses are your friends.
- Patterns can match the low and high parts of a range (a..b=4..8).

Private Functions

The defp macro defines a private function—one that can be called only within the module that declares it.

You can define private functions with multiple heads, just as you can with def. However, you cannot have some heads private and others public. That is, the following code is not valid:

```
def fun(a) when is_list(a), do: true
defp fun(a), do: false
```

The Amazing Pipe Operator: |>

I've saved the best for last, at least when it comes to functions.

You've all seen code like this:

```
people = DB.find_customers
orders = Orders.for_customers(people)
tax    = sales_tax(orders, 2016)
filing = prepare_filing(tax)
```

Bread-and-butter programming. We did it because the alternative was to write

```
filing = prepare_filing(sales_tax(Orders.for_customers(DB.find_customers), 2013))
```

and that's the kind of code that you use to get kids to eat their vegetables. Not only is it hard to read, but you have to read it inside out if you want to see the order in which things get done.

Elixir has a better way of writing it.

```
filing = DB.find_customers
          |> Orders.for_customers
          |> sales_tax(2016)
          |> prepare_filing
```

The |> operator takes the result of the expression to its left and inserts it as the first parameter of the function invocation to its right. So the list of customers the first call returns becomes the argument passed to the for_customers function. The resulting list of orders becomes the first argument to sales_tax, and the given parameter, 2016, becomes the second.

val |> f(a,b) is basically the same as calling f(val,a,b), and

```
list
|> sales_tax(2016)
|> prepare_filing
```

is the same as prepare_filing(sales_tax(list, 2016)).

In the previous example, I wrote each term in the expression on a separate line, and that's perfectly valid Elixir. But you can also chain terms on the same line.

```
iex> (1..10) |> Enum.map(&(&1*&1)) |> Enum.filter(&(&1 < 40))
[1, 4, 9, 16, 25, 36]
```

Note that I had to use parentheses in that code—the & shortcut and the pipe operator fight otherwise.

Let me repeat that—you should always use parentheses around function parameters in pipelines.

The key aspect of the pipe operator is that it lets you write code that pretty much follows your spec's form. For the sales-tax example, you might have jotted this on some paper:

- Get the customer list.
- Generate a list of their orders.
- Calculate tax on the orders.
- Prepare the filing.

To take this from a napkin spec to running code, you just put |> between the items and implement each as a function.

```
DB.find_customers
  |> Orders.for_customers
  |> sales_tax(2016)
  |> prepare_filing
```

Programming is transforming data, and the |> operator makes that transformation explicit.

And now this book's subtitle makes sense.

Modules

Modules provide namespaces for things you define. We've already seen them encapsulating named functions. They also act as wrappers for macros, structs, protocols, and other modules.

If we want to reference a function defined in a module from outside that module, we need to prefix the reference with the module's name. We don't need that prefix if code references something inside the same module as itself, as in the following example.

```
defmodule Mod do
  def func1 do
    IO.puts "in func1"
  end
  def func2 do
    func1
    IO.puts "in func2"
  end
end

Mod.func1
Mod.func2
```

func2 can call func1 directly because it is inside the same module. Outside the module, you have to use the fully qualified name, Mod.func1.

Just as you do in your favorite language, Elixir programmers use nested modules to impose structure for readability and reuse. After all, every programmer is a library writer.

To access a function in a nested module from the outside scope, prefix it with all the module names. To access it within the containing module, use either the fully qualified name or just the inner module name as a prefix.

```elixir
defmodule Outer do
  defmodule Inner do
    def inner_func do
    end
  end

  def outer_func do
    Inner.inner_func
  end
end

Outer.outer_func
Outer.Inner.inner_func
```

Module nesting in Elixir is an illusion—all modules are defined at the top level. When we define a module inside another, Elixir simply prepends the outer module name to the inner module name, putting a dot between the two. This means we can directly define a nested module.

```elixir
defmodule Mix.Tasks.Doctest do
  def run do
  end
end

Mix.Tasks.Doctest.run
```

It also means there's no particular relationship between the modules Mix and Mix.Tasks.Doctest.

Directives for Modules

Elixir has three directives that simplify working with modules. All three are executed as your program runs, and the effect of all three is *lexically scoped*—it starts at the point the directive is encountered, and stops at the end of the enclosing scope. This means a directive in a module definition takes effect from the place you wrote it until the end of the module; a directive in a function definition runs to the end of the function.

The import Directive

The import directive brings a module's functions and/or macros into the current scope. If you use a particular module a lot in your code, import can cut down the clutter in your source files by eliminating the need to repeat the module name time and again.

For example, if you import the flatten function from the List module, you'd be able to call it in your code without having to specify the module name.

```
mm/import.exs
defmodule Example do
  def func1 do
    List.flatten [1,[2,3],4]
  end
  def func2 do
    import List, only: [flatten: 1]
    flatten [5,[6,7],8]
  end
end
```

The full syntax of import is

```
import Module [, only:|except: ]
```

The optional second parameter lets you control which functions or macros are imported. You write only: or except:, followed by a list of name: arity pairs. It is a good idea to use import in the smallest possible enclosing scope and to use only: to import just the functions you need.

```
import List, only: [ flatten: 1, duplicate: 2 ]
```

Alternatively, you can give only: one of the atoms :functions or :macros, and import will bring in only functions or macros.

The alias Directive

The alias directive creates an alias for a module. One obvious use is to cut down on typing.

```
defmodule Example do
  def compile_and_go(source) do
    alias My.Other.Module.Parser, as: Parser
    alias My.Other.Module.Runner, as: Runner
    source
    |> Parser.parse()
    |> Runner.execute()
  end
end
```

We could have abbreviated these alias directives to

```
alias My.Other.Module.Parser
alias My.Other.Module.Runner
```

because the as: parameters default to the last part of the module name. We could even take this further, and do:

```
alias My.Other.Module.{Parser, Runner}
```

The require Directive

You require a module if you want to use any macros it defines. This ensures that the macro definitions are available when your code is compiled. We'll talk about require when we talk about macros on page 267.

Module Attributes

Elixir modules each have associated metadata. Each item of metadata is called an *attribute* of the module and is identified by a name. Inside a module, you can access these attributes by prefixing the name with an at sign (@).

You can give an attribute a value using the syntax

```
@name   value
```

This works only at the top level of a module—you can't set an attribute inside a function definition. You can, however, access attributes inside functions.

```
mm/attributes.exs
defmodule Example do
  @author "Dave Thomas"
  def get_author do
    @author
  end
end


IO.puts "Example was written by #{Example.get_author}"
```

You can set the same attribute multiple times in a module. If you access that attribute in a named function in that module, the value you see will be the value in effect when the function is defined.

```
mm/attributes1.exs
defmodule Example do
  @attr "one"
  def first, do: @attr
  @attr "two"
  def second, do: @attr
end
```

```
IO.puts "#{Example.first}  #{Example.second}"    # => one  two
```

These attributes are not variables in the conventional sense. Use them for configuration and metadata only. (Many Elixir programmers employ them where Java or Ruby programmers might use constants.)

Module Names: Elixir, Erlang, and Atoms

When we write modules in Elixir, they have names such as String or PhotoAlbum. We call functions in them using calls such as String.length("abc").

What's happening here is subtle. Internally, module names are just atoms. When you write a name starting with an uppercase letter, such as IO, Elixir converts it internally into an atom called Elixir.IO.

```
iex> is_atom IO
true
iex> to_string IO
"Elixir.IO"
iex> :"Elixir.IO" === IO
true
```

So a call to a function in a module is really an atom followed by a dot followed by the function name. And, indeed, we can call functions like this:

```
iex> IO.puts 123
123
iex> :"Elixir.IO".puts 123
123
```

Calling a Function in an Erlang Library

The Erlang conventions for names are different—variables start with an uppercase letter and atoms are simple lowercase names. So, for example, the Erlang module timer is called just that, the atom timer. In Elixir we write that as :timer. If you want to refer to the tc function in timer, you'd write :timer.tc. (Note the colon at the start.)

Say we want to output a floating-point number in a three-character-wide field with one decimal place. Erlang has a function for this. A search for erlang format takes us to the description of the format function in the Erlang io module.[3]

Reading the description, we see that Erlang expects us to call io.format. So, in Elixir we simply change the Erlang module name to an Elixir atom:

```
iex> :io.format("The number is ~3.1f~n", [5.678])
```

---

3.   http://erlang.org/doc/man/io.html#format-2

```
The number is 5.7
:ok
```

Finding Libraries

If you're looking for a library to use in your app, you'll want to look first for existing Elixir modules. The built-in ones are documented on the Elixir website,[4] and others are listed at hex.pm and on GitHub (search for *elixir*).

If that fails, search for a built-in Erlang library or search the Web.[5] If you find something written in Erlang, you'll be able to use it in your project (we'll cover how in the chapter on projects, on page 139). But be aware that the Erlang documentation for a library follows Erlang conventions. Variables start with uppercase letters, and identifiers starting with a lowercase letter are atoms (so Erlang would say tomato and Elixir would say :tomato). A summary of the differences between Elixir and Erlang is available online.[6]

Now that we've looked at functions, let's move on to the data they manipulate. And where better to start than with lists, the subject of the next chapter?

Your Turn

➤ *Exercise: ModulesAndFunctions-7*

Find the library functions to do the following, and then use each in iex. (If the word *Elixir* or *Erlang* appears at the end of the challenge, then you'll find the answer in that set of libraries.)

- Convert a float to a string with two decimal digits. (Erlang)
- Get the value of an operating-system environment variable. (Elixir)
- Return the extension component of a file name (so return .exs if given "dave/test.exs"). (Elixir)
- Return the process's current working directory. (Elixir)
- Convert a string containing JSON into Elixir data structures. (Just find; don't install.)
- Execute a command in your operating system's shell.

---

4. http://elixir-lang.org/docs/
5. http://erlang.org/doc/ and http://erldocs.com/R15B/ (Note that the latter is slightly out of date.)
6. http://elixir-lang.org/crash-course.html

In this chapter, you'll see:
- The recursive structure of lists
- Traversing and building lists
- Accumulators
- Implementing map and reduce

## CHAPTER 7

Lists and Recursion

When we program with lists in conventional languages, we treat them as things to be iterated—it seems natural to loop over them. So why do we have a chapter on *lists and recursion*? Because if you look at the problem in the right way, recursion is a perfect tool for processing lists.

Heads and Tails

Earlier we said a list may either be empty or consist of a head and a tail. The head contains a value and the tail is itself a list. This is a recursive definition.

We'll represent the empty list like this: [ ].

Let's imagine we could represent the split between the head and the tail using a pipe character, |. The single element list we normally write as [3] can be written as the value 3 joined to the empty list:

[3 | []]

When we see the pipe character, we say that what is on the left is the head of a list and what's on the right is the tail.

Let's look at the list [2, 3]. The head is 2, and the tail is the single-element list containing 3. And we know what that list looks like—it is our previous example. So we could write [2,3] as

[2 | [3 | []]]

At this point, part of your brain is telling you to go read today's XKCD—this list stuff can't be useful. Ignore that small voice, just for a second. We're about to do something magical. But before we do, let's add one more term, making our list [1, 2, 3]. This is the head 1 followed by the list [2, 3], which is what we derived a moment ago:

[1 | [2 | [3 | []]]]

This is valid Elixir syntax. Type it into iex.

```
iex> [ 1 | [ 2 | [ 3 | [] ] ] ]
[1, 2, 3]
```

And here's the magic. When we discussed pattern matching, we said the pattern could be a list, and the values in that list would be assigned from the right-hand side.

```
iex> [a, b, c ] = [ 1, 2, 3 ]
[1, 2, 3]
iex> a
1
iex> b
2
iex> c
3
```

We can also use the pipe character in the pattern. What's to the left of it matches the head value of the list, and what's to the right matches the tail.

```
iex> [ head | tail ] = [ 1, 2, 3 ]
[1, 2, 3]
iex> head
1
iex> tail
[2, 3]
```

Using Head and Tail to Process a List

Now we can split a list into its head and its tail, and we can construct a list from a value and a list, which become the head and tail of that new list.

So why talk about lists after we talk about modules and functions? Because lists and recursive functions go together like fish and chips. Let's look at finding the length of a list.

- The length of an empty list is 0.
- The length of a list is 1 plus the length of that list's tail.

Writing that in Elixir is easy:

lists/mylist.exs
```
defmodule MyList do
  def len([]), do: 0
  def len([head|tail]), do: 1 + len(tail)
end
```

The only tricky part is the definition of the function's second variant:

```
def len([ head | tail ]) ...
```

How iex Displays Lists

In Chapter 11, *Strings and Binaries*, on page 115, you'll see that Elixir has two representations for strings. One is the familiar sequence of characters in consecutive memory locations. Literals written with double quotes use this form.

The second form, using single quotes, represents strings as a list of integer codepoints. So the string 'cat' is the three codepoints: 99, 97, and 116.

This is a headache for iex. When it sees a list like [99,97,116] it doesn't know if it is supposed to be the string 'cat' or a list of three numbers. So it uses a heuristic. If all the values in a list represent printable characters, it displays the list as a string; otherwise it displays a list of integers.

```
iex> [99, 97, 116]
'cat'
iex> [99, 97, 116, 0]   # '0' is nonprintable
[99, 97, 116, 0]
```

In Chapter 11, *Strings and Binaries*, on page 115, we'll cover how to bypass this behavior. In the meantime, don't be surprised if a string pops up when you were expecting a list.

This is a pattern match for any nonempty list. When it does match, the variable head will hold the value of the first element of the list, and tail will hold the rest of the list. (And remember that every list is terminated by an empty list, so the tail can be [].)

Let's see this at work with the list [11, 12, 13, 14, 15]. At each step, we take off the head and add 1 to the length of the tail:

```
len([11,12,13,14,15])
= 1 + len([12,13,14,15])
= 1 + 1 + len([13,14,15])
= 1 + 1 + 1 + len([14,15])
= 1 + 1 + 1 + 1 + len([15])
= 1 + 1 + 1 + 1 + 1 + len([])
= 1 + 1 + 1 + 1 + 1 + 0
= 5
```

Let's try our code to see if theory works in practice:

```
iex> c "mylist.exs"
...mylist.exs:3: variable head is unused
[MyList]
iex> MyList.len([])
0
iex> MyList.len([11,12,13,14,15])
5
```

It works, but we have a compilation warning—we never used the variable head in the body of our function. We can fix that, and make our code more explicit, using the special variable _ (underscore), which acts as a placeholder. We can also use an underscore in front of any variable name to turn off the warning if that variable isn't used. I sometimes like to do this to document the unused parameter.

```
lists/mylist1.exs
defmodule MyList do
  def len([]),              do: 0
  def len([_head | tail]), do: 1 + len(tail)
end
```

When we compile, the warning is gone. (However, if you compile the second version of MyList, you may get a warning about "redefining module MyList." This is just Elixir being cautious.)

```
iex> c "mylist1.exs"
[MyList]
iex> MyList.len([1,2,3,4,5])
5
iex> MyList.len(["cat", "dog"])
2
```

Using Head and Tail to Build a List

Let's get more ambitious. Let's write a function that takes a list of numbers and returns a new list containing the square of each. We don't show it, but these definitions are also inside the MyList module.

```
lists/mylist1.exs
def square([]),              do: []
def square([ head | tail ]), do: [ head*head | square(tail) ]
```

There's a lot going on here. First, look at the parameter patterns for the two definitions of square. The first matches an empty list and the second matches all other lists.

Second, look at the body of the second definition:

```
def square([ head | tail ]), do: [ head*head | square(tail) ]
```

When we match a nonempty list, we return a new list whose head is the square of the original list's head and whose tail is list of squares of the tail. This is the recursive step.

Let's try it:

```
iex> c "mylist1.exs"
[MyList]
iex> MyList.square []        # this calls the 1st definition
[]
iex> MyList.square [4,5,6]    # and this calls the 2nd
[16, 25, 36]
```

Let's do something similar—a function that adds 1 to every element in the list:

lists/mylist1.exs
```
def add_1([]),               do: []
def add_1([ head | tail ]), do: [ head+1 | add_1(tail) ]
```

And call it:

```
iex> c "mylist1.exs"
[MyList]
iex> MyList.add_1 [1000]
[1001]
iex> MyList.add_1 [4,6,8]
[5, 7, 9]
```

Creating a Map Function

With both square and add_1, all the work is done in the second function definition. And that definition looks about the same for each—it returns a new list whose head is the result of either squaring or incrementing the head of its argument and whose tail is the result of calling itself recursively on the tail of the argument. Let's generalize this. We'll define a function called map that takes a list and a function and returns a new list containing the result of applying that function to each element in the original.

lists/mylist1.exs
```
def map([], _func),               do: []
def map([ head | tail ], func), do: [ func.(head) | map(tail, func) ]
```

The map function is pretty much identical to the square and add_1 functions. It returns an empty list if passed an empty list; otherwise it returns a list where the head is the result of calling the passed-in function and the tail is a recursive call to itself. Note that in the case of an empty list, we use _func as the second parameter. The underscore prevents Elixir from warning us about an unused variable.

To call this function, pass in a list and a function (defined using fn).

```
iex> c "mylist1.exs"
[MyList]
iex> MyList.map [1,2,3,4], fn (n) -> n*n end
[1, 4, 9, 16]
```

A function is just a built-in type, defined between fn and the end. Here we pass a function as the second argument (func) to map. This is invoked inside map using func.(head), which squares the value in head, using the result to build the new list.

We can call map with a different function:

```
iex> MyList.map [1,2,3,4], fn (n) -> n+1 end
[2, 3, 4, 5]
```

And another:

```
iex> MyList.map [1,2,3,4], fn (n) -> n > 2 end
[false, false, true, true]
```

And we can do the same using the & shortcut notation:

```
iex> MyList.map [1,2,3,4], &(&1 + 1)
[2, 3, 4, 5]
iex> MyList.map [1,2,3,4], &(&1 > 2)
[false, false, true, true]
```

Keeping Track of Values During Recursion

So far you've seen how to process each element in a list, but what if we want to sum all of the elements? The difference here is that we need to remember the partial sum as we process each element in turn.

In terms of a recursive structure, it's easy:

- sum([]) → 0
- sum([head | tail]) → *"total"* + sum(tail)

But the basic scheme gives us nowhere to record the total as we go along. Remember that one of our goals is to have immutable state, so we can't keep the value in a global or module-local variable.

But we *can* pass the state in a function's parameter.

```
lists/sum.exs
defmodule MyList do
  def sum([], total),            do: total
  def sum([ head | tail ], total), do: sum(tail, head+total)
end
```

Our sum function now has two parameters, the list and the total so far. In the recursive call, we pass it the list's tail and increment the total by the value of the head.

At all times, these types of functions maintain an *invariant*, a condition that is true on return from any call (or nested call). In this case, the invariant is that at any stage of the recursion, the sum of the elements in the list parameter plus the current total will equal the total of the entire list. Thus, when the list becomes empty the total will be the value we want.

When we call sum we have to remember to pass both the list and the initial total value (which will be 0):

```
iex> c "sum.exs"
[MyList]
iex> MyList.sum([1,2,3,4,5], 0)
15
iex> MyList.sum([11,12,13,14,15], 0)
65
```

Having to remember that extra zero is a little tacky, so the convention in Elixir is to hide it—our module has a public function that takes just a list, and it calls private functions to do the work.

lists/sum2.exs
```
defmodule MyList do

  def sum(list), do: _sum(list, 0)

  # private methods
  defp _sum([], total),              do: total
  defp _sum([ head | tail ], total), do: _sum(tail, head+total)
end
```

Two things to notice here: First, we use defp to define a private function. You won't be able to call these functions outside the module. Second, we chose to give our helper functions the same name as our public function, but with a leading underscore. Elixir treats them as being independent, but a human reader can see that they are clearly related.

(Had we kept the *exact* same name, they would still be different functions, as they have a different arity from the original sum function. The leading underscore simply makes it explicit. Some library code also uses do_*xxx* for these helpers.)

Your Turn

> *Exercise: ListsAndRecursion-0*

I defined our sum function to carry a partial total as a second parameter so I could illustrate how to use accumulators to build values. The sum function can also be written without an accumulator. Can you do it?

Generalizing Our Sum Function

The sum function reduces a collection to a single value. Clearly other functions need to do something similar—return the greatest/least value, the product of the elements, a string containing a concatenation of elements, and so on. How can we write a general-purpose function that reduces a collection to a value?

We know it has to take a collection. We also know we need to pass in some initial value (just like our sum/1 function passed a 0 as an initial value to its helper). Additionally, we need to pass in a function that takes the current value of the reduction along with the next element of the collection, and returns the next value of the reduction. So, it looks like our reduce function will be called with three arguments:

reduce(collection, initial_value, fun)

Now let's think about the recursive design:

- reduce([], value, _) → value
- reduce([head |tail], value, fun) → reduce(tail, fun.(head, value), fun)

reduce applies the function to the list's head and the current value, and passes the result as the new current value when reducing the list's tail.

Here's our code for reduce. See how closely it follows the design.

```
lists/reduce.exs
defmodule MyList do
  def reduce([], value, _) do
    value
  end
  def reduce([head | tail], value, func) do
    reduce(tail, func.(head, value), func)
  end
end
```

And, again, we can use the shorthand notation to pass in the function:

```
iex> c "reduce.exs"
[MyList]
iex> MyList.reduce([1,2,3,4,5], 0, &(&1 + &2))
15
iex> MyList.reduce([1,2,3,4,5], 1, &(&1 * &2))
120
```

Your Turn

➤ *Exercise: ListsAndRecursion-1*

Write a `mapsum` function that takes a list and a function. It applies the function to each element of the list and then sums the result, so

```
iex> MyList.mapsum [1, 2, 3], &(&1 * &1)
14
```

➤ *Exercise: ListsAndRecursion-2*

Write a `max(list)` that returns the element with the maximum value in the list. (This is slightly trickier than it sounds.)

➤ *Exercise: ListsAndRecursion-3*

An Elixir single-quoted string is actually a list of individual character codes. Write a `caesar(list, n)` function that adds `n` to each list element, wrapping if the addition results in a character greater than z.

```
iex> MyList.caesar('ryvkve', 13)
?????? :)
```

More Complex List Patterns

Not every list problem can be easily solved by processing one element at a time. Fortunately, the join operator, |, supports multiple values to its left. Thus, you could write

```
iex> [ 1, 2, 3 | [ 4, 5, 6 ]]
[1, 2, 3, 4, 5, 6]
```

The same thing works in patterns, so you can match multiple individual elements as the head. For example, the following program swaps pairs of values in a list.

lists/swap.exs
```
defmodule Swapper do
  def swap([]), do: []
  def swap([ a, b | tail ]), do: [ b, a | swap(tail) ]
  def swap([_]), do: raise "Can't swap a list with an odd number of elements"
end
```

We can play with it in iex:

```
iex> c "swap.exs"
[Swapper]
iex> Swapper.swap [1,2,3,4,5,6]
[2, 1, 4, 3, 6, 5]
iex> Swapper.swap [1,2,3,4,5,6,7]
** (RuntimeError) Can't swap a list with an odd number of elements
```

The third definition of swap matches a list with a single element. This will happen if we get to the end of the recursion and have only one element left. As we take two values off the list on each cycle, the initial list must have had an odd number of elements.

Lists of Lists

Let's imagine we had recorded temperatures and rainfall at a number of weather stations. Each reading looks like this:

```
[ timestamp, location_id, temperature, rainfall ]
```

Our code is passed a list containing a number of these readings, and we want to report on the conditions for one particular location, number 27.

```
lists/weather.exs
defmodule WeatherHistory do

  def for_location_27([]), do: []
  def for_location_27([ [time, 27, temp, rain ] | tail]) do
    [ [time, 27, temp, rain] | for_location_27(tail) ]
  end
  def for_location_27([ _ | tail]), do: for_location_27(tail)

end
```

This is a standard *recurse until the list is empty* stanza. But look at our function definition's second clause. Where we'd normally match into a variable called head, here the pattern is

```
for_location_27([ [ time, 27, temp, rain ] | tail])
```

For this to match, the head of the list must itself be a four-element list, and the second element of this sublist must be 27. This function will execute only for entries from the desired location. But when we do this kind of filtering, we also have to remember to deal with the case when our function doesn't match. That's what the third line does. We could have written

```
for_location_27([ [ time, _, temp, rain ] | tail])
```

but in reality we don't care *what* is in the head at this point.

In the same module we define some simple test data:

```
lists/weather.exs
def test_data do
  [
    [1366225622, 26, 15, 0.125],
    [1366225622, 27, 15, 0.45],
    [1366225622, 28, 21, 0.25],
    [1366229222, 26, 19, 0.081],
    [1366229222, 27, 17, 0.468],
    [1366229222, 28, 15, 0.60],
    [1366232822, 26, 22, 0.095],
    [1366232822, 27, 21, 0.05],
    [1366232822, 28, 24, 0.03],
    [1366236422, 26, 17, 0.025]
  ]
end
```

We can use that to play with our function in iex. To make this easier, I'm using the import function. This adds the functions in WeatherHistory to our local name scope. After calling import we don't have to put the module name in front of every function call.

```
iex> c "weather.exs"
[WeatherHistory]
iex> import WeatherHistory
nil
iex> for_location_27(test_data)
[[1366225622, 27, 15, 0.45], [1366229222, 27, 17, 0.468],
 [1366232822, 27, 21, 0.05]]
```

Our function is specific to a particular location, which is pretty limiting. We'd like to be able to pass in the location as a parameter. We can use pattern matching for this.

```
lists/weather2.exs
defmodule WeatherHistory do

  def for_location([], _target_loc), do: []

➤ def for_location([ [time, target_loc, temp, rain ] | tail], target_loc) do
    [ [time, target_loc, temp, rain] | for_location(tail, target_loc) ]
  end

  def for_location([ _ | tail], target_loc), do: for_location(tail, target_loc)

end
```

Now the second function fires only when the location extracted from the list head equals the target location passed as a parameter.

But we can improve on this. Our filter doesn't care about the other three fields in the head—it just needs the location. But we do need the value of the head itself to create the output list. Fortunately, Elixir pattern matching is recursive and we can match patterns inside patterns.

```
lists/weather3.exs
defmodule WeatherHistory do

  def for_location([], target_loc), do: []

➤ def for_location([ head = [_, target_loc, _, _ ] | tail], target_loc) do
    [ head | for_location(tail, target_loc) ]
  end

  def for_location([ _ | tail], target_loc), do: for_location(tail, target_loc)

end
```

The key change here is this line:

```
def for_location([ head = [_, target_loc, _, _ ] | tail], target_loc)
```

Compare that with the previous version:

```
def for_location([ [ time, target_loc, temp, rain ] | tail], target_loc)
```

In the new version, we use placeholders for the fields we don't care about. But we also match the entire four-element array into the parameter head. It's as if we said "match the head of the list where the second element is matched to target_loc and then match that whole head with the variable head." We've extracted an individual component of the sublist as well as the entire sublist.

In the original body of for_location, we generated our result list using the individual fields:

```
def for_location([ [ time, target_loc, temp, rain ] | tail], target_loc)
  [ [ time, target_loc, temp, rain ] | for_location(tail, target_loc) ]
end
```

In the new version, we can just use the head, making it a lot more clear:

```
def for_location([ head = [_, target_loc, _, _ ] | tail], target_loc)  do
  [ head | for_location(tail, target_loc) ]
end
```

Your Turn

➤ *Exercise: ListsAndRecursion-4*
Write a function MyList.span(from, to) that returns a list of the numbers from from up to to.

The List Module in Action

The List module provides a set of functions that operate on lists.

```
#
# Concatenate lists
#
iex> [1,2,3] ++ [4,5,6]
[1, 2, 3, 4, 5, 6]
#
# Flatten
#
iex> List.flatten([[[1], 2], [[[3]]]])
[1, 2, 3]
#
# Folding (like reduce, but can choose direction)
#
iex> List.foldl([1,2,3], "", fn value, acc -> "#{value}(#{acc})" end)
"3(2(1()))"
iex> List.foldr([1,2,3], "", fn value, acc -> "#{value}(#{acc})" end)
"1(2(3()))"
#
# Updating in the middle (not a cheap operation)
#
iex> list = [ 1, 2, 3 ]
[ 1, 2, 3 ]
iex> List.replace_at(list, 2, "buckle my shoe")
[1, 2, "buckle my shoe"]
#
# Accessing tuples within lists
#
iex> kw = [{:name, "Dave"}, {:likes, "Programming"}, {:where, "Dallas", "TX"}]
[{:name, "Dave"}, {:likes, "Programming"}, {:where, "Dallas", "TX"}]
iex> List.keyfind(kw, "Dallas", 1)
{:where, "Dallas", "TX"}
iex> List.keyfind(kw, "TX", 2)
{:where, "Dallas", "TX"}
iex> List.keyfind(kw, "TX", 1)
nil
iex> List.keyfind(kw, "TX", 1, "No city called TX")
"No city called TX"
iex> kw = List.keydelete(kw, "TX", 2)
[name: "Dave", likes: "Programming"]
iex> kw = List.keyreplace(kw, :name, 0, {:first_name, "Dave"})
[first_name: "Dave", likes: "Programming"]
```

Get Friendly with Lists

Lists are the natural data structure to use when you have a stream of values to handle. You'll use them to parse data, handle collections of values, and record the results of a series of function calls. It's worth spending a while getting comfortable with them.

Next we'll look at the various dictionary types, including maps. These let us organize data into collections of key/value pairs.

In this chapter, you'll see:
• The two and a half dictionary data types
• Pattern matching and updating maps
• Structs
• Nested data structures

## CHAPTER 8

Maps, Keyword Lists, Sets, and Structs

A dictionary is a data type that associates keys with values.

We've already looked briefly at the dictionary types: maps and keyword lists. In this short chapter we'll cover how to use them with pattern matching and how to update them. Finally we'll look at the Keyword module, which implements a specialized dictionary intended for storing function and program options, and the MapSet module, which implements sets.

First, though, let's answer a common question—how do we choose an appropriate dictionary type for a particular need?

How to Choose Between Maps and Keyword Lists

Ask yourself these questions (in this order):

• Do I want to pattern-match against the contents (for example, matching a dictionary that has a key of :name somewhere in it)?

  If so, use a map.

• Will I want more than one entry with the same key?

  If so, you'll have to use the Keyword module.

• Do I need to guarantee the elements are ordered?

  If so, again, use the Keyword module.

• And, if you've reached this point:

  Use a map.

Keyword Lists

Keyword lists are typically used in the context of options passed to functions.

```
maps/keywords.exs
defmodule Canvas do

  @defaults [ fg: "black", bg: "white", font: "Merriweather" ]

  def draw_text(text, options \\ []) do
    options = Keyword.merge(@defaults, options)
    IO.puts "Drawing text #{inspect(text)}"
    IO.puts "Foreground: #{options[:fg]}"
    IO.puts "Background: #{Keyword.get(options, :bg)}"
    IO.puts "Font:       #{Keyword.get(options, :font)}"
    IO.puts "Pattern:    #{Keyword.get(options, :pattern, "solid")}"
    IO.puts "Style:      #{inspect Keyword.get_values(options, :style)}"
  end

end

Canvas.draw_text("hello", fg: "red", style: "italic", style: "bold")

# =>
#   Drawing text "hello"
#   Foreground: red
#   Background: white
#   Font:       Merriweather
#   Pattern:    solid
#   Style:      ["italic", "bold"]
```

For simple access, you can use the access operator, *kwlist[key]*. In addition, all the functions of the Keyword[1] and Enum[2] modules are available.

Maps

Maps are the go-to key/value data structure in Elixir. They have good performance at all sizes.

Let's play with the Map API:[3]

```
iex> map = %{ name: "Dave", likes: "Programming", where: "Dallas" }
%{likes: "Programming", name: "Dave", where: "Dallas"}
iex> Map.keys map
[:likes, :name, :where]
iex> Map.values map
["Programming", "Dave", "Dallas"]
iex> map[:name]
"Dave"
iex> map.name
```

---

1.   http://elixir-lang.org/docs/master/elixir/Keyword.html
2.   http://elixir-lang.org/docs/master/elixir/Enum.html
3.   http://elixir-lang.org/docs/master/elixir/Map.html

```
"Dave"
iex> map1 = Map.drop map, [:where, :likes]
%{name: "Dave"}
iex> map2 = Map.put map, :also_likes, "Ruby"
%{also_likes: "Ruby", likes: "Programming", name: "Dave", where: "Dallas"}
iex> Map.keys map2
[:also_likes, :likes, :name, :where]
iex> Map.has_key? map1, :where
false
iex> { value, updated_map } = Map.pop map2, :also_likes
{"Ruby", %{likes: "Programming", name: "Dave", where: "Dallas"}}
iex> Map.equal? map, updated_map
true
```

Pattern Matching and Updating Maps

The question we most often ask of our maps is, "Do you have the following keys (and maybe values)?" For example, given the map:

```
person = %{ name: "Dave", height: 1.88 }
```

- Is there an entry with the key :name?

  ```
  iex> %{ name: a_name } = person
  %{height: 1.88, name: "Dave"}
  iex> a_name
  "Dave"
  ```

- Are there entries for the keys :name and :height?

  ```
  iex> %{ name: _, height: _ } = person
  %{height: 1.88, name: "Dave"}
  ```

- Does the entry with key :name have the value "Dave"?

  ```
  iex> %{ name: "Dave" } = person
  %{height: 1.88, name: "Dave"}
  ```

Our map does not have the key :weight, so the following pattern match fails:

```
iex> %{ name: _, weight: _ } = person
** (MatchError) no match of right hand side value: %{height: 1.88, name: "Dave"}
```

It's worth noting how the first pattern match destructured the map, extracting the value associated with the key :name. We can use this in many ways. Here's one example. The for construct lets us iterate over a collection, filtering as we go. We cover it when we talk about enumerating on page 109. The following example uses for to iterate over a list of people. Destructuring is used to extract the height value, which is used to filter the results.

```
maps/query.exs
people = [
  %{ name: "Grumpy",     height: 1.24 },
  %{ name: "Dave",       height: 1.88 },
  %{ name: "Dopey",      height: 1.32 },
  %{ name: "Shaquille",  height: 2.16 },
  %{ name: "Sneezy",     height: 1.28 }
]

IO.inspect(for person = %{ height: height } <- people,
                           height > 1.5,
           do: person)
```

This produces

```
[%{height: 1.88, name: "Dave"}, %{height: 2.16, name: "Shaquille"}]
```

In this code, we feed a list of maps to our comprehension. The generator clause binds each map (as a whole) to person and binds the height from that map to height. The filter selects only those maps where the height exceeds 1.5, and the do block prints the whole map.

Clearly pattern matching is just pattern matching, so this maps capability works equally well in cond expressions, function head matching, and any other circumstances in which patterns are used.

```
maps/book_room.exs
defmodule HotelRoom do

  def book(%{name: name, height: height})
  when height > 1.9 do
    IO.puts "Need extra long bed for #{name}"
  end

  def book(%{name: name, height: height})
  when height < 1.3 do
    IO.puts "Need low shower controls for #{name}"
  end

  def book(person) do
    IO.puts "Need regular bed for #{person.name}"
  end

end

people |> Enum.each(&HotelRoom.book/1)

#=> Need low shower controls for Grumpy
#   Need regular bed for Dave
#   Need regular bed for Dopey
```

```
#   Need extra long bed for Shaquille
#   Need low shower controls for Sneezy
```

Pattern Matching Can't Bind Keys

Maps do not allow you to bind a value to a key during pattern matching. Thus, you can write this:

```
iex> %{ 2 => state } = %{ 1 => :ok, 2 => :error }
%{1 => :ok, 2 => :error}
iex> state
:error
```

but not this:

```
iex> %{ item => :ok } = %{ 1 => :ok, 2 => :error }
** (CompileError) iex:5: illegal use of variable item in map key…
```

Pattern Matching Can Match Variable Keys

When we looked at basic pattern matching, we saw that the pin operator on page 19 could be used to use the value already in a variable on the left-hand side of a match. We can do the same with the keys of a map:

```
iex> data = %{ name: "Dave", state: "TX", likes: "Elixir" }
%{likes: "Elixir", name: "Dave", state: "TX"}
iex> for key <- [ :name, :likes ] do
...>    %{ ^key => value } = data
...>    value
...> end
["Dave", "Elixir"]
```

Updating a Map

In the previous chapter we saw how lists are updated through a combination of copying and changing the head.

With maps, we can add new key/value entries and update existing entries without traversing the whole structure. But as with all values in Elixir, a map is immutable, and so the result of the update is a new map.

The simplest way to update a map is with this syntax:

```
new_map = %{ old_map | key => value, … }
```

This creates a new map that is a copy of the old, but the values associated with the keys on the right of the pipe character are updated:

```
iex> m = %{ a: 1, b: 2, c: 3 }
%{a: 1, b: 2, c: 3}
iex> m1 = %{ m | b: "two", c: "three" }
```

```
%{a: 1, b: "two", c: "three"}
iex> m2 = %{ m1 | a: "one" }
%{a: "one", b: "two", c: "three"}
```

However, this syntax will not add a new key to a map. To do this, you have to use the Map.put_new/3 function.

Structs

When Elixir sees %{ ... } it knows it is looking at a map. But it doesn't know much more than that. In particular, it doesn't know what you intend to do with the map, whether only certain keys are allowed, or whether some keys should have default values.

That's fine for anonymous maps. But what if we want to create a typed map—a map that has a fixed set of fields and default values for those fields, and that you can pattern-match by type as well as content.

Enter the *struct*.

A struct is just a module that wraps a limited form of map. It's limited because the keys must be atoms and because these maps don't have Dict capabilities.

The name of the module becomes the name of the map type. Inside the module, you use the defstruct macro to define the map's characteristics.

```
maps/defstruct.exs
defmodule Subscriber do
  defstruct name: "", paid: false, over_18: true
end
```

Let's play with this in iex:

```
$ iex defstruct.exs
iex> s1 = %Subscriber{}
%Subscriber{name: "", over_18: true, paid: false}
iex> s2 = %Subscriber{ name: "Dave" }
%Subscriber{name: "Dave", over_18: true, paid: false}
iex> s3 = %Subscriber{ name: "Mary", paid: true }
%Subscriber{name: "Mary", over_18: true, paid: true}
```

The syntax for creating a struct is the same as the syntax for creating a map—you simply add the module name between the % and the {.

You access the fields in a struct using dot notation or pattern matching:

```
iex> s3.name
"Mary"
iex> %Subscriber{name: a_name} = s3
%Subscriber{name: "Mary", over_18: true, paid: true}
```

```
iex> a_name
"Mary"
```

And updates follow suit:

```
iex> s4 = %Subscriber{ s3 | name: "Marie"}
%Subscriber{name: "Marie", over_18: true, paid: true}
```

Why are structs wrapped in a module? The idea is that you are likely to want to add struct-specific behaviour.

```
maps/defstruct1.exs
defmodule Attendee do
  defstruct name: "", paid: false, over_18: true

  def may_attend_after_party(attendee = %Attendee{}) do
    attendee.paid && attendee.over_18
  end

  def print_vip_badge(%Attendee{name: name}) when name !=  "" do
    IO.puts "Very cheap badge for #{name}"
  end

  def print_vip_badge(%Attendee{}) do
    raise "missing name for badge"
  end
end
```

```
$ iex defstruct1.exs
iex> a1 = %Attendee{name: "Dave", over_18: true}
%Attendee{name: "Dave", over_18: true, paid: false}
iex> Attendee.may_attend_after_party(a1)
false
iex> a2 = %Attendee{a1 | paid: true}
%Attendee{name: "Dave", over_18: true, paid: true}
iex> Attendee.may_attend_after_party(a2)
true
iex> Attendee.print_vip_badge(a2)
Very cheap badge for Dave
:ok
iex> a3 = %Attendee{}
%Attendee{name: "", over_18: true, paid: false}
iex> Attendee.print_vip_badge(a3)
** (RuntimeError) missing name for badge
     defstruct1.exs:13: Attendee.print_vip_badge/1
```

Notice how we could call the functions in the Attendee module to manipulate the associated struct.

Structs also play a large role when implementing polymorphism, which we'll see when we look at protocols on page 293.

Nested Dictionary Structures

The various dictionary types let us associate keys with values. But those values can themselves be dictionaries. For example, we may have a bug-reporting system. We could represent this using the following:

```
maps/nested.exs
defmodule Customer do
  defstruct name: "", company: ""
end

defmodule BugReport do
  defstruct owner: %Customer{}, details: "", severity: 1
end
```

Let's create a simple report:

```
iex> report = %BugReport{owner: %Customer{name: "Dave", company: "Pragmatic"},
...>                     details: "broken"}
%BugReport{details: "broken",
         owner: %Customer{company: "Pragmatic", name: "Dave"},
         severity: 1}
```

The owner attribute of the report is itself a Customer struct.

We can access nested fields using regular dot notation:

```
iex> report.owner.company
"Pragmatic"
```

But now our customer complains the company name is incorrect—it should be PragProg. Let's fix it:

```
iex> report = %BugReport{ report | owner:
...>                              %Customer{ report.owner | company: "PragProg" }}
%BugReport{details: "broken",
 owner: %Customer{company: "PragProg", name: "Dave"},
 severity: 1}
```

Ugly stuff! We had to update the overall bug report's owner attribute with an updated customer structure. This is verbose, hard to read, and error prone.

Fortunately, Elixir has a set of nested dictionary-access functions. One of these, put_in, lets us set a value in a nested structure:

```
iex> put_in(report.owner.company, "PragProg")
%BugReport{details: "broken",
 owner: %Customer{company: "PragProg", name: "Dave"},
 severity: 1}
```

This isn't magic—it's simply a macro that generates the long-winded code we'd have to have written otherwise.

The update_in function lets us apply a function to a value in a structure.

```
iex> update_in(report.owner.name, &("Mr. " <> &1))
%BugReport{details: "broken",
  owner: %Customer{company: "PragProg", name: "Mr. Dave"},
```

```
    severity: 1}
```

The other two nested access functions are get_in and get_and_update_in. The documentation in iex contains everything you need for these. However, both of these functions support a cool trick: nested access.

Nested Accessors and Nonstructs

If you are using the nested accessor functions with maps or keyword lists, you can supply the keys as atoms:

```
iex> report = %{ owner: %{ name: "Dave", company: "Pragmatic" }, severity: 1}
%{owner: %{company: "Pragmatic", name: "Dave"}, severity: 1}
iex> put_in(report[:owner][:company], "PragProg")
%{owner: %{company: "PragProg", name: "Dave"}, severity: 1}
iex> update_in(report[:owner][:name], &("Mr. " <> &1))
%{owner: %{company: "Pragmatic", name: "Mr. Dave"}, severity: 1}
```

Dynamic (Runtime) Nested Accessors

The nested accessors we've seen so far are macros—they operate at compile time. As a result, they have some limitations:

- The number of keys you pass a particular call is static.
- You can't pass the set of keys as parameters between functions.

These are a natural consequence of the way the macros bake their parameters into code at compile time.

To overcome this, get_in, put_in, update_in, and get_and_update_in can all take a list of keys as a separate parameter. Adding this parameter changes them from macros to function calls, so they become dynamic.

	Macro	Function
get_in	*no*	(dict, keys)
put_in	(path, value)	(dict, keys, value)
update_in	(path, fn)	(dict, keys, fn)
get_and_update_in	(path, fn)	(dict, keys, fn)

Here's a simple example:

maps/dynamic_nested.exs
```
nested = %{
    buttercup: %{
      actor: %{
        first: "Robin",
        last:  "Wright"
      },
      role: "princess"
```

```
      },
    westley: %{
      actor: %{
        first: "Carey",
        last:  "Ewes"       # typo!
      },
      role: "farm boy"
    }
}

IO.inspect get_in(nested, [:buttercup])
# => %{actor: %{first: "Robin", last: "Wright"}, role: "princess"}

IO.inspect get_in(nested, [:buttercup, :actor])
# => %{first: "Robin", last: "Wright"}

IO.inspect get_in(nested, [:buttercup, :actor, :first])
# => "Robin"

IO.inspect put_in(nested, [:westley, :actor, :last], "Elwes")
# => %{buttercup: %{actor: %{first: "Robin", last: "Wright"}, role: "princess"},
# =>     westley: %{actor: %{first: "Carey", last: "Elwes"}, role: "farm boy"}}
```

There's a cool trick that the dynamic versions of both get_in and get_and_update_in
support—if you pass a function as a key, that function is invoked to return
the corresponding values.

maps/get_in_func.exs
```
authors = [
  %{ name: "José",  language: "Elixir" },
  %{ name: "Matz",  language: "Ruby" },
  %{ name: "Larry", language: "Perl" }
]

languages_with_an_r = fn (:get, collection, next_fn) ->
    for row <- collection do
      if String.contains?(row.language, "r") do
        next_fn.(row)
      end
    end
end

IO.inspect get_in(authors, [languages_with_an_r, :name])
#=> [ "José", nil, "Larry" ]
```

Sets

There is currently just one implementation of sets, the MapSet.

```
iex> set1 = Enum.into 1..5, MapSet.new
#MapSet<[1, 2, 3, 4, 5]>
```

```
iex> MapSet.member? set1, 3
true
iex> set2 = Enum.into 3..8, MapSet.new
#MapSet<[3, 4, 5, 6, 7, 8]>
iex> MapSet.union set1, set2
#MapSet<[7, 6, 4, 1, 8, 2, 3, 5]>
iex> MapSet.difference set1, set2
#MapSet<[1, 2]>
iex> MapSet.difference set2, set1
#MapSet<[6, 7, 8]>
iex> MapSet.intersection set1, set2
#MapSet<[3, 4, 5]>
```

With Great Power Comes Great Temptation

The dictionary types are clearly a powerful tool—you'll use them all the time. But you might also be tempted to abuse them. Structs in particular might lead you into the darkness because you can associate functions with them in their module definitions. At some point, the old object-orientation neurons still active in the nether regions of your brain might burst into life and you might think, "Hey, this is a bit like a class definition." And you'd be right. You *can* write something akin to object-oriented code using structs (or maps) and modules.

This is a bad idea. Not because objects are intrinsically bad, but because you'll be mixing paradigms and diluting the benefits a functional approach gives you.

Stay pure, young coder. Stay pure.

As a way of refocusing you away from the dark side, the next chapter is a mini diversion into the benefits of separating functions and the data they work on. And we disguise it in a discussion of types.

## CHAPTER 9

An Aside—What Are Types?

The preceding two chapters described the basics of lists and maps. But you may have noticed that, although I talked about them as types, I didn't really say what I meant.

The first thing to understand is that the primitive data types are not necessarily the same as the types they can represent.

For example, a primitive Elixir list is just an ordered list of values. We can use the [...] literal to create a list, and the | operator to deconstruct and build lists.

Then there's another layer. Elixir has the List module, which provides a set of functions that operate on lists. Often these functions simply use recursion and the | operator to add this extra functionality.

In my mind, there's a difference between the primitive list and the functionality of the List module. The primitive list is an implementation, whereas the List module adds a layer of abstraction. Both implement types, but the type is different. Primitive lists, for example, don't have a flatten function.

Maps are also a primitive type. And, like lists, they have an Elixir module that implements a richer, derived map type.

The Keyword type is an Elixir module. But it is implemented as a list of tuples:

```
options = [ {:width, 72}, {:style, "light"}, {:style, "print"} ]
```

Clearly this is still a list, and all the list functions will work on it. But Elixir adds functionality to give you dictionary-like behaviour.

```
iex> options = [ {:width, 72}, {:style, "light"}, {:style, "print"} ]
[width: 72, style: "light", style: "print"]
iex> List.last options
{:style, "print"}
```

```
iex> Keyword.get_values options, :style
["light", "print"]
```

In a way, this is a form of the duck typing that is talked about in dynamic object-oriented languages.[1] The Keyword module doesn't have an underlying primitive data type. It simply assumes that any value it works on is a list that has been structured a certain way.

This means the APIs for collections in Elixir are fairly broad. Working with a keyword list, you have access to the APIs in the primitive list type, and the List and Keyword modules. You also get Enum and Collectable, which we talk about next.

---

1. http://en.wikipedia.org/wiki/Duck_typing

## CHAPTER 10

Processing Collections—Enum and Stream

Elixir comes with a number of types that act as collections. We've already seen lists and maps. Ranges, files, and even functions can also act as collections. And as we'll discuss when we look at protocols on page 293, you can also define your own.

Collections differ in their implementation. But they all share something: you can iterate through them. Some of them share an additional trait: you can add things to them.

Technically, things that can be iterated are said to implement the Enumerable protocol.

Elixir provides two modules that have a bunch of iteration functions. The Enum module is the workhorse for collections. You'll use it all the time. I strongly recommend getting to know it.

The Stream module lets you enumerate a collection lazily. This means that the next value is calculated only when it is needed. You'll use this less often, but when you do it's a lifesaver.

I don't want to fill this book with a list of all the APIs. You'll find the definitive (and up-to-date) list online.[1] Instead, I'll illustrate some common uses and let you browse the documentation for yourself. (But please do remember to do so. Much of Elixir's power comes from these libraries.)

Enum—Processing Collections

The Enum module is probably the most used of all the Elixir libraries. Employ it to iterate, filter, combine, split, and otherwise manipulate collections. Here are some common tasks:

---

1. http://elixir-lang.org/docs/

- Convert any collection into a list:

```
iex> list = Enum.to_list 1..5
[1, 2, 3, 4, 5]
```

- Concatenate collections:

```
iex> Enum.concat([1,2,3], [4,5,6])
[1, 2, 3, 4, 5, 6]
iex> Enum.concat [1,2,3], 'abc'
[1, 2, 3, 97, 98, 99]
```

- Create collections whose elements are some function of the original:

```
iex> Enum.map(list, &(&1 * 10))
[10, 20, 30, 40, 50]
iex> Enum.map(list, &String.duplicate("*", &1))
["*", "**", "***", "****", "*****"]
```

- Select elements by position or criteria:

```
iex> Enum.at(10..20, 3)
13
iex> Enum.at(10..20, 20)
nil
iex> Enum.at(10..20, 20, :no_one_here)
:no_one_here
iex> Enum.filter(list, &(&1 > 2))
[3, 4, 5]
iex> require Integer     # to get access to is_even
nil
iex> Enum.filter(list, &Integer.is_even/1)
[2, 4]
iex> Enum.reject(list, &Integer.is_even/1)
[1, 3, 5]
```

- Sort and compare elements:

```
iex> Enum.sort ["there", "was", "a", "crooked", "man"]
["a", "crooked", "man", "there", "was"]
iex> Enum.sort ["there", "was", "a", "crooked", "man"],
...>        &(String.length(&1) <= String.length(&2))
["a", "was", "man", "there", "crooked"]
iex(4)> Enum.max ["there", "was", "a", "crooked", "man"]
"was"
iex(5)> Enum.max_by ["there", "was", "a", "crooked", "man"], &String.length/1
"crooked"
```

- Split a collection:

```
iex> Enum.take(list, 3)
[1, 2, 3]
iex> Enum.take_every list, 2
```

```
[1, 3, 5]
iex> Enum.take_while(list, &(&1 < 4))
[1, 2, 3]
iex> Enum.split(list, 3)
{[1, 2, 3], [4, 5]}
iex> Enum.split_while(list, &(&1 < 4))
{[1, 2, 3], [4, 5]}
```

- Join a collection:

```
iex> Enum.join(list)
"12345"
iex> Enum.join(list, ", ")
"1, 2, 3, 4, 5"
```

- Predicate operations:

```
iex> Enum.all?(list, &(&1 < 4))
false
iex> Enum.any?(list, &(&1 < 4))
true
iex> Enum.member?(list, 4)
true
iex> Enum.empty?(list)
false
```

- Merge collections:

```
iex> Enum.zip(list, [:a, :b, :c])
[{1, :a}, {2, :b}, {3, :c}]
iex> Enum.with_index(["once", "upon", "a", "time"])
[{"once", 0}, {"upon", 1}, {"a", 2}, {"time", 3}]
```

- Fold elements into a single value:

```
iex> Enum.reduce(1..100, &(&1+&2))
5050
iex> Enum.reduce(["now", "is", "the", "time"],fn word, longest ->
...>        if String.length(word) > String.length(longest) do
...>            word
...>        else
...>            longest
...>        end
...> end)
"time"
iex> Enum.reduce(["now", "is", "the", "time"], 0, fn word, longest ->
...>        if    String.length(word) > longest,
...>        do:   String.length(word),
...>        else: longest
...> end)
4
```

- Deal a hand of cards:

```
iex> import Enum
iex> deck = for rank <- '23456789TJQKA', suit <- 'CDHS', do: [suit,rank]
['C2', 'D2', 'H2', 'S2', 'C3', 'D3', ... ]
iex> deck |> shuffle |> take(13)
['DQ', 'S6', 'HJ', 'H4', 'C7', 'D6', 'SJ', 'S9', 'D7', 'HA', 'S4', 'C2', 'CT']
iex> hands = deck |> shuffle |> chunk(13)
[['D8', 'CQ', 'H2', 'H3', 'HK', 'H9', 'DK', 'S9', 'CT', 'ST', 'SK', 'D2', 'HA'],
 ['C5', 'S3', 'CK', 'HQ', 'D3', 'D4', 'CA', 'C8', 'S6', 'DQ', 'H5', 'S2', 'C4'],
 ['C7', 'C6', 'C2', 'D6', 'D7', 'SA', 'SQ', 'H8', 'DT', 'C3', 'H7', 'DA', 'HT'],
 ['S5', 'S4', 'C9', 'S8', 'D5', 'H4', 'S7', 'SJ', 'HJ', 'D9', 'DJ', 'CJ', 'H6']]
```

A Note on Sorting

In our example of sort, we used

```
iex> Enum.sort ["there", "was", "a", "crooked", "man"],
...>        &(String.length(&1) <= String.length(&2))
```

It's important to use <= and not just < if you want the sort to be *stable*.

Your Turn

➤ *Exercise: ListsAndRecursion-5*

Implement the following Enum functions using no library functions or list comprehensions: all?, each, filter, split, and take. You may need to use an if statement to implement filter. The syntax for this is

```
if condition do
  expression(s)
else
  expression(s)
end
```

➤ *Exercise: ListsAndRecursion-6*

(Hard) Write a flatten(list) function that takes a list that may contain any number of sublists, which themselves may contain sublists, to any depth. It returns the elements of these lists as a flat list.

```
iex> MyList.flatten([ 1, [ 2, 3, [4] ], 5, [[[6]]]])
[1,2,3,4,5,6]
```

Hint: You may have to use Enum.reverse to get your result in the correct order.

Streams—Lazy Enumerables

In Elixir, the Enum module is greedy. This means that when you pass it a collection, it potentially consumes all the contents of that collection. It also means the result will typically be another collection. Look at the following pipeline:

```
enum/pipeline.exs
[ 1, 2, 3, 4, 5 ]
|> Enum.map(&(&1*&1))
|> Enum.with_index
|> Enum.map(fn {value, index} -> value - index end)
|> IO.inspect   #=> [1,3,7,13,21]
```

The first map function takes the original list and creates a new list of its squares. with_index takes this list and returns a list of tuples. The next map then subtracts the index from the value, generating a list that gets passed to IO.inspect.

So, this pipeline generates four lists on its way to outputting the final result.

Let's look at something different. Here's some code that reads lines from a file and returns the longest.

```
enum/longest_line.exs
IO.puts File.read!("/usr/share/dict/words")
        |> String.split
        |> Enum.max_by(&String.length/1)
```

In this case, we read the whole dictionary into memory (on my machine that's 2.4MB), then split into a list of words (236,000 of them) before processing it to find the longest (which happens to be *formaldehydesulphoxylate*).

In both of these examples, our code is suboptimal because each call to Enum is self-contained. Each call takes a collection and returns a collection.

What we really want is to process the elements in the collection as we need them. We don't need to store intermediate results as full collections; we just need to pass the current element from function to function. And that's what streams do.

A Stream Is a Composable Enumerator

Here's a simple example of creating a Stream:

```
iex> s = Stream.map [1, 3, 5, 7], &(&1 + 1)
#Stream<[enum: [1, 3, 5, 7], funs: [#Function<37.75994740/1 in Stream.map/2>] ]>
```

If we'd called Enum.map, we'd have seen the result [2,4,6,8] come back immediately. Instead we get back a stream value that contains a specification of what we intended.

How do we get the stream to start giving us results? Treat it as a collection and pass it to a function in the Enum module:

```
iex> s = Stream.map [1, 3, 5, 7], &(&1 + 1)
#Stream<...>
iex> Enum.to_list s
[2, 4, 6, 8]
```

Because streams are enumerable, you can also pass a stream to a stream function. Because of this, we say that streams are *composable*.

```
iex> squares = Stream.map [1, 2, 3, 4], &(&1*&1)
#Stream<[enum: [1, 2, 3, 4],
        funs: [#Function<32.133702391 in Stream.map/2>] ]>

iex> plus_ones = Stream.map squares, &(&1+1)
#Stream<[enum: [1, 2, 3, 4],
        funs: [#Function<32.133702391 in Stream.map/2>,
               #Function<32.133702391 in Stream.map/2>] ]>

iex> odds = Stream.filter plus_ones, fn x -> rem(x,2) == 1 end
#Stream<[enum: [1, 2, 3, 4],
        funs: [#Function<26.133702391 in Stream.filter/2>,
               #Function<32.133702391 in Stream.map/2>,
               #Function<32.133702391 in Stream.map/2>] ]>

iex> Enum.to_list odds
[5, 17]
```

Of course, in real life we'd have written this as

```
enum/stream1.exs
[1,2,3,4]
|> Stream.map(&(&1*&1))
|> Stream.map(&(&1+1))
|> Stream.filter(fn x -> rem(x,2) == 1 end)
|> Enum.to_list
```

Note that we're never creating intermediate lists—we're just passing successive elements of each of the collections to the next in the chain. The Stream values shown in the previous iex session give a hint of how this works—chained streams are represented as a list of functions, each of which is applied in turn to each element of the stream as it is processed.

Streams aren't only for lists. More and more Elixir modules now support streams. For example, here's our longest-word code written using streams:

```
enum/stream2.exs
IO.puts File.open!("/usr/share/dict/words")
        |> IO.stream(:line)
        |> Enum.max_by(&String.length/1)
```

The magic here is the call to IO.stream, which converts an IO device (in this case the open file) into a stream that serves one line at a time. In fact, this is such a useful concept that there's a shortcut:

```
enum/stream3.exs
IO.puts File.stream!("/usr/share/dict/words") |> Enum.max_by(&String.length/1)
```

The good news is that there is no intermediate storage. The bad news is that it runs about two times slower than the previous version. However, consider the case where we were reading data from a remote server or from an external sensor (maybe temperature readings). Successive lines might arrive slowly, and they might go on for ever. With the Enum implementation we'd have to wait for all the lines to arrive before we started processing. With streams we can process them as they arrive.

Infinite Streams

Because streams are lazy, there's no need for the whole collection to be available up front. For example, if I write

```
iex> Enum.map(1..10_000_000, &(&1+1)) |> Enum.take(5)
[2, 3, 4, 5, 6]
```

it takes about 8 seconds before I see the result. Elixir is creating a 10-million-element list, then taking the first five elements from it. If instead I write

```
iex> Stream.map(1..10_000_000, &(&1+1)) |> Enum.take(5)
[2, 3, 4, 5, 6]
```

the result comes back instantaneously. The take call just needs five values, which it gets from the stream. Once it has them, there's no more processing.

In these examples the stream is bounded, but it can equally well go on forever. To do that, we'll need to create streams based on functions.

Creating Your Own Streams

Streams are implemented solely in Elixir libraries—there is no specific runtime support. However, this doesn't mean you want to drop down to the very lowest level and create your own streamable types. The actual implementation is complex (in the same way that string theory and dating rituals are complex). Instead, you probably want to use some helpful wrapper functions to do the heavy lifting. There are a number of these, including cycle, repeatedly, iterate, unfold, and resource. (If you needed proof that the internal implementation is tricky, consider the fact that these last two names give you almost no hint of their power.)

Let's start with the three simplest: cycle, repeatedly, and iterate.

Stream.cycle

Stream.cycle takes an enumerable and returns an infinite stream containing that enumerable's elements. When it gets to the end, it repeats from the beginning, indefinitely. Here's an example that generates the rows in an HTML table with alternating *green* and *white* classes:

```
iex> Stream.cycle(~w{ green white }) |>
...> Stream.zip(1..5) |>
...> Enum.map(fn {class, value} ->
...>      ~s{<tr class="#{class}"><td>#{value}</td></tr>\n} end) |>
...> IO.puts
<tr class="green"><td>1</td></tr>
<tr class="white"><td>2</td></tr>
<tr class="green"><td>3</td></tr>
<tr class="white"><td>4</td></tr>
<tr class="green"><td>5</td></tr>
```

Stream.repeatedly

Stream.repeatedly takes a function and invokes it each time a new value is wanted.

```
iex> Stream.repeatedly(fn -> true end) |> Enum.take(3)
[true, true, true]
iex> Stream.repeatedly(&:random.uniform/0) |> Enum.take(3)
[0.7230402056221108, 0.94581636451987, 0.5014907142064751]
```

Stream.iterate

Stream.iterate(start_value, next_fun) generates an infinite stream. The first value is start_value. The next value is generated by applying next_fun to this value. This continues for as long as the stream is being used, with each value being the result of applying next_fun to the previous value.

Here are some examples:

```
iex> Stream.iterate(0, &(&1+1)) |> Enum.take(5)
[0, 1, 2, 3, 4]
iex> Stream.iterate(2, &(&1*&1)) |> Enum.take(5)
[2, 4, 16, 256, 65536]
iex> Stream.iterate([], &[&1]) |> Enum.take(5)
[[], [[]], [[[]]], [[[[]]]], [[[[[]]]]]]
```

Stream.unfold

Now we can get a little more adventurous. Stream.unfold is related to iterate, but you can be more explicit both about the values output to the stream and about the values passed to the next iteration. You supply an initial value and a function. The function uses the argument to create two values, returned as a tuple. The first is the value to be returned by this iteration of the stream, and the second is the value to be passed to the function on the next iteration of the stream. If the function returns nil, the stream terminates.

This sounds abstract, but unfold is quite useful—it is a general way of creating a potentially infinite stream of values where each value is some function of the previous state.

The key is the generating function. Its general form is

```
fn state -> { stream_value, new_state } end
```

For example, here's a stream of Fibonacci numbers:

```
iex> Stream.unfold({0,1}, fn {f1,f2} -> {f1, {f2, f1+f2}} end) |> Enum.take(15)
[0, 1, 1, 2, 3, 5, 8, 13, 21, 34, 55, 89, 144, 233, 377]
```

Here the *state* is a tuple containing the current and the next number in the sequence. We seed it with the initial state of {0, 1}. The value each iteration of the stream returns is the first of the state values. The new state moves one down the sequence, so an initial state of {f1,f2} becomes a new state of {f2,f1+f2}.

Stream.resource

At this point you might be wondering how streams can interact with external resources. We've already seen how you can turn a file's contents into a stream of lines, but how could you implement this yourself? You'd need to open the file when the stream first starts, return successive lines, and then close the file at the end. Or maybe you want to turn a database result-set cursor into a stream of values. You'd have to execute the query when the stream starts, return each row as stream values, and close the query at the end. And that's where Stream.resource comes in.

Stream.resource builds upon Stream.unfold. It makes two changes.

The first argument to unfold is the initial value to be passed to the iteration function. But if that value is a resource, we don't want to open it until the stream starts delivering values, and that might not happen until long after we create the stream. To get around this, resource takes not a value, but a function that returns the value. That's the first change.

Second, when the stream is done with the resource, we may need to close it. That's what the third argument to Stream.resource does—it takes the final accumulator value and does whatever is needed to deallocate the resource.

Here's an example from the library documentation:

```
Stream.resource(fn -> File.open!("sample") end,
            fn file ->
              case IO.read(file, :line) do
                data when is_binary(data) -> {[data], file}
                _ -> {:halt, file}
              end
            end,
            fn file -> File.close(file) end)
```

The first function opens the file when the stream becomes active, and passes it to the second function. This reads the file, line by line, returning either a line and the file as a tuple, or a :halt tuple at the end of the file. The third function closes the file.

Let's finish with a different kind of resource: time. We'll implement a timer that counts down the number of seconds until the start of the next minute. It uses a stream resource to do this. The allocation function returns the number of seconds left until the next minute starts. It does this each time the stream is evaluated, so we'll get a countdown that varies depending on when it is called.

The iteration function looks at the time left. If zero, it returns {:halt, 0}; otherwise it sleeps for a second and returns the current countdown as a string, along with the decremented counter.

In this case there's no resource deallocation, so the third function does nothing.

Here's the code:

```
enum/countdown.exs
defmodule Countdown do

  def sleep(seconds) do
    receive do
      after seconds*1000 -> nil
    end
  end

  def say(text) do
    spawn fn -> :os.cmd('say #{text}') end
  end
```

```elixir
def timer do
  Stream.resource(
    fn ->             # the number of seconds to the start of the next minute
      {_h,_m,s} = :erlang.time
      60 - s - 1
    end,

    fn                # wait for the next second, then return its countdown
      0 ->
        {:halt, 0}

      count ->
        sleep(1)
        { [inspect(count)], count - 1 }
    end,

    fn _ -> end   # nothing to deallocate
  )
  end
end
```

(The eagle-eyed among you will have noticed a function called say in the Countdown module. This executes the shell command say, which, on OS X, speaks its argument. You could substitute espeak on Linux and ptts on Windows.)

Let's play with the code.

```
$ iex countdown.exs
iex> counter = Countdown.timer
#Function<17.133702391 in Stream.resource/3>
iex> printer = counter |> Stream.each(&IO.puts/1)
#Stream[enum: #Function<17.133702391 in Stream.resource/3>,
 funs: [#Function<0.133702391 in Stream.each/2>] ]>
iex> speaker = printer |> Stream.each(&Countdown.say/1)
#Stream[enum: #Function<17.133702391 in Stream.resource/3>,
 funs: [#Function<0.133702391 in Stream.each/2>,
  #Function<0.133702391 in Stream.each/2>] ]>
```

So far, we've built a stream that creates time events, prints the countdown value, and speaks it. But there's been no output, as we haven't yet asked the stream for any values. Let's do that now:

```
iex> speaker |> Enum.take(5)
37      ** numbers are output once
36      ** per second. Even cooler,the
35      ** computer says
34      ** "thirty seven", "thirty six"…
33
["37", "36", "35", "34", "33"]
```

Cool—we must have started it around 22 seconds into a minute, so the countdown starts at 37. Let's use the same stream again, a few seconds later:

```
iex> speaker |> Enum.take(3)
29
28
27
["29", "28", "27"]
```

Wait some more seconds, and this time let it run to the top of the minute:

```
iex> speaker |> Enum.to_list
6
5
4
3
2
1
["6", "5", "4", "3","2", "1"]
```

This is clearly not great code, as it fails to correct the sleep time for any delays introduced by our code. But it illustrates a very cool point. Lazy streams let you deal with resources that are asynchronous to your code, and the fact that they are initialized every time they are used means they're effectively side-effect-free. Every time we pipe our stream to an Enum function, we get a fresh set of values, computed at that time.

Streams in Practice

In the same way that functional programming requires you to look at problems in a new way, streams ask you to look at iteration and collections afresh. Not every situation where you are iterating requires a stream. But consider using a stream when you want to defer processing until you need the data, and when you need to deal with large numbers of things without necessarily generating them all at once.

The Collectable Protocol

The Enumerable protocol lets you iterate over the elements in a type—given a collection, you can get the elements. Collectable is in some sense the opposite—it allows you to build a collection by inserting elements into it.

Not all collections are collectable. Ranges, for example, cannot have new entries added to them.

The collectable API is pretty low-level, so you'll typically access it via Enum.into and when using comprehensions (which we cover in the next section). For example, we can inject the elements of a range into an empty list using

```
iex> Enum.into 1..5, []
[1, 2, 3, 4, 5]
```

If the list is not empty, the new elements are tacked onto the end:

```
iex> Enum.into 1..5, [100, 101 ]
[100, 101, 1, 2, 3, 4, 5]
```

Output streams are collectable, so the following code lazily copies standard input to standard output:

```
iex> Enum.into IO.stream(:stdio, :line), IO.stream(:stdio, :line)
```

Comprehensions

When you're writing functional code, you often map and filter collections of things. To make your life easier (and your code easier to read), Elixir provides a general-purpose shortcut for this: the *comprehension*.

The idea of a comprehension is fairly simple: given one or more collections, extract all combinations of values from each, optionally filter the values, and then generate a new collection using the values that remain.

The general syntax for comprehensions is deceptively simple:

result = for *generator or filter…* [, into: *value*], do: *expression*

Let's see a couple of basic examples before we get into the details.

```
iex> for x <- [ 1, 2, 3, 4, 5 ], do: x * x
[1, 4, 9, 16, 25]
iex> for x <- [ 1, 2, 3, 4, 5 ], x < 4, do: x * x
[1, 4, 9]
```

A generator specifies how you want to extract values from a collection.

pattern <- enumerable_thing

Any variables matched in the pattern are available in the rest of the comprehension (including the block). For example, x <- [1,2,3] says that we want to first run the rest of the comprehension with x set to 1. Then we run it with x set to 2, and so on. If we have two generators, their operations are nested, so

```
x <- [1,2], y <- [5,6]
```

will run the rest of the comprehension with x=1, y=5; x=1, y=6; x=2, y=5; and x=2, y=6. We can use those values of x and y in the do block.

```
iex> for x <- [1,2], y <- [5,6], do:  x * y
[5, 6, 10, 12]
iex> for x <- [1,2], y <- [5,6], do:  {x,  y}
[{1, 5}, {1, 6}, {2, 5}, {2, 6}]
```

You can use variables from generators in later generators:

```
iex> min_maxes = [{1,4}, {2,3}, {10, 15}]
[{1, 4}, {2, 3}, {10, 15}]
iex> for {min,max} <- min_maxes, n <- min..max, do: n
[1, 2, 3, 4, 2, 3, 10, 11, 12, 13, 14, 15]
```

A filter is a predicate. It acts as a gatekeeper for the rest of the comprehension—if the condition is false, then the comprehension moves on to the next iteration without generating an output value.

For example, the code that follows uses a comprehension to list pairs of numbers from 1 to 8 whose product is a multiple of 10. It uses two generators (to cycle through the pairs of numbers) and two filters. The first filter allows only pairs in which the first number is at least the value of the second. The second filter checks to see if the product is a multiple of 10.

```
iex> first8 = [ 1,2,3,4,5,6,7,8 ]
[1, 2, 3, 4, 5, 6, 7, 8]
iex> for x <- first8, y <- first8, x >= y, rem(x*y, 10)==0, do: { x, y }
[{5, 2}, {5, 4}, {6, 5}, {8, 5}]
```

This comprehension iterates 64 times, with x=1, y=1; x=1, y=2; and so on. However, the first filter cuts the iteration short when x is less than y. This means the second filter runs only 36 times.

Because the first term in a generator is a pattern, we can use it to deconstruct structured data. Here's a comprehension that swaps the keys and values in a keyword list.

```
iex> reports = [ dallas: :hot, minneapolis: :cold, dc: :muggy, la: :smoggy ]
[dallas: :hot, minneapolis: :cold, dc: :muggy, la: :smoggy]
iex> for { city, weather } <- reports, do: { weather, city }
[hot: :dallas, cold: :minneapolis, muggy: :dc, smoggy: :la]
```

Comprehensions Work on Bits, Too

A bitstring (and, by extension, a binary or a string) is simply a collection of ones and zeroes. So it's probably no surprise that comprehensions work on bits, too. What might be surprising is the syntax:

```
iex> for << ch <- "hello" >>, do: ch
'hello'
iex> for << ch <- "hello" >>, do: <<ch>>
["h", "e", "l", "l", "o"]
```

Here the generator is enclosed in << and >>, indicating a binary. In the first case, the do block returns the integer code for each character, so the resulting list is [104, 101, 108, 108, 111], which iex displays as 'hello'.

In the second case, we convert the code back into a string, and the result is a list of those one-character strings.

Again, the thing to the left of the <- is a pattern, and so we can use binary pattern matching. Let's convert a string into the octal representation of its characters:

```
iex> for << << b1::size(2), b2::size(3), b3::size(3) >> <- "hello" >>,
...> do: "0#{b1}#{b2}#{b3}"
["0150", "0145", "0154", "0154", "0157"]
```

Scoping and Comprehensions

All variable assignments inside a comprehension are local to that comprehension—you will not affect the value of a variable in the outer scope.

```
iex> name = "Dave"
"Dave"
iex> for name <- [ "cat", "dog" ], do: String.upcase(name)
["CAT", "DOG"]
iex> name
"Dave"
iex>
```

The Value Returned by a Comprehension

In our examples so far, the comprehension has returned a list. The list contains the values returned by the do expression for each iteration of the comprehension.

This behavior can be changed with the into: parameter. This takes a collection that is to receive the results of the comprehension. For example, we can populate a map using

```
iex> for x <- ~w{ cat dog }, into: %{}, do: { x, String.upcase(x) }
%{"cat" => "CAT", "dog" => "DOG"}
```

It might be more clear to use Map.new in this case:

```
iex> for x <- ~w{ cat dog }, into: Map.new, do: { x, String.upcase(x) }
%{"cat" => "CAT", "dog" => "DOG"}
```

The collection doesn't have to be empty:

```
iex> for x <- ~w{ cat dog }, into: %{"ant" => "ANT"}, do: { x, String.upcase(x) }
%{"ant" => "ANT", "cat" => "CAT", "dog" => "DOG"}
```

In Chapter 22, *Protocols—Polymorphic Functions*, on page 293, we'll look at protocols, which let us specify common behaviors across different types. The into: option takes values that implement the Collectable protocol. These include lists, binaries, functions, maps, files, hash dicts, hash sets, and IO streams, so we can write things such as

```
iex> for x <- ~w{ cat dog }, into: IO.stream(:stdio,:line), do: "<<#{x}>>\n"
<<cat>>
<<dog>>
%IO.Stream{device: :standard_io, line_or_bytes: :line, raw: false}
```

Your Turn

➤ *Exercise: ListsAndRecursion-7*

In the last exercise of Chapter 7, *Lists and Recursion*, on page 69, you wrote a span function. Use it and list comprehensions to return a list of the prime numbers from 2 to *n*.

➤ *Exercise: ListsAndRecursion-8*

The Pragmatic Bookshelf has offices in Texas (TX) and North Carolina (NC), so we have to charge sales tax on orders shipped to these states. The rates can be expressed as a keyword list:[2]

```
tax_rates = [ NC: 0.075, TX: 0.08 ]
```

Here's a list of orders:

```
orders = [
    [ id: 123, ship_to: :NC, net_amount: 100.00 ],
    [ id: 124, ship_to: :OK, net_amount:  35.50 ],
    [ id: 125, ship_to: :TX, net_amount:  24.00 ],
    [ id: 126, ship_to: :TX, net_amount:  44.80 ],
    [ id: 127, ship_to: :NC, net_amount:  25.00 ],
    [ id: 128, ship_to: :MA, net_amount:  10.00 ],
    [ id: 129, ship_to: :CA, net_amount: 102.00 ],
    [ id: 130, ship_to: :NC, net_amount:  50.00 ] ]
```

Write a function that takes both lists and returns a copy of the orders, but with an extra field, total_amount, which is the net plus sales tax. If a shipment is not to NC or TX, there's no tax applied.

Moving Past Divinity

L. Peter Deutsch once penned, "To iterate is human, to recurse divine." And that's certainly the way I felt when I first started coding Elixir. The joy of

---

2. I wish it were that simple....

pattern-matching lists in sets of recursive functions drove my designs. After a while, I realized that perhaps I was taking this too far.

In reality, most of our day-to-day work is better handled using the various enumerators built into Elixir. They make your code smaller, easier to understand, and probably more efficient.

Part of the process of learning to be effective in Elixir is working out for yourself when to use recursion and when to use enumerators. I recommend enumerating when you can.

Next we'll look at string handling in Elixir (and Erlang).

CHAPTER 11

Strings and Binaries

We've been happily using strings without really discussing them. Let's rectify that.

String Literals

Elixir has two kinds of string: single-quoted and double-quoted. They differ significantly in their internal representation. But they also have many things in common.

- Strings can hold characters in UTF-8 encoding.

- They may contain escape sequences:

\a	BEL (0x07)	\b	BS (0x08)			\d	DEL (0x7f)
\e	ESC (0x1b)	\f	FF (0x0c)			\n	NL (0x0a)
\r	CR (0x0d)	\s	SP (0x20)			\t	TAB (0x09)
\v	VT (0x0b)	\uhhh	1–6 hex digits	\xhh	2 hex digits		

- They allow interpolation on Elixir expressions using the syntax #{…}.

  ```
  iex> name = "dave"
  "dave"
  iex> "Hello, #{String.capitalize name}!"
  "Hello, Dave!"
  ```

- Characters that would otherwise have special meaning can be escaped with a backslash.

- They support *heredocs*.

Heredocs

Any string can span several lines. To illustrate this, we'll use both IO.puts and IO.write. We use write for the multiline string because puts always appends a newline, and we want to see the contents without this.

```
IO.puts "start"
IO.write "
   my
   string
"
IO.puts "end"
```

produces:

```
start

   my
   string
end
```

Notice how the multiline string retains the leading and trailing newlines and the leading spaces on the intermediate lines.

The *heredoc* notation fixes this. Triple the string delimiter (''' or """) and indent the trailing delimiter to the same margin as your string contents, and you get this:

```
IO.puts "start"
IO.write """
   my
   string
   """
IO.puts "end"
```

produces:

```
start
my
string
end
```

Heredocs are used extensively to add documentation to functions and modules.

Sigils

Like Ruby, Elixir has an alternative syntax for some literals. We've already seen it with regular expressions, where we wrote ~r{...}. In Elixir, these ~-style literals are called *sigils* (a symbol with magical powers).

A sigil starts with a tilde, followed by an upper- or lowercase letter, some delimited content, and perhaps some options. The delimiters can be <...>, {...}, [...], (...), |...|, /.../, "...", and '...'.

The letter determines the sigil's type:

~C   A character list with no escaping or interpolation

~c   A character list, escaped and interpolated just like a single-quoted string

~R   A regular expression with no escaping or interpolation

~r   A regular expression, escaped and interpolated

~S   A string with no escaping or interpolation

~s   A string, escaped and interpolated just like a double-quoted string

~W   A list of whitespace-delimited words, with no escaping or interpolation

~w   A list of whitespace-delimited words, with escaping and interpolation

Here are some examples, using a variety of delimiters.

```
iex> ~C[1\n2#{1+2}]
'1\\n2\#{1+2}'
iex> ~c"1\n2#{1+2}"
'1\n23'
iex> ~S[1\n2#{1+2}]
"1\\n2\#{1+2}"
iex> ~s/1\n2#{1+2}/
"1\n23"
iex> ~W[the c#{'a'}t sat on the mat]
["the", "c\#{'a'}t", "sat", "on", "the", "mat"]
iex> ~w[the c#{'a'}t sat on the mat]
["the", "cat", "sat", "on", "the", "mat"]
```

The ~W and ~w sigils take an optional type specifier, a, c, or s, which determines whether it returns atoms, a list, or strings of characters. (We've already seen the ~r options.)

```
iex> ~w[the c#{'a'}t sat on the mat]a
[:the, :cat, :sat, :on, :the, :mat]
iex> ~w[the c#{'a'}t sat on the mat]c
['the', 'cat', 'sat', 'on', 'the', 'mat']
iex> ~w[the c#{'a'}t sat on the mat]s
["the", "cat", "sat", "on", "the", "mat"]
```

The delimiter can be any nonword character. If it is (, [, {, or <, then the terminating delimiter is the corresponding closing character. Otherwise the terminating delimiter is the next nonescaped occurrence of the opening delimiter.

Elixir does not check the nesting of delimiters, so the sigil ~s{a{b} is the three-character string a{b.

If the opening delimiter is three single or three double quotes, the sigil is treated as a heredoc.

```
iex> ~w"""
...> the
...> cat
...> sat
...> """
["the", "cat", "sat"]
```

If you want to specify modifiers with heredoc sigils (most commonly you'd do this with ~r), add them after the trailing delimiter.

```
iex> ~r"""
...> hello
...> """i
~r/hello\n/i
```

One of the interesting things about sigils is that you can define your own. We talk about this in Part III, on page 307.

The Name "strings"

Before we get further into this, I need to explain something. In most other languages, you'd call 'cat' and "cat" both *strings*. And that's what I've been doing so far. But Elixir has a different convention.

In Elixir, the convention is that we call only double-quoted strings "strings." The single-quoted form is a character list.

This is important. The single- and double-quoted forms are very different, and libraries that work on strings work only on the double-quoted form.

Let's explore the differences in more detail.

Single-Quoted Strings—Lists of Character Codes

Single-quoted strings are represented as a list of integer values, each value corresponding to a codepoint in the string. For this reason, we refer to them as *character lists* (or *char lists*).

```
iex> str = 'wombat'
'wombat'
iex> is_list str
true
iex> length str
6
iex> Enum.reverse str
'tabmow'
```

This is confusing: iex *says* it is a list, but it shows the value as a string. That's because iex prints a list of integers as a string if it believes each number in the list is a printable character. You can try this for yourself.

```
iex> [ 67, 65, 84 ]
'CAT'
```

You can look at the internal representation in a number of ways:

```
iex> str = 'wombat'
'wombat'
iex> :io.format "~w~n", [ str ]
[119,111,109,98,97,116]
:ok
iex> List.to_tuple str
{119, 111, 109, 98, 97, 116}
iex> str ++ [0]
[119, 111, 109, 98, 97, 116, 0]
```

The ~w in the format string forces str to be written as an Erlang term—the underlying list of integers. The ~n is a newline.

The last example creates a new character list with a null byte at the end. iex no longer thinks all the bytes are printable, and so returns the underlying character codes.

If a character list contains characters Erlang considers nonprintable, you'll see the list representation.

```
iex> '∂x/∂y'
[8706, 120, 47, 8706, 121]
```

Because a character list is a list, we can use the usual pattern matching and List functions.

```
iex> 'pole' ++ 'vault'
'polevault'
iex> 'pole' -- 'vault'
'poe'
iex> List.zip [ 'abc', '123' ]
[{97, 49}, {98, 50}, {99, 51}]
iex> [ head | tail ] = 'cat'
'cat'
iex> head
99
iex> tail
'at'
iex> [ head | tail ]
'cat'
```

Why is the head of 'cat' 99 and not *c*? Remember that a char list is just a list of integer character codes, so each individual entry is a number. It happens that 99 is the code for a lowercase *c*.

In fact, the notation ?c returns the integer code for the character c. This is often useful when employing patterns to extract information from character lists. Here's a simple module that parses the character-list representation of an optionally signed decimal number.

```
strings/parse.exs
defmodule Parse do

  def number([ ?- | tail ]), do: _number_digits(tail, 0) * -1
  def number([ ?+ | tail ]), do: _number_digits(tail, 0)
  def number(str),           do: _number_digits(str,  0)

  defp _number_digits([], value), do: value
  defp _number_digits([ digit | tail ], value)
  when digit in '0123456789' do
    _number_digits(tail, value*10 + digit - ?0)
  end
  defp _number_digits([ non_digit | _ ], _) do
    raise "Invalid digit '#{[non_digit]}'"
  end
end
```

Let's try it in iex.

```
iex> c("parse.exs")
[Parse]
iex> Parse.number('123')
123
iex> Parse.number('-123')
-123
iex> Parse.number('+123')
123
iex> Parse.number('+9')
9
iex> Parse.number('+a')
** (RuntimeError) Invalid digit 'a'
```

Your Turn

➤ *Exercise: StringsAndBinaries-1*

Write a function that returns true if a single-quoted string contains only printable ASCII characters (space through tilde).

➤ *Exercise: StringsAndBinaries-2*

Write an anagram?(word1, word2) that returns true if its parameters are ana-grams.

➤ *Exercise: StringsAndBinaries-3*

Try the following in iex:

```
iex> [ 'cat' | 'dog' ]
['cat',100,111,103]
```

Why does iex print 'cat' as a string, but 'dog' as individual numbers?

➤ *Exercise: StringsAndBinaries-4*

(Hard) Write a function that takes a single-quoted string of the form *number* [+-*/] *number* and returns the result of the calculation. The indi-vidual numbers do not have leading plus or minus signs.

```
calculate('123 + 27') # => 150
```

Binaries

The binary type represents a sequence of bits.

A binary literal looks like << *term,...* >>.

The simplest term is just a number from 0 to 255. The numbers are stored as successive bytes in the binary.

```
iex> b = << 1, 2, 3 >>
<<1, 2, 3>>
iex> byte_size b
3
iex> bit_size b
24
```

You can specify modifiers to set any term's size (in bits). This is useful when working with binary formats such as media files and network packets.

```
iex> b = << 1::size(2), 1::size(3) >>    # 01 001
<<9::size(5)>>                           # = 9 (base 10)
iex> byte_size b
1
iex> bit_size b
5
```

You can store integers, floats, and other binaries in binaries.

```
iex> int = << 1 >>
<<1>>
```

```
iex> float = << 2.5 :: float >>
<<64, 4, 0, 0, 0, 0, 0, 0>>
iex> mix = << int :: binary, float :: binary >>
<<1, 64, 4, 0, 0, 0, 0, 0, 0>>
```

Let's finish an initial look at binaries with an example of bit extraction. An IEEE 754 float has a sign bit, 11 bits of exponent, and 52 bits of mantissa. The exponent is biased by 1023, and the mantissa is a fraction with the top bit assumed to be 1. So we can extract the fields and then use :math.pow, which performs exponentiation, to reassemble the number:

```
iex> << sign::size(1), exp::size(11), mantissa::size(52) >> = << 3.14159::float >>
iex> (1 + mantissa / :math.pow(2, 52)) * :math.pow(2, exp-1023)
3.14159
```

Double-Quoted Strings Are Binaries

Whereas single-quoted strings are stored as char lists, the contents of a double-quoted string (*dqs*) are stored as a consecutive sequence of bytes in UTF-8 encoding. Clearly this is more efficient in terms of memory and certain forms of access, but it does have two implications.

First, because UTF-8 characters can take more than a single byte to represent, the size of the binary is not necessarily the length of the string.

```
iex> dqs = "∂x/∂y"
"∂x/∂y"
iex> String.length dqs
5
iex> byte_size dqs
9
iex> String.at(dqs, 0)
"∂"
iex> String.codepoints(dqs)
["∂", "x", "/", "∂", "y"]
iex> String.split(dqs, "/")
["∂x", "∂y"]
```

Second, because you're no longer using lists, you need to learn and work with the binary syntax alongside the list syntax in your code.

Strings and Elixir Libraries

When Elixir library documentation uses the word *string* (and most of the time it uses the word *binary*), it means double-quoted strings.

The String module defines functions that work with double-quoted strings.

at(str, offset)

> Returns the grapheme at the given offset (starting at 0). Negative offsets count from the end of the string.

```
iex> String.at("∂og", 0)
"∂"
iex> String.at("∂og", -1)
"g"
```

capitalize(str)

> Converts str to lowercase, and then capitalizes the first character.

```
iex> String.capitalize "école"
"École"
iex> String.capitalize "ÎÎÎÎÎ"
"Îîîîî"
```

codepoints(str)

> Returns the codepoints in str.

```
iex> String.codepoints("José's ∂øg")
["J", "o", "s", "é", "'", "s", " ", "∂", "ø", "g"]
```

downcase(str)

> Converts str to lowercase.

```
iex> String.downcase "ØRSteD"
"ørsted"
```

duplicate(str, n)

> Returns a string containing n copies of str.

```
iex> String.duplicate "Ho! ", 3
"Ho! Ho! Ho! "
```

ends_with?(str, suffix | [suffixes])

> True if str ends with any of the given suffixes.

```
iex> String.ends_with? "string", ["elix", "stri", "ring"]
true
```

first(str)

> Returns the first grapheme from str.

```
iex> String.first "∂og"
"∂"
```

graphemes(str)

> Returns the graphemes in the string. This is different from the codepoints function, which lists combining characters separately. The following

example uses a combining diaeresis along with the letter "e" to represent "ë". (It might not display properly on your ereader.)

```
iex> String.codepoints "noe\u0308l"
["n", "o", "e", "¨", "l"]
iex> String.graphemes "noe\u0308l"
["n", "o", "ë", "l"]
```

last(str)

Returns the last grapheme from str.

```
iex> String.last "∂og"
"g"
```

length(str)

Returns the number of graphemes in str.

```
iex> String.length "∂x/∂y"
5
```

ljust(str, new_length, padding \\ " ")

Returns a new string, at least new_length characters long, containing str left-justified and padded with padding.

```
iex> String.ljust("cat", 5)
"cat  "
```

lstrip(str)

Removes leading whitespace from str.

```
iex> String.lstrip "\t\f    Hello\t\n"
"Hello\t\n"
```

lstrip(str, character)

Removes leading copies of character (an integer codepoint) from str.

```
iex> String.lstrip "!!!SALE!!!", ?!
"SALE!!!"
```

next_codepoint(str)

Splits str into its leading codepoint and the rest, or nil if str is empty. This may be used as the basis of an iterator.

```
defmodule MyString do
  def each(str, func), do: _each(String.next_codepoint(str), func)

  defp _each({codepoint, rest}, func) do
    func.(codepoint)
    _each(String.next_codepoint(rest), func)
  end
```

```
    defp _each(nil, _), do: []
  end

  MyString.each "∂og", fn c -> IO.puts c end
```

produces:

```
∂
o
g
```

next_grapheme(str)

Same as next_codepoint, but returns graphemes (and :no_grapheme on completion).

printable?(str)

Returns true if str contains only printable characters.

```
iex> String.printable? "José"
true
iex> String.printable? "\x{0000} a null"
false
```

replace(str, pattern, replacement, options \\ [global: true, insert_replaced: nil])

Replaces pattern with replacement in str under control of options.

If the :global option is true, all occurrences of the pattern are replaced; otherwise only the first is replaced.

If :insert_replaced is a number, the pattern is inserted into the replacement at that offset. If the option is a list, it is inserted multiple times.

```
iex> String.replace "the cat on the mat", "at", "AT"
"the cAT on the mAT"
iex> String.replace "the cat on the mat", "at", "AT", global: false
"the cAT on the mat"
iex> String.replace "the cat on the mat", "at", "AT", insert_replaced: 0
"the catAT on the matAT"
iex> String.replace "the cat on the mat", "at", "AT", insert_replaced: [0,2]
"the catATat on the matATat"
```

reverse(str)

Reverses the graphemes in a string.

```
iex> String.reverse "pupils"
"slipup"
iex> String.reverse "∑f÷∂"
"∂÷f∑"
```

rjust(str, new_length, padding \\ 32)

Returns a new string, at least new_length characters long, containing str right-justified and padded with padding.

```
iex> String.rjust("cat", 5, ?>)
">>cat"
```

rstrip(str)

Removes trailing whitespace from str.

```
iex> String.rstrip(" line \r\n")
" line"
```

rstrip(str, character)

Removes trailing occurrences of character from str.

```
iex> String.rstrip "!!!SALE!!!", ?!
"!!!SALE"
```

slice(str, offset, len)

Returns a len character substring starting at offset (measured from the end of str if negative).

```
iex> String.slice "the cat on the mat", 4, 3
"cat"
iex> String.slice "the cat on the mat", -3, 3
"mat"
```

split(str, pattern \\ nil, options \\ [global: true])

Splits str into substrings delimited by pattern. If :global is false, only one split is performed. pattern can be a string, a regular expression, or nil. In the latter case, the string is split on whitespace.

```
iex> String.split "   the cat on the mat   "
["the", "cat", "on", "the", "mat"]
iex> String.split "the cat on the mat", "t"
["", "he ca", " on ", "he ma", ""]
iex> String.split "the cat on the mat", ~r{[ae]}
["th", " c", "t on th", " m", "t"]
iex> String.split "the cat on the mat", ~r{[ae]}, parts: 2
["th", " cat on the mat"]
```

starts_with?(str, prefix | [prefixes])

True if str starts with any of the given prefixes.

```
iex> String.starts_with? "string", ["elix", "stri", "ring"]
true
```

strip(str)

Strips leading and trailing whitespace from str.

```
iex> String.strip "\t  Hello    \r\n"
"Hello"
```

strip(str, character)

Strips leading and trailing instances of character from str.

```
iex> String.strip "!!!SALE!!!", ?!
"SALE"
```

upcase(str)

```
iex> String.upcase "José Ørstüd"
"JOSÉ ØRSTÜD"
```

valid_character?(str)

Returns true if str is a single-character string containing a valid codepoint.

```
iex> String.valid_character? "∂"
true
icx> String.valid_character? "∂og"
false
```

Your Turn

➤ *Exercise: StringsAndBinaries-5*

Write a function that takes a list of dqs and prints each on a separate line, centered in a column that has the width of the longest string. Make sure it works with UTF characters.

```
iex> center(["cat", "zebra", "elephant"])
  cat
 zebra
elephant
```

Binaries and Pattern Matching

The first rule of binaries is "if in doubt, specify the type of each field." Available types are binary, bits, bitstring, bytes, float, integer, utf8, utf16, and utf32. You can also add qualifiers:

- size(*n*): The size in bits of the field.

- signed or unsigned: For integer fields, should it be interpreted as signed?

- endianness: big, little, or native.

Use hyphens to separate multiple attributes for a field:

```
<< length::unsigned-integer-size(12), flags::bitstring-size(4) >>  = data
```

However, unless you're doing a lot of work with binary file or protocol formats, the most common use of all this scary stuff is to process UTF-8 strings.

String Processing with Binaries

When we process lists, we use patterns that split the head from the rest of the list. With binaries that hold strings, we can do the same kind of trick. We have to specify the type of the head (UTF-8), and make sure the tail remains a binary.

```
strings/utf-iterate.ex
defmodule Utf8 do
  def each(str, func) when is_binary(str), do: _each(str, func)

  defp _each(<< head :: utf8, tail :: binary >>, func) do
    func.(head)
    _each(tail, func)
  end

  defp _each(<<>>, _func), do: []
end

Utf8.each "∂og", fn char -> IO.puts char end
```

produces:

```
8706
111
103
```

The parallels with list processing are clear, but the differences are significant. Rather than use [head | tail], we use << head::utf8, tail::binary >>. And rather than terminate when we reach the empty list, [], we look for an empty binary, <<>>.

Your Turn

➤ *Exercise: StringsAndBinaries-6*

Write a function to capitalize the sentences in a string. Each sentence is terminated by a period and a space. Right now, the case of the characters in the string is random.

```
iex> capitalize_sentences("oh. a DOG. woof. ")
"Oh. A dog. Woof. "
```

➤ *Exercise: StringsAndBinaries-7*

Chapter 7 had an exercise about calculating sales tax on page 112. We now have the sales information in a file of comma-separated id, ship_to, and amount values. The file looks like this:

```
id,ship_to,net_amount
123,:NC,100.00
124,:OK,35.50
125,:TX,24.00
126,:TX,44.80
127,:NC,25.00
128,:MA,10.00
129,:CA,102.00
120,:NC,50.00
```

Write a function that reads and parses this file and then passes the result to the sales_tax function. Remember that the data should be formatted into a keyword list, and that the fields need to be the correct types (so the id field is an integer, and so on).

You'll need the library functions File.open, IO.read(file, :line), and IO.stream(file).

Familiar Yet Strange

String handling in Elixir is the result of a long evolutionary process in the underlying Erlang environment. If we were starting from scratch, things would probably look a little different. But once you get over the slightly strange way that strings are matched using binaries, you'll find that it works out well. In particular, pattern matching makes it very easy to look to strings that start with a particular sequence, which in turn makes simple parsing tasks a pleasure to write.

You may have noticed that we're a long way into the book and haven't yet talked about control-flow constructs such as if and case. This is deliberate: we use them less often in Elixir than in more conventional languages. However, we still need them, so they are the subject of the next chapter.

In this chapter, you'll see:
- if and unless
- cond (a multiway if)
- case (a pattern-matching switch)
- Exceptions

## CHAPTER 12

Control Flow

Elixir code tries to be declarative, not imperative.

In Elixir we write lots of small functions, and a combination of guard clauses and pattern matching of parameters replaces most of the control flow seen in other languages.

However, Elixir does have a small set of control-flow constructs. The reason I've waited so long to introduce them is that I want you to try not to use them much. You definitely will, and should, drop the occasional if or case into your code. But before you do, consider more functional alternatives. The benefit will become obvious as you write more code—functions written without explicit control flow tend to be shorter and more focused. They're easier to read, test, and reuse. If you end up with a 10- or 20-line function in an Elixir program, it is pretty much guaranteed that it will contain one of the constructs in this chapter and that you can simplify it.

So, forewarned, let's go.

if and unless

In Elixir, if and its evil twin, unless, take two parameters: a condition and a keyword list, which can contain the keys do: and else:. If the condition is truthy, the if expression evaluates the code associated with the do: key; otherwise it evaluates the else: code. The else: branch may be absent.

```
iex> if 1 == 1, do: "true part", else: "false part"
"true part"

iex> if 1 == 2, do: "true part", else: "false part"
"false part"
```

Just as it does with function definitions, Elixir provides some syntactic sugar. You can write the first of the previous examples as follows:

```
iex> if 1 == 1 do
...>    "true part"
...> else
...>    "false part"
...> end
true part
```

unless is similar:

```
iex> unless 1 == 1, do: "error", else: "OK"
"OK"
iex> unless 1 == 2, do: "OK", else: "error"
"OK"
iex> unless 1 == 2 do
...>    "OK"
...> else
...>    "error"
...> end
"OK"
```

The value of if and unless is the value of the expression that was evaluated.

cond

The cond macro lets you list out a series of conditions, each with associated code. It executes the code corresponding to the first truthy conditions.

In the game of FizzBuzz, children count up from 1. If the number is a multiple of three, they say "Fizz." For multiples of five, they say "Buzz." For multiples of both, they say "FizzBuzz." Otherwise, they say the number.

In Elixir, we could code this as follows:

control/fizzbuzz.ex
```
Line 1  defmodule FizzBuzz do

          def upto(n) when n > 0, do: _upto(1, n, [])

     5    defp _upto(_current, 0, result),  do: Enum.reverse result

          defp _upto(current, left, result) do
            next_answer =
              cond do
    10          rem(current, 3) == 0 and rem(current, 5) == 0 ->
                  "FizzBuzz"
                rem(current, 3) == 0 ->
                  "Fizz"
                rem(current, 5) == 0 ->
```

```
15          "Buzz"
            true ->
              current
          end
        _upto(current+1, left-1, [ next_answer | result ])
20    end
    end
```

The cond starts on line 8. We assign the value of the cond expression to
next_answer. Inside the cond, we have four alternatives—the current number is
a multiple of 3 and 5, just 3, just 5, or neither. Elixir examines each in turn
and returns the value of the expression following the -> for the first true one.
The _upto function then recurses to find the next value. Note the use of true ->
to handle the case where none of the previous conditions match. This is the
equivalent of the else or default stanza of a more traditional case statement.

There's a minor problem, though. The result list we build always has the most
recent value as its head. When we finish, we'll end up with a list that has the
answers in reverse order. That's why in the anchor case (when left is zero),
we reverse the result before returning it. This is a very common pattern. And
don't worry about performance—list reversal is highly optimized.

Let's try the code in iex:

```
iex> c("fizzbuzz.ex")
[FizzBuzz]
iex> FizzBuzz.upto(20)
[1, 2, "Fizz", 4, "Buzz", "Fizz", 7, 8, "Fizz", "Buzz", 11, "Fizz",
.. 13, 14, "FizzBuzz", 16, 17, "Fizz", 19, "Buzz"]
```

In this case, we could do something different and remove the call to reverse.
If we process the numbers in reverse order (so we start at n and end at 1),
the resulting list will be in the correct order.

control/fizzbuzz1.ex
```
defmodule FizzBuzz do

  def upto(n) when n > 0, do: _downto(n, [])

  defp _downto(0, result),  do: result
  defp _downto(current, result) do
    next_answer =
      cond do
        rem(current, 3) == 0 and rem(current, 5) == 0 ->
          "FizzBuzz"
        rem(current, 3) == 0 ->
          "Fizz"
        rem(current, 5) == 0 ->
          "Buzz"
```

```
        true ->
          current
      end
    _downto(current-1, [ next_answer | result ])
  end
end
```

This code is quite a bit cleaner than the previous version. However, it is also slightly less idiomatic—readers will expect to traverse the numbers in a natural order and reverse the result.

There's a third option. FizzBuzz transforms a number into a string. We like to code things as transformations, so let's use Enum.map to transform the range of numbers from 1 to n to the corresponding FizzBuzz words.

control/fizzbuzz2.ex

```
defmodule FizzBuzz do
  def upto(n) when n > 0 do
    1..n |> Enum.map(&fizzbuzz/1)
  end

  defp fizzbuzz(n) do
    cond do
      rem(n, 3) == 0 and rem(n, 5) == 0 ->
        "FizzBuzz"
      rem(n, 3) == 0 ->
        "Fizz"
      rem(n, 5) == 0 ->
        "Buzz"
      true ->
        n
    end
  end
end
```

This section is intended to show you how cond works, but you'll often find that it's better not to use it, and instead to take advantage of pattern matching in function calls. The choice is yours.

control/fizzbuzz3.ex

```
defmodule FizzBuzz do
  def upto(n) when n > 0 do
    1..n |> Enum.map(&fizzbuzz/1)
  end

  defp fizzbuzz(n), do: _fizzword(n, rem(n, 3), rem(n, 5))

  defp _fizzword(_n, 0, 0), do: "FizzBuzz"
  defp _fizzword(_n, 0, _), do: "Fizz"
  defp _fizzword(_n, _, 0), do: "Buzz"
```

```
  defp _fizzword( n, _, _), do: n
end
```

case

case lets you test a value against a set of patterns, executes the code associated with the first one that matches, and returns the value of that code. The patterns may include guard clauses.

For example, the File.open function returns a two-element tuple. If the open is successful, it returns {:ok, file}, where file is an identifier for the open file. If the open fails, it returns {:error, reason}. We can use case to take the appropriate action when we open a file. (In this case the code opens its own source file.)

control/case.ex
```
case File.open("case.ex") do
{ :ok, file } ->
  IO.puts "First line: #{IO.read(file, :line)}"
{ :error, reason } ->
  IO.puts "Failed to open file: #{reason}"
end
```

produces: First line: case File.open("case.ex") do

If we change the file name to something that doesn't exist and then rerun the code, we instead get: Failed to open file: enoent.

We can use the full power of nested pattern matches:

control/case1.exs
```
defmodule Users do
  dave = %{ name: "Dave", state: "TX", likes: "programming" }

  case dave do
    %{state: some_state} = person ->
      IO.puts "#{person.name} lives in #{some_state}"
    _ ->
      IO.puts "No matches"
  end
end
```

We've seen how to employ guard clauses to refine the pattern used when matching functions. We can do the same with case.

control/case2.exs
```
dave = %{name: "Dave", age: 27}

case dave do
  person = %{age: age} when is_number(age) and age >= 21 ->
    IO.puts "You are cleared to enter the Foo Bar, #{person.name}"
```

```
    _   ->
      IO.puts "Sorry, no admission"
end
```

Raising Exceptions

First, the official warning: exceptions in Elixir are *not* control-flow structures. Instead, Elixir exceptions are intended for things that should never happen in normal operation. That means the database going down or a name server failing to respond could be considered exceptional. Failing to open a configuration file whose name is fixed could be seen as exceptional. However, failing to open a file whose name a user entered is not. (You could anticipate that a user might mistype it every now and then.)

Raise an exception with the raise function. At its simplest, you pass it a string and it generates an exception of type RuntimeError.

```
iex> raise "Giving up"
** (RuntimeError) Giving up
```

You can also pass the type of the exception, along with other optional attributes. All exceptions implement at least the message attribute.

```
iex> raise RuntimeError
** (RuntimeError) runtime error
iex> raise RuntimeError, message: "override message"
** (RuntimeError) override message
```

You use exceptions far less in Elixir than in other languages—the design philosophy is that errors should propagate back up to an external, supervising process. We'll cover this when we talk about OTP Supervisors on page 227.

Elixir has all the usual exception-catching mechanisms. To emphasize how little you should use them, I've described them in an appendix on page 317.

Designing with Exceptions

If File.open succeeds, it returns {:ok, file}, where file is the service that gives you access to the file. If it fails, it returns {:error, reason}. So, for code that knows a file open might not succeed and that wants to handle the fact, you might write

```
case File.open(user_file_name) do
{:ok, file} ->
  process(file)
{:error, message} ->
  IO.puts :stderr, "Couldn't open #{user_file_name}: #{message}"
end
```

If instead you expect the file to open successfully every time, you could raise an exception on failure.

```
case File.open("config_file") do
{:ok, file} ->
  process(file)
{:error, message} ->
  raise "Failed to open config file: #{message}"
end
```

Or you could let Elixir raise an exception for you and write

```
{ :ok, file } = File.open("config_file")
process(file)
```

If the pattern match on the first line fails, Elixir will raise a MatchError exception. It won't be as informative as our version that handled the error explicitly, but if the error should never happen, this form is probably good enough (at least until it triggers the first time and the operations folks say they'd like more information).

An even better way to handle this is to use File.open!. The trailing exclamation point in the method name is an Elixir convention—if you see it, you know the function will raise an exception on error, and that exception will be meaningful. So we could simply write

```
file = File.open!("config_file")
```

and get on with our lives.

Doing More with Less

Elixir has just a few forms of control flow: if, unless, cond, case, and (perhaps) raise. But surprisingly, this doesn't matter in practice. Elixir programs are rich and expressive without a lot of branching code. And they're easier to work with as a result.

That concludes our basic tour of Elixir. Now let's start putting it all together and implement a full project.

Your Turn

➤ *Exercise: ControlFlow-1*
Rewrite the FizzBuzz example using case.

➤ *Exercise: ControlFlow-2*
We now have three different implementations of FizzBuzz. One uses cond, one uses case, and one uses separate functions with guard clauses.

Take a minute to look at all three. Which do you feel best expresses the problem. Which will be easiest to maintain?

The case style and the implementation using guard clauses are different from control structures in most other languages. If you feel that one of these was the best implementation, can you think of ways to remind yourself to investigate these options as you write Elixir code in the future?

➤ *Exercise: ControlFlow-3*

Many built-in functions have two forms. The *xxx* form returns the tuple {:ok, data} and the *xxx!* form returns data on success but raises an exception otherwise. However, some functions don't have the *xxx!* form.

Write an ok! function that takes an arbitrary parameter. If the parameter is the tuple {:ok, data}, return the data. Otherwise, raise an exception containing information from the parameter.

You could use your function like this:

```
file = ok! File.open("somefile")
```

In this chapter, you'll see:
  • Project structure
  • The mix build tool
  • ExUnit testing framework
  • DocTests

## CHAPTER 13

Organizing a Project

Let's stop hacking and get serious.

You'll want to organize your source code, write tests, and handle any dependencies. And you'll want to follow Elixir conventions, because that way you'll get support from the tools.

In this chapter we'll look at mix, the Elixir build tool. We'll investigate the directory structure it uses and see how to manage external dependencies. And we'll end up using ExUnit to write tests for our code (and to validate the examples in our code's documentation). To motivate this, we'll write a tool that downloads and lists the n oldest issues from a GitHub project. Along the way, we'll need to find some libraries and make some design decisions typical of an Elixir project. We'll call our project issues.

The Project: Fetch Issues from GitHub

GitHub provides a nice web API for fetching issues.[1] Simply issue a GET request to

https://api.github.com/repos/*user*/*project*/issues

and you'll get back a JSON list of issues. We'll reformat this, sort it, and filter out the oldest n, presenting the result as a table:

```
  #  |  created_at           |  title
-----+-----------------------+------------------------------------------
 889 |  2013-03-16T22:03:13Z |  MIX_PATH environment variable (of sorts)
 892 |  2013-03-20T19:22:07Z |  Enhanced mix test --cover
 893 |  2013-03-21T06:23:00Z |  mix test time reports
 898 |  2013-03-23T19:19:08Z |  Add mix compile --warnings-as-errors
```

---

1. http://developer.github.com/v3/

How Our Code Will Do It

Our program will run from the command line. We'll need to pass in a GitHub user name, a project name, and an optional count. This means we'll need some basic command-line parsing.

We'll need to access GitHub as an HTTP client, so we'll have to find a library that gives us the client side of HTTP. The response that comes back will be in JSON, so we'll need a library that handles JSON, too. We'll need to be able to sort the resulting structure. And finally, we'll need to lay out selected fields in a table.

We can think of this data transformation in terms of a production line. Raw data enters at one end and is transformed by each of the stations in turn.

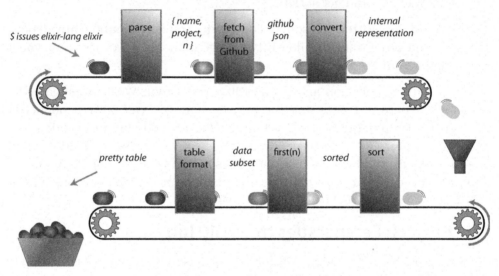

Here we see data, starting at *command line* and ending at *pretty table*. At each stage, it undergoes a transformation (parse, fetch, and so on). These transformations are the functions we write. We'll cover each one in turn.

Task: Use Mix to Create Our New Project

Mix is a command-line utility that manages Elixir projects. Use it to create new projects, manage a project's dependencies, run tests, and run your code. If you have Elixir installed, you also have mix. Try running it now:

```
$ mix help
mix                     # Run the default task (current: mix run)
mix archive             # List all archives
mix archive.build       # Archive this project into a .ez file
  :         :                   :              :
```

```
mix new            # Create a new Elixir project
mix run            # Run the given file or expression
mix test           # Run a project's tests
iex -S mix         # Start IEx and run the default task
```

This is a list of the standard *tasks* that come with mix. (Your list may be a little different, depending on your version of Elixir.) For more information on a particular task, use mix help *taskname*.

```
$ mix help deps
```

```
List all dependencies and their status.
```

```
Dependencies must be specified in the `mix.exs` file in one of
the following formats:
  . . .
```

You can also write your own mix tasks, both for a project and to share between projects.[2]

Create the Project Tree

Each Elixir project lives in its own directory tree. If you use mix to manage this tree, then you'll need to follow the mix conventions (which are also the conventions of the Elixir community). We'll use these conventions in the rest of this chapter.

We'll call our project issues, so it will go in a directory named issues. We'll create this directory using mix.

At the command line, navigate to a place where you want this new project to live, and type

```
$ mix new issues
* creating README.md
    :          :
* creating test
* creating test/test_helper.exs
* creating test/issues_test.exs

Your mix project was created successfully.
You can use mix to compile it, test it, and more:

    cd issues
    mix test

Run `mix help` for more commands.
```

---

2.   http://elixir-lang.org/getting_started/mix_otp/1.html

In tree form, the newly created files and directories look like this:

```
issues
├── .gitignore
├── README.md
├── config
│   └── config.exs
├── lib
│   └── issues.ex
├── mix.exs
└── test
    ├── issues_test.exs
    └── test_helper.exs
```

Change into the issues/ directory. This is a good time to set up version control. I use Git, so I do

```
$ git init
$ git add .
$ git commit -m "Initial commit of new project"
```

(I don't want to clutter the book with version-control stuff, so that's the last time I'll mention it. Make sure you follow your own version-control practices as we go along.)

Our new project contains three directories and seven files.

.gitignore

Lists the files and directories generated as by-products of the build and not to be saved in the repository.

README.md

A place to put a description of your project (in Markdown format). If you store your project on GitHub, this file's contents will appear on the project's home page.

config/

Eventually we'll put some application-specific configuration here.

lib/

This is where our project's source lives. Mix has already added a top-level module (issues.ex in our case).

mix.exs

This source file contains our project's configuration options. We will be adding stuff to this as our project progresses.

test/

> A place to store our tests. Mix has already created a helper file and a stub for unit tests of the issues module.

Now our job is to add our code. But before we do, let's think a little about the implementation.

Transformation: Parse the Command Line

Let's start with the command line. We really don't want to couple the handling of command-line options into the main body of our program, so let's write a separate module to interface between what the user types and what our program does. By convention this module is called *Project*.CLI (so our code would be in Issues.CLI). Also by convention, the main entry point to this module will be a function called run that takes an array of command-line arguments.

Where should we put this module?

Elixir has a convention. Inside the lib/ directory, create a subdirectory with the same name as the project (so we'd create the directory lib/issues/). This directory will contain the main source for our application, one module per file. And each module will be namespaced inside the Issues module—the module naming follows the directory naming.

In this case, the module we want to write is Issues.CLI—it is the CLI module nested inside the Issues module. Let's reflect that in the directory structure and put cli.ex in the lib/issues directory:

```
lib
├── issues
│   └── cli.ex
└── issues.ex
```

Elixir comes bundled with an option-parsing library,[3] so we will use that. We'll tell it that -h and --help are possible switches, and anything else is an argument. It returns a tuple, where the first element is a keyword list of the options and the second is a list of the remaining arguments. Our initial CLI module looks like the following.

---

3.   http://elixir-lang.org/docs/stable/elixir/OptionParser.html

```
project/0/issues/lib/issues/cli.ex
defmodule Issues.CLI do

  @default_count 4

  @moduledoc """
  Handle the command line parsing and the dispatch to
  the various functions that end up generating a
  table of the last _n_ issues in a github project
  """

  def run(argv) do
    parse_args(argv)
  end

  @doc """
  `argv` can be -h or --help, which returns :help.

  Otherwise it is a github user name, project name, and (optionally)
  the number of entries to format.

  Return a tuple of `{ user, project, count }`, or `:help` if help was given.
  """
  def parse_args(argv) do
    parse = OptionParser.parse(argv, switches: [ help: :boolean],
                                     aliases: [ h:     :help    ])
    case  parse  do

    { [ help: true ], _, _ }
      -> :help

    { _, [ user, project, count ], _ }
      -> { user, project, count }

    { _, [ user, project ], _ }
      -> { user, project, @default_count }

    _ -> :help

    end
  end
end
```

Step: Write Some Basic Tests

At this point, I get a little nervous if I don't have some tests. Fortunately, Elixir comes with a wonderful (and simple) testing framework called ExUnit.

Have a look at the file test/issues_test.exs.

```
project/0/issues/test/issues_test.exs
defmodule IssuesTest do
  use ExUnit.Case
  doctest Issues

  test "the truth" do
    assert 1 + 1 == 2
  end
end
```

It acts as a template for all the test files you write. I just copy and paste the boilerplate into separate test files as I need them. So let's write tests for our CLI module, putting those tests into the file test/cli_test.exs. We'll test that the option parser successfully detects the -h and --help options, and that it returns the arguments otherwise. We'll also check that it supplies a default value for the count if only two arguments are given.

```
project/1/issues/test/cli_test.exs
defmodule CliTest do
  use ExUnit.Case
  doctest Issues

  import Issues.CLI, only: [ parse_args: 1 ]

  test ":help returned by option parsing with -h and --help options" do
    assert parse_args(["-h",     "anything"]) == :help
    assert parse_args(["--help", "anything"]) == :help
  end

  test "three values returned if three given" do
    assert parse_args(["user", "project", "99"]) == { "user", "project", 99 }
  end

  test "count is defaulted if two values given" do
    assert parse_args(["user", "project"]) == { "user", "project", 4 }
  end
end
```

These tests all use the basic assert macro that ExUnit provides. This macro is clever—if an assertion fails, it can extract the values from the expression you pass it, giving you a nice error message.

To run our tests, we'll use the mix test task.

```
issues$ mix test
Compiled lib/issues.ex
Compiled lib/issues/cli.ex
Generated issues app
..

Failures:

  1) test three values returned if three given (CliTest)
     test/cli_test.exs:11
     Assertion with == failed
     code: parse_args(["user", "project", "99"]) == {"user", "project", 99}
     lhs:  {"user", "project", "99"}
     rhs:  {"user", "project", 99}
     stacktrace:
       test/cli_test.exs:12

.
Finished in 0.01 seconds
4 tests, 1 failures
```

Three of the four tests ran successfully. However, when we pass a count as the third parameter, it blows up. See how the assertion shows you its type (== in this case), the line of code that failed, and the two values that we compared. You can see the difference between the left-hand side (lhs), which is the value returned by parse_args, and the expected value (the rhs). We were expecting to get a number as the count, but we got a string.

That's easily fixed. The built-in function String.to_integer converts a binary (a string) into an integer.

project/1/issues/lib/issues/cli.ex

```
  def parse_args(argv) do
    parse = OptionParser.parse(argv, switches: [ help: :boolean],
                                     aliases:  [ h:     :help   ])
    case parse do

    { [ help: true ], _,              _ } -> :help
➤   { _, [ user, project, count ], _ } -> { user, project,
➤                                           String.to_integer(count) }
    { _, [ user, project ],          _ } -> { user, project, @default_count }
    _                                     -> :help
    end
  end
```

Your Turn

➤ *Exercise: OrganizingAProject-1*

Do what I did. Honest. Create the project and write and test the option parser. It's one thing to read about it, but you'll be doing this a lot, so you may as well start now.

Transformation: Fetch from GitHub

Now let's continue down our data-transformation chain. Having parsed our arguments, we need to transform them by fetching data from GitHub. So we'll extend our run function to call a process function, passing it the value returned from the parse_args function. We could have written this:

```
process(parse_args(argv))
```

But to understand this code, you have to read it right to left. I prefer to make the chain more explicit using the Elixir pipe operator:

project/1/issues/lib/issues/cli.ex
```
def run(argv) do
  argv
  |> parse_args
  |> process
end
```

We need two variants of the process function. One handles the case where the user asked for help and parse_args returned :help. The second handles the case where a user, project, and count are returned.

project/1/issues/lib/issues/cli.ex
```
def process(:help) do
  IO.puts """
  usage:  issues <user> <project> [ count | #{@default_count} ]
  """
  System.halt(0)
end

def process({user, project, _count}) do
  Issues.GithubIssues.fetch(user, project)
end
```

We can use mix to run our function. Let's first see if help gets displayed.

```
$ mix run -e 'Issues.CLI.run(["-h"])'
usage:  issues <user> <project> [ count | 4 ]
```

You pass mix run an Elixir expression, which gets evaluated in the context of your application. Mix will recompile your application, as it is out of date before executing the expression.

If we pass it user and project names, however, it'll blow up because we haven't written that code yet.

```
% mix run -e 'Issues.CLI.run(["elixir-lang", "elixir"])'
** (UndefinedFunctionError) undefined function: Issues.GithubIssues.fetch/2
    GithubIssues.fetch("elixir-lang", "elixir")
```

Let's write that code now. Our program will act as an HTTP client, accessing GitHub through its web API. So, it looks like we'll need an external library.

Task: Use Libraries

Elixir comes with a bunch of libraries preinstalled. Some are written in Elixir, and others in Erlang.

The first port of call is http://elixir-lang.org/docs/, the Elixir documentation. Often you'll find a built-in library that does what you want.

Next, check if any standard Erlang libraries do what you need. This isn't a simple task. Visit http://erlang.org/doc/ and look in the left sidebar for *Application Groups*. There you'll find libraries sorted by top-level category.

If you find what you're looking for in either of these two places, you're all set, because all these libraries are already available to your application. But if the built-in libraries don't have what you need, you'll have to add an external dependency.

Finding an External Library

Package managers: Ruby has RubyGems, Python has pip, Node.js has npm.

And Elixir has *hex*.

Visit http://hex.pm and search its list of packages that integrate nicely with a mix-based project.

If all else fails, Google and GitHub are your friends. Search for terms such as *elixir http client* or *erlang distributed logger*, and you're likely to turn up the libraries you need.

In our case, we need an HTTP client. We find that Elixir has nothing built in, but hex.pm has a number of HTTP client libraries.

To me, HTTPoison looks like a good option. So how do we include it in our project?

Adding a Library to Your Project

Mix takes the view that all external libraries should be copied into the project's directory structure. The good news is that it handles all this for us—we just need to list the dependencies, and it does the rest. Remember the mix.exs file at the top level of our project? Here is that original version.

```
project/0/issues/mix.exs
defmodule Issues.Mixfile do
  use Mix.Project


  def project do
    [ app:             :issues,
      version:         "0.0.1",
      elixir:          "~> 1.2",
      build_embedded:  Mix.env == :prod,
      start_permanent: Mix.env == :prod,
      deps:            deps ]
  end


  # Configuration for the OTP application
  # Type `mix help compile.app` for more information
  def application do
    [applications: [:logger]]
  end


  # Dependencies can be Hex packages:
  #
  #   {:mydep, "~> 0.3.0"}
  #
  # Or git/path repositories:
  #
  #   {:mydep, git: "https://github.com/elixir-lang/mydep.git", tag: "0.1.0"}
  #
  # Type "mix help deps" for more examples and options
  defp deps do
    []
  end
end
```

We add new dependencies to the deps function. As the HTTPoison package is in hex.pm, that's very straightforward. We just give the name and the version we want.

```
project/1/issues/mix.exs
defp deps do
  [
    { :httpoison, "~> 0.8" }
  ]
end
```

In this case, we give the version as "~> 0.8". This matches any version of HTTPoison with a major version of 0 and a minor version of 8 or greater. In iex, type h Version for more details.

Once your mix.exs file is updated, you're ready to have mix manage your dependencies.

Use mix deps to list the dependencies and their status:

```
$ mix deps
* httpoison (package)
  the dependency is not available, run `mix deps.get`
```

Download the dependencies with mix deps.get:

```
$ mix deps.get
Running dependency resolution
Dependency resolution completed successfully
  certifi: v0.3.0
  hackney: v1.4.7
  httpoison: v0.8.0
  idna: v1.0.2
  mimerl: v1.0.2
  ssl_verify_hostname: v1.0.5
* Getting httpoison (Hex package)
  . . .
```

Run mix deps again:

```
$ mix deps
* idna (Hex package) (rebar)
  locked at 1.0.2 (idna)
  the dependency build is outdated, please run "mix deps.compile"


  . . .


* httpoison (Hex package) (mix)
  locked at 0.8.0 (httpoison)
  the dependency build is outdated, please run "mix deps.compile"
```

This shows that the HTTPoison library is installed but that it hasn't yet been compiled. Mix also remembers the exact version of each library it installs in the file mix.lock. This means that at any point in the future you can get the same version of the library you use now.

Don't worry that the library isn't compiled—mix will automatically compile it the first time we need it.

If you look at your project tree, you'll find a new directory called deps containing your dependencies. Note that these dependencies are themselves just projects, so you can browse their source and read their documentation.

Your Turn

➤ *Exercise: OrganizingAProject-2*
Add the dependency to your project and install it.

Back to the Transformation

So, back to our problem. We have to write the function GithubIssues.fetch, which transforms a user name and project into a data structure containing that project's issues. The HTTPoison page on GitHub gives us a clue,[4] and we write a new module, Issues.GithubIssues:

```elixir
defmodule Issues.GithubIssues do
  @user_agent  [ {"User-agent", "Elixir dave@pragprog.com"} ]

  def fetch(user, project) do
    issues_url(user, project)
    |> HTTPoison.get(@user_agent)
    |> handle_response
  end

  def issues_url(user, project) do
    "https://api.github.com/repos/#{user}/#{project}/issues"
  end

  def handle_response({ :ok, %{status_code: 200, body: body}}), do: { :ok,    body }
  def handle_response({ ___, %{status_code: ___, body: body}}), do: { :error, body }
end
```

We simply call get on the GitHub URL. (We also have to pass in a user-agent header to keep the GitHub API happy.) What comes back is a structure. If we have a successful response, we return a tuple whose first element is :ok, along with the body. Otherwise we return an :error tuple, also with the body.

But there's one more thing. If you look at the HTTPoison GitHub page, you'll see that the example code calls HTTPoison.start. That's because HTTPoison actually runs as a separate application, outside your main process. A lot of developers will copy this code, calling start inline like this. I did myself, until José Valim set me straight—there's a better way. Back in our mix.exs file, there's a function called application.

```elixir
# Configuration for the OTP application
# Type `mix help compile.app` for more information
def application do
  [applications: [:logger]]
```

---

4.   https://github.com/edgurgel/httpoison

end

OTP is the framework that manages suites of running applications. The application function configures the contents of these suites. By default, this app function starts the Elixir logger. But we can use it to start extra applications. We tell mix about starting HTTPoison here. (I found this counterintuitive at first. Erlang—and, by extension, Elixir—programs are often structured as suites of cooperating subapplications. Frequently, the code that would be a library in another language is a subapplication in Elixir. It might help to think of these as components or services.)

project/1/issues/mix.exs
```
def application do
  [ applications: [ :logger, :httpoison ] ]
end
```

Don't worry about the details here—we'll be talking about this extensively in Part II of this book.

We can play with this in iex. Use the -S mix option to run mix before dropping into interaction mode. Because this is the first time we've tried to run our code since installing the dependencies, you'll see them get compiled:

```
$ iex -S mix
Erlang/OTP 18 [erts-7.1] [source] [64-bit] [smp:4:4] [async-threads:10]...

==> idna (compile)
Compiled src/idna_ucs.erl
Compiled src/idna.erl
    :         :
Generated issues app

iex(1)>
```

Let's try it out:

```
iex> Issues.GithubIssues.fetch("elixir-lang", "elixir")
{:ok,
 "[{\"url\":\"https://api.github.com/repos/elixir-lang/elixir/issues/4126\",
  \"labels_url\":\"https://api.github.com/repos/elixir-lang/elixir/...",
  \"comments_url\":\"https://api.github.com/repos/elixir-lang/elixir/...",
  \"events_url\":\"https://api.github.com/repos/elixir-lang/elixir/...",
  \"html_url\":\"https://github.com/elixir-lang/elixir/issues/4126\",
  \"id\":124284664,\"number\":4126,
  \"title\":\"#put_in function with structs raises . . .
```

This is the body of the Github response. It's a tuple with the first element set to :ok. The second element is a single long string containing the data encoded in JSON format.

Transformation: Convert Response

We'll need a JSON library to convert the response into a data structure. Searching hex.pm, I found the poison library[5] (no relation to HTTPoison), so let's add its dependency to our mix.exs file.

```
project/2/issues/mix.exs
defp deps do
  [
    httpoison: "~> 0.8",
    poison:    "~> 1.5"
  ]
end
```

Run mix deps.get, and you'll end up with poison installed.

To convert the body from a string, we call the Poison.Parser.parse! function when we return the message from the GitHub API:

```
project/3/issues/lib/issues/github_issues.ex
  def handle_response({:ok, %{status_code: 200, body: body}}) do
➤   { :ok, Poison.Parser.parse!(body) }
  end

  def handle_response({_, %{status_code: ___, body: body}}) do
➤   { :error, Poison.Parser.parse!(body) }
  end
```

We also have to deal with a possible error response from the fetch, so back in the CLI module we write a function that decodes the body and returns it on a success response; the function extracts the error from the body and displays it otherwise.

```
  def process({user, project, _count}) do
    Issues.GithubIssues.fetch(user, project)
➤   |> decode_response
  end

  def decode_response({:ok, body}), do: body

  def decode_response({:error, error}) do
    {_, message} = List.keyfind(error, "message", 0)
    IO.puts "Error fetching from Github: #{message}"
    System.halt(2)
  end
```

---

5.   https://github.com/devinus/poison

The JSON that GitHub returns for a successful response is a list with one element per GitHub issue. That element is itself a list of key/value tuples. To make these easier (and more efficient) to work with, we'll convert our list of lists into a list of Elixir maps, which give you fast access by key to a list of key/value pairs.[6]

We'll do that by piping our data through this function:

```
def convert_to_list_of_maps(list) do
  list
  |> Enum.map(&Enum.into(&1, Map.new))
end
```

Our process function now looks like this:

```
    def process({user, project, _count}) do
      Issues.GithubIssues.fetch(user, project)
      |> decode_response
➤     |> convert_to_list_of_maps
    end
```

Dependencies That Aren't in Hex

The dependencies you need are likely in hex, so mix will probably find them automatically. However, sometimes you'll need to go further afield. The good news is that mix can also load dependencies from other sources. The most common is GitHub.

HTTPoison uses a library called Hackney. In earlier versions of the book, hackney wasn't in hex.pm, so I had to add the following dependency to my mix.exs:

```
def deps do
  [ { . . . },
    { :hackney, github: "benoitc/hackney" }
  ]
end
```

Application Configuration

Before we move on, there's one little tweak I'd like to make. The issues_url function hardcodes the GitHub URL. Let's make this configurable.

Remember that when we created the project using mix new, it added a config/ directory containing config.exs. That file stores application-level configuration.

It should start with the line

```
use Mix.Config
```

---

6. http://elixir-lang.org/docs/stable/elixir/Map.html

We then write configuration information for each of the applications in our project. Here we're configuring the Issues application, so we write the following code.

```
project/3/issues/config/config.exs
use Mix.Config
config :issues, github_url: "https://api.github.com"
```

Each config line adds one or more key/value pairs to the given application's environment. If you have multiple lines for the same application, they accumulate, with duplicate keys in later lines overriding values from earlier ones.

In our code, we use the Application.get_env function to return a value from the environment.

```
project/3/issues/lib/issues/github_issues.ex
# use a module attribute to fetch the value at compile time
@github_url Application.get_env(:issues, :github_url)

def issues_url(user, project) do
  "#{@github_url}/repos/#{user}/#{project}/issues"
end
```

Because the application environment is commonly used in Erlang code, you'll find yourself using the configuration facility to configure code you import, as well as code you write.

Sometimes you may want to vary the configuration, perhaps depending on your application's environment. One way is to use the import_config function, which reads configuration from a file. If your config.exs contains

```
use Mix.Config
```

```
import_config "#{Mix.env}.exs"
```

then Elixir will read dev.exs, test.exs, or prod.exs, depending on your environment.

You can override the default config file name (config/config.exs) using the --config option to elixir.

Transformation: Sort Data

Look at our original "design."

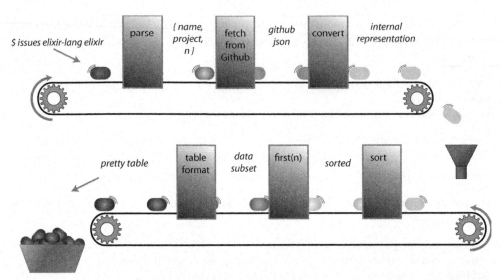

We're making good progress—we've coded all of the top conveyor belt. Our next transformation is to sort the data on its created_at field. And this can just use a standard Elixir library function, sort/2. We *could* create a new module for this, but it would be pretty lonely. For now we'll put the function in the CLI module and keep an eye out for opportunities to move it out if we add related functions later.

So now our CLI module contains

```
def process({user, project, count}) do
  Issues.GithubIssues.fetch(user, project)
  |> decode_response
  |> convert_to_list_of_maps
  |> sort_into_ascending_order
end

def sort_into_ascending_order(list_of_issues) do
  Enum.sort list_of_issues,
            fn i1, i2 -> i1["created_at"] <= i2["created_at"] end
end
```

That sort_into_ascending_order function worries me a little—I get the comparison the wrong way around about 50% of the time, so let's write a little CLI test.

```
project/3/issues/test/cli_test.exs
test "sort ascending orders the correct way" do
  result = sort_into_ascending_order(fake_created_at_list(["c", "a", "b"]))
  issues = for issue <- result, do: issue["created_at"]
  assert issues == ~w{a b c}
end

defp fake_created_at_list(values) do
```

```
  data = for value <- values,
         do: [{"created_at", value}, {"other_data", "xxx"} ]
  convert_to_list_of_maps data
end
```

Update the import line at the top of the test:

```
import Issues.CLI, only: [ parse_args: 1,
                           sort_into_ascending_order: 1,
                           convert_to_list_of_maps: 1 ]
```

and run it:

```
$ mix test
.....
Finished in 0.00 seconds
5 tests, 0 failures
```

Lookin' fine; mighty fine.

Transformation: Take First *n* Items

Our next transformation is to extract the first *count* entries from the list. Resisting the temptation to write the function ourselves,[7] we discover the built-in Enum.take:

```
def process({user, project, count}) do
  Issues.GithubIssues.fetch(user, project)
  |> decode_response
  |> convert_to_list_of_maps
  |> sort_into_ascending_order
  |> Enum.take(count)
end
```

Your Turn

> *Exercise: OrganizingAProject-3*
> Bring your version of this project in line with the code here.

> *Exercise: OrganizingAProject-4*
> (Tricky) Before reading the next section, see if you can write the code to format the data into columns, like the sample output at the start of the chapter. This is probably the longest piece of Elixir code you'll have written. Try to do it without using if or cond.

---

7. How *would* you write such a function?

Transformation: Format the Table

All that's left from our design is to create the formatted table. This would be a nice interface:

```elixir
def process({user, project, count}) do
  Issues.GithubIssues.fetch(user, project)
  |> decode_response
  |> convert_to_list_of_maps
  |> sort_into_ascending_order
  |> Enum.take(count)
➤ |> print_table_for_columns(["number", "created_at", "title"])
end
```

We pass the formatter the list of columns to include in the table, and it writes the table to standard output.

The formatter doesn't add any new project- or design-related techniques, so we'll just list it on the next page.

project/4/issues/lib/issues/table_formatter.ex

```elixir
defmodule Issues.TableFormatter do

  import Enum, only: [ each: 2, map: 2, map_join: 3, max: 1 ]

  def print_table_for_columns(rows, headers) do
    with data_by_columns = split_into_columns(rows, headers),
         column_widths   = widths_of(data_by_columns),
         format          = format_for(column_widths)
    do
      puts_one_line_in_columns(headers, format)
      IO.puts(separator(column_widths))
      puts_in_columns(data_by_columns, format)
    end
  end

  def split_into_columns(rows, headers) do
    for header <- headers do
      for row <- rows, do: printable(row[header])
    end
  end

  def printable(str) when is_binary(str), do: str
  def printable(str), do: to_string(str)

  def widths_of(columns) do
    for column <- columns, do: column |> map(&String.length/1) |> max
  end

  def format_for(column_widths) do
```

```
    map_join(column_widths, " | ", fn width -> "~-#{width}s" end) <> "~n"
  end

  def separator(column_widths) do
    map_join(column_widths, "-+-", fn width -> List.duplicate("-", width) end)
  end

  def puts_in_columns(data_by_columns, format) do
    data_by_columns
    |> List.zip
    |> map(&Tuple.to_list/1)
    |> each(&puts_one_line_in_columns(&1, format))
  end

  def puts_one_line_in_columns(fields, format) do
    :io.format(format, fields)
  end
end
```

And here are the tests for it.

project/4/issues/test/table_formatter_test.exs

```
defmodule TableFormatterTest do
  use ExUnit.Case          # bring in the test functionality
  import ExUnit.CaptureIO  # And allow us to capture stuff sent to stdout

  alias Issues.TableFormatter, as: TF

  def simple_test_data do
    [ [ c1: "r1 c1", c2: "r1 c2",  c3: "r1 c3", c4: "r1+++c4" ],
      [ c1: "r2 c1", c2: "r2 c2",  c3: "r2 c3", c4: "r2 c4"   ],
      [ c1: "r3 c1", c2: "r3 c2",  c3: "r3 c3", c4: "r3 c4"   ],
      [ c1: "r4 c1", c2: "r4++c2", c3: "r4 c3", c4: "r4 c4"   ] ]
  end

  def headers, do: [ :c1, :c2, :c4 ]

  def split_with_three_columns,
    do: TF.split_into_columns(simple_test_data, headers)

  test "split_into_columns" do
    columns = split_with_three_columns
    assert      length(columns) == length(headers)
    assert List.first(columns) == ["r1 c1", "r2 c1", "r3 c1", "r4 c1"]
    assert  List.last(columns) == ["r1+++c4", "r2 c4", "r3 c4", "r4 c4"]
  end

  test "column_widths" do
    widths = TF.widths_of(split_with_three_columns)
    assert widths == [ 5, 6, 7 ]
  end
```

```
test "correct format string returned" do
  assert TF.format_for([9, 10, 11]) == "~-9s | ~-10s | ~-11s~n"
end

test "Output is correct" do
  result = capture_io fn ->
    TF.print_table_for_columns(simple_test_data, headers)
  end
  assert result == """
c1    | c2     | c4
------+--------+--------
r1 c1 | r1 c2  | r1+++c4
r2 c1 | r2 c2  | r2 c4
r3 c1 | r3 c2  | r3 c4
r4 c1 | r4++c2 | r4 c4
  """
  end
end
```

(Although you can't see it here, the output we compare against in the last test contains trailing whitespace.)

Rather than clutter the process function in the CLI module with a long module name, I chose to use import to make the print function available without a module qualifier. This goes near the top of cli.ex.

```
import Issues.TableFormatter, only: [ print_table_for_columns: 2 ]
```

This code also uses a wonderful Elixir testing feature. By importing ExUnit.CaptureIO, we get access to the capture_io function. This runs the code passed to it, but captures anything written to standard output, returning it as a string.

Task: Make a Command-Line Executable

Although we can run our code by calling the run function via mix, it isn't really friendly for other users. So let's create something we can run from the command line.

Mix can package our code, along with its dependencies, into a single file that can be run on any Unix-based platform. This uses Erlang's *escript* utility, which can run precompiled programs stored as a Zip archive. In our case, the program will be run as issues.

When escript runs a program, it looks in your mix.exs file for the option escript. This should return a keyword list of escript configuration settings. The most important of these is main_module:, which must be set to the name of a module containing a main function. It passes the command-line arguments to this main function as a list of character lists (not binaries). As this seems to be a command-line concern, we'll put the main function in Issues.CLI. Here's the update to mix.exs:

```
project/4/issues/mix.exs
defmodule Issues.Mixfile do
  use Mix.Project

  def project do
➤    [ app:             :issues,
      escript:          escript_config,
      version:          "0.0.1",
      elixir:           "~> 1.2",
      build_embedded:   Mix.env == :prod,
      start_permanent:  Mix.env == :prod,
      deps:             deps ]
  end

  # Configuration for the OTP application
  def application do
    [
      applications: [ :logger, :httpoison ]
    ]
  end

  defp deps do
    [
      httpoison: "~> 0.5",
      poison:    "~> 1.5"
    ]
  end

➤  defp escript_config do
➤    [ main_module: Issues.CLI ]
➤  end
end
```

Now let's add a main function to our CLI. In fact, all we need to do is rename
the existing run function:

```
project/4/issues/lib/issues/cli.ex
def main(argv) do
  argv
    |> parse_args
    |> process
end
```

Then we package our program using mix:

```
$ mix escript.build
Generated escript issues
```

Now we can run the app locally. We can also send it to a friend—it will run
on any computer that has Erlang installed.

```
$ ./issues elixir-lang elixir 3
numb | created_at          | title
-----+---------------------+-------------------------------------------------
3328 | 2015-05-14T15:00:37Z | Support delayed evaluation of code in .iex.exs
3400 | 2015-06-17T13:04:45Z | Float.round is inconsistent
3413 | 2015-06-21T07:58:03Z | Remove Float.to_string/2 and Float.to_char_list/2…
```

Task: Add Some Logging

Imagine a large Elixir application—dozens of processes potentially running across a number of nodes. You'd really want a standard way to keep track of significant events as it runs. Enter the Elixir logger.

The default mix.exs starts the logger for your application.

```
project/5/issues/mix.exs
def application do
  [
    applications: [ :logger, :httpoison ]
  ]
end
```

The logger supports four levels of message—in increasing order of severity they are debug, info, warn, and error. You select the level of logging in two ways.

First, you can determine at compile time the minimum level of logging to include. Logging below this level is not even compiled into your code. The compile-time level is set in the config/config.exs file:

```
project/5/issues/config/config.exs
use Mix.Config
config :issues, github_url: "https://api.github.com"
➤ config :logger, compile_time_purge_level: :info
```

Next, you can change the minimum log level at runtime by calling Logger.configure. (Clearly, this cannot enable log levels that you excluded at compile time.)

After all this configuration, it's time to add some logging.

The basic logging functions are Logger.debug, .info, .warn, and .error. Each function takes either a string or a zero-arity function:

```
Logger.debug "Order total #{total(order)}"
Logger.debug fn -> "Order total #{total(order)}" end
```

Why have the function version? Perhaps the calculation of the order total is expensive. In the first version, we'll always call it to interpolate the value into our string, even if the runtime log level is set to ignore debug-level messages. In the function variant, though, the total function will be invoked only if the log message is needed.

Anyway, here's a version of our fetch function with some logging:

```
project/5/issues/lib/issues/github_issues.ex
defmodule Issues.GithubIssues do

➤  require Logger

   @user_agent [ {"User-agent", "Elixir dave@pragprog.com"} ]

   def fetch(user, project) do
➤    Logger.info "Fetching user #{user}'s project #{project}"
     issues_url(user, project)
     |> HTTPoison.get(@user_agent)
     |> handle_response
   end

   def handle_response({:ok, %{status_code: 200, body: body}}) do
➤    Logger.info "Successful response"
➤    Logger.debug fn -> inspect(body) end
     { :ok, Poison.Parser.parse!(body) }
   end

   def handle_response({_, %{status_code: status, body: body}}) do
➤    Logger.error "Error #{status} returned"
     { :error, Poison.Parser.parse!(body) }
   end

   # use a module attribute to fetch the value at compile time
   @github_url Application.get_env(:issues, :github_url)

   def issues_url(user, project) do
     "#{@github_url}/repos/#{user}/#{project}/issues"
   end

end
```

Note the use of require Logger at the top of the module. If you forget this (and I do every time), you'll get an error when you make the first call to Logger.

We can play with the new code in iex:

```
iex> Issues.CLI.process {"elixir-lang", "elixir", 1}
21:58:27.577 [info] Fetching user elixir-lang's project elixir
21:58:28.175 [info] Successful response
numb | created_at          | title
-----+---------------------+------------------------------------------------
2396 | 2014-06-12T15:02:23Z | Elixir version checking for installed archives
:ok
```

Notice that the debug-level message is not displayed.

Task: Test the Comments

When I document my functions, I like to include examples of the function being used—comments saying things such as, "Feed it these arguments, and you'll get this result." In the Elixir world, a common way to do this is to show the function being used in an iex session.

Here's an example. Our TableFormatter holds a number of self-contained functions that we can document.

`project/5/issues/lib/issues/table_formatter.ex`
```elixir
defmodule Issues.TableFormatter do

  import Enum, only: [ each: 2, map: 2, map_join: 3, max: 1 ]

  @doc """
  Takes a list of row data, where each row is a Map, and a list of
  headers. Prints a table to STDOUT of the data from each row
  identified by each header. That is, each header identifies a column,
  and those columns are extracted and printed from the rows.0

  We calculate the width of each column to fit the longest element
  in that column.
  """
  def print_table_for_columns(rows, headers) do
    with data_by_columns = split_into_columns(rows, headers),
         column_widths   = widths_of(data_by_columns),
         format          = format_for(column_widths)
    do
         puts_one_line_in_columns(headers, format)
         IO.puts(separator(column_widths))
         puts_in_columns(data_by_columns, format)
    end
  end

  @doc """
  Given a list of rows, where each row contains a keyed list
  of columns, return a list containing lists of the data in
  each column. The `headers` parameter contains the
  list of columns to extract

  ## Example

      iex> list = [Enum.into([{"a", "1"},{"b", "2"},{"c", "3"}], %{}),
      ...>         Enum.into([{"a", "4"},{"b", "5"},{"c", "6"}], %{})]
      iex> Issues.TableFormatter.split_into_columns(list, [ "a", "b", "c" ])
      [ ["1", "4"], ["2", "5"], ["3", "6"] ]

  """
  def split_into_columns(rows, headers) do
```

```
    for header <- headers do
      for row <- rows, do: printable(row[header])
    end
end

@doc """
Return a binary (string) version of our parameter.
## Examples
    iex> Issues.TableFormatter.printable("a")
    "a"
    iex> Issues.TableFormatter.printable(99)
    "99"
"""
def printable(str) when is_binary(str), do: str
def printable(str), do: to_string(str)

@doc """
Given a list containing sublists, where each sublist contains the data for
a column, return a list containing the maximum width of each column

## Example
    iex> data = [ [ "cat", "wombat", "elk"], ["mongoose", "ant", "gnu"]]
    iex> Issues.TableFormatter.widths_of(data)
    [ 6, 8 ]
"""
def widths_of(columns) do
  for column <- columns, do: column |> map(&String.length/1) |> max
end

@doc """
Return a format string that hard codes the widths of a set of columns.
We put `" | "` between each column.

## Example
    iex> widths = [5,6,99]
    iex> Issues.TableFormatter.format_for(widths)
    "~-5s | ~-6s | ~-99s~n"
"""
def format_for(column_widths) do
  map_join(column_widths, " | ", fn width -> "~-#{width}s" end) <> "~n"
end

@doc """
Generate the line that goes below the column headings. It is a string of
hyphens, with + signs where the vertical bar between the columns goes.

## Example
    iex> widths = [5,6,9]
    iex> Issues.TableFormatter.separator(widths)
    "------+--------+----------"
```

```
  """
  def separator(column_widths) do
    map_join(column_widths, "-+-", fn width -> List.duplicate("-", width) end)
  end

  @doc """
  Given a list containing rows of data, a list containing the header selectors,
  and a format string, write the extracted data under control of the format string.
  """
  def puts_in_columns(data_by_columns, format) do
    data_by_columns
    |> List.zip
    |> map(&Tuple.to_list/1)
    |> each(&puts_one_line_in_columns(&1, format))
  end

  def puts_one_line_in_columns(fields, format) do
    :io.format(format, fields)
  end
end
```

Note how some of the documentation contains sample iex sessions.

Now we write a test that validates that each of the iex sessions returns the values shown in the @doc string. We create a new test file, test/doc_test.exs, containing this:

project/5/issues/test/doc_test.exs
```
defmodule DocTest do
  use ExUnit.Case
  doctest Issues.TableFormatter
end
```

We can now run this:

```
$ mix test test/doc_test.exs
......
Finished in 0.00 seconds
5 tests, 0 failures
```

And, of course, these tests are integrated into the overall test suite:

```
$ mix test
.............
Finished in 0.01 seconds
13 tests, 0 failures
```

Let's force an error to see what happens:

```
@doc """
Return a binary (string) version of our parameter.
```

```
## Examples

    iex> Issues.TableFormatter.printable("a")
    "a"
    iex> Issues.TableFormatter.printable(99)
    "99.0"
"""
def printable(str) when is_binary(str), do: str
def printable(str), do: to_string(str)
```

And run the tests again:

```
$  mix test test/doc_test.exs
.........
  1) test doc at Issues.TableFormatter.printable/1 (3) (DocTest)
     Doctest failed
     code: " Issues.TableFormatter.printable(99) should equal \"99.0\""
     lhs:   "\"99\""
     stacktrace:
       lib/issues/table_formatter.ex:52: Issues.TableFormatter (module)
Finished in 0.01 seconds
6 tests, 1 failures
```

Task: Create Project Documentation

Java has Javadoc, Ruby has RDoc, and Elixir has ExDoc—a documentation tool that describes your project, showing the modules, the things defined in them, and any documentation you've written for them.

Using it is easy. First, add the ExDoc dependency to your mix.exs file. You'll also need to add an output formatter—I use earmark, a pure-Elixir Markdown-to-HTML convertor.

```
defp deps do
  [
    httpoison:   "~> 0.8",
    poison:      "~> 1.5",
➤   ex_doc:      "~> 0.11",
➤   earmark:     ">= 0.0.0"
  ]
end
```

While you're in the mix.exs, you can add a project name and (if your project is in GitHub) a URL. The latter allows ExDoc to provide live links to your source code. These parameters go in the project function:

```
  def project do
    [ app:        :issues,
      version:    "0.0.1",
➤     name:       "Issues",
```

➤   *source_url:* *"https://github.com/pragdave/issues",*
       deps: deps]
    end

Then run `mix deps.get`.

To generate the documentation, just run

```
$ mix docs
Docs generated with success.
Open up docs/index.html in your browser to read them.
```

The first time you run it, this will install ExDoc. That involves compiling some C code, so you'll need a development environment on your machine.

Open docs/index.html in your browser, then use the sidebar on the left to search or drill down through your modules. Here's what I see for the start of the documentation for TableFormatter:

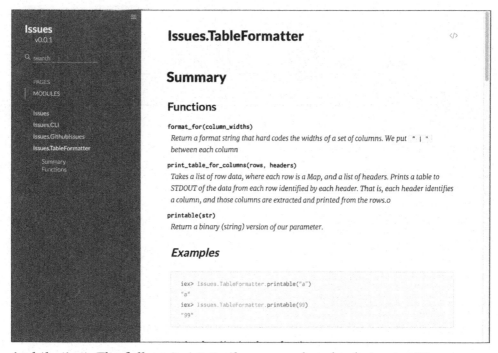

And that's it. The full project is in the source download at project/5/issues.

Coding by Transforming Data

I wanted to show you how Elixir projects are written—the tools we use and the processes we follow. I wanted to illustrate how lots of small functions can transform data, how specifying that transformation acts as an outline for the program, and how easy testing can be in Elixir.

But mostly I wanted to show how enjoyable Elixir development is, and how thinking about the world in terms of data and its transformation is a productive way to code.

Let's look at our original outline:

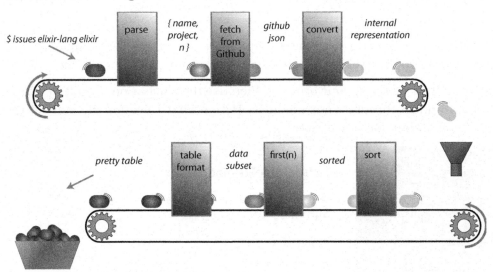

And then at the CLI.process function:

```elixir
def process({user, project, count}) do
  Issues.GithubIssues.fetch(user, project)
  |> decode_response
  |> convert_to_list_of_maps
  |> sort_into_ascending_order
  |> Enum.take(count)
  |> print_table_for_columns(["number", "created_at", "title"])
end
```

This is a cool way to code.

Next we'll turn our attention to concurrent programming, a key strength of Elixir.

Your Turn

➤ *Exercise: OrganizingAProject-6*

In the United States, the National Oceanic and Atmospheric Administration provides hourly XML feeds of conditions at 1,800 locations.[8] For example,

---

8.   http://w1.weather.gov/xml/current_obs

the feed for a small airport close to where I'm writing this is at http://w1.weather.gov/xml/current_obs/KDTO.xml.

Write an application that fetches this data, parses it, and displays it in a nice format.

(Hint: You might not have to download a library to handle XML parsing.)

Part II

Concurrent Programming

You want to write concurrent programs. That's probably why you're reading this book.

Let's look at Elixir's actor-based concurrency model. Then we'll dig into OTP, the Erlang management architecture that helps you create applications that are highly scalable and very reliable.

## CHAPTER 14

Working with Multiple Processes

One of Elixir's key features is the idea of packaging code into small chunks that can be run independently and concurrently.

If you've come from a conventional programming language, this may worry you. Concurrent programming is "known" to be difficult, and there's a performance penalty to pay when you create lots of processes.

Elixir doesn't have these issues, thanks to the architecture of the Erlang VM on which it runs.

Elixir uses the *actor* model of concurrency. An actor is an independent process that shares nothing with any other process. You can spawn new processes, send them messages, and receive messages back. And that's it (apart from some details about error handling and monitoring, which we cover later).

In the past, you may have had to use threads or operating-system processes to achieve concurrency. Each time, you probably felt you were opening Pandora's box—there was so much that could go wrong. But that worry just evaporates in Elixir. In fact, Elixir developers are so comfortable creating new processes, they'll often do it at times when you'd have created an *object* in a language such as Java.

One more thing—when we talk about processes in Elixir, we are not talking about native operating-system processes. These are too slow and bulky. Instead, Elixir uses process support in Erlang. These processes will run across all your CPUs (just like native processes), but they have very little overhead. As we'll cover a bit later, it's very easy to create hundreds of thousands of Elixir processes on even a modest computer.

A Simple Process

Here's a module that defines a function we'd like to run as a separate process.

```
spawn/spawn-basic.ex
defmodule SpawnBasic do
  def greet do
    IO.puts "Hello"
  end
end
```

Yup, that's it. There's nothing special—it's just regular code.

Let's fire up iex and play:

```
iex> c("spawn-basic.ex")
[SpawnBasic]
```

First let's call it as a regular function:

```
iex> SpawnBasic.greet
Hello
:ok
```

Now let's run it in a separate process:

```
iex> spawn(SpawnBasic, :greet, [])
Hello
#PID<0.42.0>
```

The spawn function kicks off a new process. It comes in many forms, but the two simplest ones let you run an anonymous function and run a named function in a module, passing a list of arguments. (We used the latter here.)

The spawn returns a *Process Identifier*, normally called a PID. This uniquely identifies the process it creates. (This identifier could be unique among all processes in the world, but here it's just unique in our application.)

When we call spawn, it creates a new process to run the code we specify. We don't know exactly when it will execute—we know only that it is eligible to run.

In this example, we can see that our function ran and output "Hello" prior to iex reporting the PID returned by spawn. But you can't rely on this. Instead you'll use messages to synchronize your processes' activity.

Sending Messages Between Processes

Let's rewrite our example to use messages. The top level will send greet a message containing a string, and the greet function will respond with a greeting containing that message.

In Elixir we send a message using the send function. It takes a PID and the message to send (an Elixir value, which we also call a *term*) on the right. You can send anything you want, but most Elixir developers seem to use atoms and tuples.

We wait for messages using receive. In a way, this acts just like case, with the message body as the parameter. Inside the block associated with the receive call, you can specify any number of patterns and associated actions. Just as with case, the action associated with the first pattern that matches the function is run.

Here's the updated version of our greet function.

```
spawn/spawn1.ex
defmodule Spawn1 do
  def greet do
    receive do
      {sender, msg} ->
        send sender, { :ok, "Hello, #{msg}" }
    end
  end
end

# here's a client
pid = spawn(Spawn1, :greet, [])
send pid, {self, "World!"}

receive do
  {:ok, message} ->
    IO.puts message
end
```

The function uses receive to wait for a message, and then matches the message in the block. In this case, the only pattern is a two-element tuple, where the first element is the original sender's PID and the second is the message. In the corresponding action, we use send sender, ... to send a formatted string back to the original message sender. We package that string into a tuple, with :ok as its first element.

Outside the module, we call spawn to create a process, and send it a tuple:

```
send pid, { self, "World!" }
```

The function self returns its caller's PID. Here we use it to pass our PID to the greet function so it will know where to send the response.

We then wait for a response. Notice that we do a pattern match on {:ok, message}, extracting the second element of the tuple, which contains the actual text.

We can run this in iex:

```
iex> c("spawn1.ex")
Hello, World!
[Spawn1]
```

Very cool. The text was sent, and greet responded with the full greeting.

Handling Multiple Messages

Let's try sending a second message.

spawn/spawn2.ex
```
defmodule Spawn2 do
  def greet do
    receive do
      {sender, msg} ->
        send sender, { :ok, "Hello, #{msg}" }
    end
  end
end


# here's a client
pid = spawn(Spawn2, :greet, [])

send pid, {self, "World!"}

receive do
  {:ok, message} ->
    IO.puts message
end

send pid, {self, "Kermit!"}
receive do
  {:ok, message} ->
    IO.puts message
end
```

Run it in iex:

```
iex> c("spawn2.ex")
Hello World!
.... just sits there ....
```

The first message is sent back, but the second is nowhere to be seen. What's worse, iex just hangs, and we have to use ^C (the control-C key sequence) to get out of it.

That's because our greet function handles only a single message. Once it has processed the receive, it exits. As a result, the second message we send it is never processed. The second receive at the top level then just hangs, waiting for a response that will never come.

Let's at least fix the hanging part. We can tell receive that we want to time out if a response is not received in so many milliseconds. This uses a pseudo-pattern called after.

```
spawn/spawn3.ex
defmodule Spawn3 do
  def greet do
    receive do
      {sender, msg} ->
        send sender, { :ok, "Hello, #{msg}" }
    end
  end
end

# here's a client
pid = spawn(Spawn3, :greet, [])

send pid, {self, "World!"}
receive do
  {:ok, message} ->
    IO.puts message
end

send pid, {self, "Kermit!"}
receive do
  {:ok, message} ->
    IO.puts message
  after 500 ->
    IO.puts "The greeter has gone away"
end

iex> c("spawn3.ex")
Hello World!
... short pause ...
The greeter has gone away
[Spawn3]
```

But how would we make our greet function handle multiple messages? Our natural reaction is to make it loop, doing a receive on each iteration. Elixir doesn't have loops, but it does have recursion.

```
spawn/spawn4.ex
defmodule Spawn4 do
  def greet do
    receive do
      {sender, msg} ->
        send sender, { :ok, "Hello, #{msg}" }
        greet
    end
  end
end

# here's a client
pid = spawn(Spawn4, :greet, [])
send pid, {self, "World!"}
receive do
  {:ok, message} ->
    IO.puts message
end

send pid, {self, "Kermit!"}
receive do
  {:ok, message} ->
    IO.puts message
  after 500 ->
    IO.puts "The greeter has gone away"
end
```

Run this, and both messages are processed:

```
iex> c("spawn4.ex")
Hello World!
Hello Kermit!
[Spawn4]
```

Recursion, Looping, and the Stack

The recursive greet function might have worried you a little. Every time it receives a message, it ends up calling itself. In many languages, that adds a new frame to the stack. After a large number of messages, you might run out of memory.

This doesn't happen in Elixir, as it implements *tail-call optimization*. If the last thing a function does is call itself, there's no need to make the call. Instead, the runtime simply jumps back to the start of the function. If the recursive call has arguments, then these replace the original parameters.

But beware—the recursive call *must* be the very last thing executed. For example, the following code is not tail recursive:

```
def factorial(0), do: 1
```

```
def factorial(n), do: n * factorial(n-1)
```

Although the recursive call is physically the last thing in the function, it is not the last thing executed. The function has to multiply the value it returns by n.

To make it tail recursive, we need to move the multiplication into the recursive call, and this means adding an accumulator:

```
spawn/fact_tr.ex
defmodule TailRecursive do
  def factorial(n),   do: _fact(n, 1)
  defp _fact(0, acc), do: acc
  defp _fact(n, acc), do: _fact(n-1, acc*n)
end
```

Process Overhead

At the start of the chapter, I somewhat cavalierly said Elixir processes were very low overhead. Now it is time to back that up. Let's write some code that creates *n* processes. The first will send a number to the second. It will increment that number and pass it to the third. This will continue until we get to the last process, which will pass the number back to the top level.

```
spawn/chain.ex
Line 1  defmodule Chain do
     -    def counter(next_pid) do
     -      receive do
     -        n ->
     5          send next_pid, n + 1
     -      end
     -    end
     -
     -    def create_processes(n) do
    10      last = Enum.reduce 1..n, self,
     -               fn (_,send_to) ->
     -                 spawn(Chain, :counter, [send_to])
     -               end
     -
    15      send last, 0     # start the count by sending a zero to the last process
     -
     -      receive do        # and wait for the result to come back to us
     -        final_answer when is_integer(final_answer) ->
     -          "Result is #{inspect(final_answer)}"
    20      end
     -    end
     -
     -    def run(n) do
     -      IO.puts inspect :timer.tc(Chain, :create_processes, [n])
```

```
25      end
  -   end
```

The counter function on line 2 is the code that will be run in separate processes. It is passed the PID of the next process in the chain. When it receives a number, it increments it and sends it on to that next process.

The create_processes function is probably the densest piece of Elixir we've encountered so far. Let's break it down.

It is passed the number of processes to create. Each process has to be passed the PID of the previous process so that it knows who to send the updated number to. All this is done on line 11.

The reduce call will iterate over the range 1..n. Each time around, it will pass an accumulator as the second parameter to its function. We set the initial value of that accumulator to self, our PID.

In the function, we spawn a new process that runs the counter function, using the third parameter of spawn to pass in the accumulator's current value (initially self). The value spawn returns is the PID of the newly created process, which becomes the accumulator's value for the next iteration.

Putting it another way, each time we spawn a new process, we pass it the previous process's PID in the send_to parameter.

The value that the reduce function returns is the accumulator's final value, which is the PID of the last process created.

On the next line we set the ball rolling by passing 0 to the last process. It will increment it and pass 1 to the second-to-last process. This goes on until the very first process we created passes the result back to us. We use the receive block to capture this, and format it into a nice message.

Our receive block contains a new feature. We've already seen how guard clauses can constrain pattern matching and function calling. The same guard clauses can be used to qualify the pattern in a receive block.

Why do we need this, though? It turns out there's a bug in some versions of Elixir.[1] When you compile and run a program using iex -S mix, a residual message is left lying around from the compilation process (it records a process's termination). We ignore that message by telling the receive clause that we're interested only in simple integers.

---

1.   https://github.com/elixir-lang/elixir/issues/1050

The run function starts the whole thing off. It uses a built-in Erlang library, tc, which can time a function's execution. We pass it the module, name, and parameters, and it responds with a tuple. The first element is the execution time in microseconds and the second is the result the function returns.

We'll run this code from the command line rather than from iex. (You'll see why in a second.) These results are on my 2011 MacBook Air (2.13GHz Core 2 Duo and 4GB RAM).

```
$ elixir -r chain.ex -e "Chain.run(10)"
{4015, "Result is 10"}
```

We asked it to run 10 processes, and it came back in 4 ms. The answer looks correct. Let's try 100 processes.

```
$ elixir -r chain.ex -e "Chain.run(100)"
{4562, "Result is 100"}
```

Only a small increase in the time. There's probably some startup latency on the first process creation. Onward! Let's try 1,000.

```
$ elixir -r chain.ex -e "Chain.run(1_000)"
{8458, "Result is 1000"}
```

Now 10,000.

```
$ elixir -r chain.ex -e "Chain.run(10_000)"
{66769, "Result is 10000"}
```

Ten thousand processes created and executed in 66 ms. Let's try for 400,000.

```
$ elixir -r chain.ex -e "Chain.run(400_000)"
=ERROR REPORT==== 25-Apr-2013::15:16:14 ===
Too many processes
** (SystemLimitError) a system limit has been reached
```

It looks like the virtual machine won't support 400,000 processes. Fortunately, this is not a hard limit—we just bumped into a default value. We can increase this using the VM's +P parameter. We pass this parameter to the VM using the --erl parameter to elixir. (This is why I chose to run from the command line.)

```
$ elixir --erl "+P 1000000"  -r chain.ex -e "Chain.run(400_000)"
{2249466, "Result is 400000"}
```

One last run, this time with 1,000,000 processes.

```
$ elixir --erl "+P 1000000"  -r chain.ex -e "Chain.run(1_000_000)"
{5470945, "Result is 1000000"}
```

We ran a million processes (sequentially) in about 5½ seconds. And, as this graph shows, the time per process was pretty much linear once we overcame the startup time.

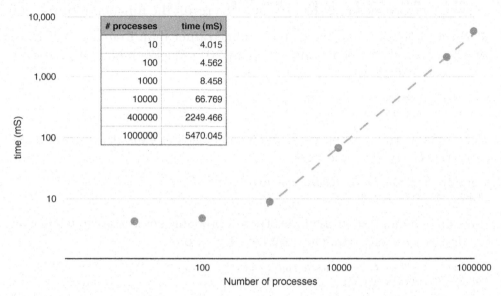

# processes	time (mS)
10	4.015
100	4.562
1000	8.458
10000	66.769
400000	2249.466
1000000	5470.045

This kind of performance is stunning, and it changes the way we design code. We can now create hundreds of little helper processes. And each process can contain its own state—in a way, processes in Elixir are like objects in an object-oriented system (but they have a better sense of humor).

Your Turn

➤ *Exercise: WorkingWithMultipleProcesses-1*
Run this code on your machine. See if you get comparable results.

➤ *Exercise: WorkingWithMultipleProcesses-2*
Write a program that spawns two processes and then passes each a unique token (for example, "fred" and "betty"). Have them send the tokens back.

– Is the order in which the replies are received deterministic in theory? In practice?
– If either answer is no, how could you make it so?

When Processes Die

Who gets told when a process dies? By default, no one. Obviously the VM knows and can report it to the console, but your code will be oblivious unless you explicitly tell Elixir you want to get involved.

Here's the default case: we spawn a function that uses the Erlang timer library to sleep for 500 ms. It then exits with a status of 99.

The code that spawns it sits in a receive. If it receives a message, it reports that fact; otherwise, after one second it lets us know that nothing happened.

```
spawn/link1.exs
defmodule Link1 do
  import :timer, only: [ sleep: 1 ]

  def sad_function do
    sleep 500
    exit(:boom)
  end
  def run do
    spawn(Link1, :sad_function, [])
    receive do
      msg ->
        IO.puts "MESSAGE RECEIVED: #{inspect msg}"
    after 1000 ->
        IO.puts "Nothing happened as far as I am concerned"
    end
  end
end
```

```
Link1.run
```

(Think about how you'd have written this in your old programming language.)

We can run this from the console:

```
$ elixir -r link1.exs
Nothing happened as far as I am concerned
```

As far as the top level was concerned, the spawned process exiting caused no activity.

Linking Two Processes

If we want two processes to share in each other's pain, we can *link* them. When processes are linked, each can receive information when the other exits. The spawn_link call spawns a process and links it to the caller in one operation.

```
spawn/link2.exs
defmodule Link2 do
  import :timer, only: [ sleep: 1 ]

  def sad_function do
    sleep 500
    exit(:boom)
  end
```

```
    def run do
➤     spawn_link(Link2, :sad_function, [])
      receive do
        msg ->
          IO.puts "MESSAGE RECEIVED: #{inspect msg}"
        after 1000 ->
          IO.puts "Nothing happened as far as I am concerned"
      end
    end
  end
```

```
Link2.run
```

The runtime reports the abnormal termination:

```
$ elixir -r link2.exs
** (EXIT from #PID<0.35.0>) :boom
```

So our child process died, and it killed the entire application. That's the default behaviour of linked processes—when one exits abnormally, it kills the other.

What if you want to handle the death of another process? Well, you probably don't want to do this. Elixir uses the OTP framework for constructing process trees, and OTP includes the concept of process supervision. An incredible amount of effort has been spent getting this right, so I recommend using it most of the time. (We cover this in Chapter 17, *OTP: Supervisors*, on page 227.)

However, you can tell Elixir to convert the exit signals from a linked process into a message you can handle. Do this by *trapping the exit*.

spawn/link3.exs
```
defmodule Link3 do
  import :timer, only: [ sleep: 1 ]

  def sad_function do
    sleep 500
    exit(:boom)
  end
  def run do
➤   Process.flag(:trap_exit, true)
    spawn_link(Link3, :sad_function, [])
    receive do
      msg ->
        IO.puts "MESSAGE RECEIVED: #{inspect msg}"
      after 1000 ->
        IO.puts "Nothing happened as far as I am concerned"
    end
  end
end
```

```
Link3.run
```

This time we see an :EXIT message when the spawned process terminates:

```
$ elixir -r link3.exs
MESSAGE RECEIVED: {:EXIT, #PID<0.41.0>, :boom}
```

It doesn't matter why a process exits—it may simply finish processing, it may explicitly exit, or it may raise an exception—the same :EXIT message is received. Following an error, however, it contains details of what went wrong.

Monitoring a Process

Linking joins the calling process and another process—each receives notifications about the other. By contrast, *monitoring* lets a process spawn another and be notified of its termination, but without the reverse notification—it is one-way only.

When you monitor a process, you receive a :DOWN message when it exits or fails, or if it doesn't exist.

You can use spawn_monitor to turn on monitoring when you spawn a process, or you can use Process.monitor to monitor an existing process. However, if you use Process.monitor (or link to an existing process), there is a potential race condition—if the other process dies before your monitor call completes, you may not receive a notification. The spawn_link and spawn_monitor versions are atomic, however, so you'll always catch a failure.

spawn/monitor1.exs
```
defmodule Monitor1 do
  import :timer, only: [ sleep: 1 ]

  def sad_function do
    sleep 500
    exit(:boom)
  end

  def run do
    res = spawn_monitor(Monitor1, :sad_function, [])
    IO.puts inspect res
    receive do
      msg ->
        IO.puts "MESSAGE RECEIVED: #{inspect msg}"
    after 1000 ->
        IO.puts "Nothing happened as far as I am concerned"
    end
  end
end
```

```
Monitor1.run
```

Run it, and the results are similar to the spawn_link version:

```
$ elixir -r monitor1.exs
{#PID<0.37.0>,#Reference<0.0.0.53>}
MESSAGE RECEIVED: {:DOWN,#Reference<0.0.0.53>,:process,#PID<0.37.0>,:boom}
```

(The Reference record in the message is the identity of the monitor that was created. The spawn_monitor call also returns it, along with the PID.)

So, when do you use links and when should you choose monitors?

It depends on your processes' semantics. If the intent is that a failure in one process should terminate another, then you need links. If instead you need to know when some other process exits for any reason, choose monitors.

Your Turn

The Erlang function timer.sleep(time_in_ms) suspends the current process for a given time. You might want to use it to force some scenarios in the following exercises. The key with the exercises is to get used to the different reports you'll see when you're developing code.

> *Exercise: WorkingWithMultipleProcesses-3*
> Use spawn_link to start a process, and have that process send a message to the parent and then exit immediately. Meanwhile, sleep for 500 ms in the parent, then receive as many messages as are waiting. Trace what you receive. Does it matter that you weren't waiting for the notification from the child when it exited?

> *Exercise: WorkingWithMultipleProcesses-4*
> Do the same, but have the child raise an exception. What difference do you see in the tracing?

> *Exercise: WorkingWithMultipleProcesses-5*
> Repeat the two, changing spawn_link to spawn_monitor.

Parallel Map—The "Hello, World" of Erlang

Devin Torres reminded me that every book in the Erlang space must, by law, include a definition of a parallel map function. Regular map returns the list that results from applying a function to each element of a collection. The parallel version does the same, but it applies the function to each element in a separate process.

```
spawn/pmap.exs
defmodule Parallel do
  def pmap(collection, fun) do
    me = self
    collection
    |> Enum.map(fn (elem) ->
         spawn_link fn -> (send me, { self, fun.(elem) }) end
       end)
    |> Enum.map(fn (pid) ->
         receive do { ^pid, result } -> result end
       end)
  end
end
```

Our method contains two transformations (look for the |> operator). The first transformation maps collection into a list of PIDs, where each PID in the list runs the given function on an individual list element. If the collection contains 1,000 items, we'll run 1,000 processes.

The second transformation converts the list of PIDs into the results returned by the processes corresponding to each PID in the list. Note how it uses ^pid in the receive block to get the result for each PID in turn. Without this we'd get back the results in random order.

But does it work?

```
iex> c("pmap.exs")
[Parallel]
iex> Parallel.pmap 1..10, &(&1 * &1)
[1,4,9,16,25,36,49,64,81,100]
```

That's pretty sweet, but it gets better, as we'll cover when we look at tasks and agents on page 255.

Your Turn

➤ *Exercise: WorkingWithMultipleProcesses-6*
In the pmap code, I assigned the value of self to the variable me at the top of the method and then used me as the target of the message returned by the spawned processes. Why use a separate variable here?

➤ *Exercise: WorkingWithMultipleProcesses-7*
Change the ^pid in pmap to _pid. This means the receive block will take responses in the order the processes send them. Now run the code again. Do you see any difference in the output? If you're like me, you don't, but the program clearly contains a bug. Are you scared by this? Can you find a way to reveal the problem (perhaps by passing in a different function,

by sleeping, or by increasing the number of processes)? Change it back to ^pid and make sure the order is now correct.

A Fibonacci Server

Let's round out this chapter with an example program. Its task is to calculate *fib(n)* for a list of *n*, where *fib(n)* is the nth Fibonacci number. (The Fibonacci sequence starts 0, 1. Each subsequent number is the sum of the preceding two numbers in the sequence.)[2] I chose this not because it is something we all do every day, but because the naïve calculation of Fibonacci numbers 10 through 37 takes a measurable number of seconds on typical computers.

The twist is that we'll write our program to calculate different Fibonacci numbers in parallel. To do this, we'll write a trivial server process that does the calculation, and a scheduler that assigns work to a calculation process when it becomes free. The following diagram shows the message flow.

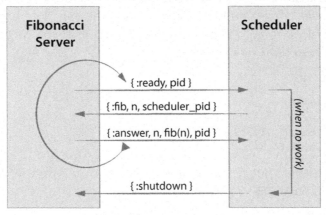

When the calculator is ready for the next number, it sends a :ready message to the scheduler. If there is still work to do, the scheduler sends it to the calculator in a :fib message; otherwise it sends the calculator a :shutdown. When a calculator receives a :fib message, it calculates the given Fibonacci number and returns it in an :answer. If it gets a :shutdown, it simply exits.

Here's the Fibonacci calculator module:

```
spawn/fib.exs
defmodule FibSolver do

  def fib(scheduler) do
    send scheduler, { :ready, self }
```

---

2. http://en.wikipedia.org/wiki/Fibonacci_number

```
    receive do
      { :fib, n, client } ->
        send client, { :answer, n, fib_calc(n), self }
        fib(scheduler)
      { :shutdown } ->
        exit(:normal)
    end
end
```

```
# very inefficient, deliberately
defp fib_calc(0), do: 0
defp fib_calc(1), do: 1
defp fib_calc(n), do: fib_calc(n-1) + fib_calc(n-2)
end
```

The public API is the fib function, which takes the scheduler PID. When it starts, it sends a :ready message to the scheduler and then waits for a message back.

If it gets a :fib message, it calculates the answer and sends it back to the client. It then loops by calling itself recursively. This will send another :ready message, telling the client it is ready for more work.

If it gets a :shutdown it simply exits.

The Task Scheduler

The scheduler is a little more complex, as it is designed to handle both a varying number of server processes and an unknown amount of work.

spawn/fib.exs
```
defmodule Scheduler do

  def run(num_processes, module, func, to_calculate) do
    (1..num_processes)
    |> Enum.map(fn(_) -> spawn(module, func, [self]) end)
    |> schedule_processes(to_calculate, [])
  end

  defp schedule_processes(processes, queue, results) do
    receive do
      {:ready, pid} when length(queue) > 0 ->
        [ next | tail ] = queue
        send pid, {:fib, next, self}
        schedule_processes(processes, tail, results)

      {:ready, pid} ->
        send pid, {:shutdown}
        if length(processes) > 1 do
          schedule_processes(List.delete(processes, pid), queue, results)
        else
          Enum.sort(results, fn {n1,_}, {n2,_}  -> n1 <= n2 end)
        end

      {:answer, number, result, _pid} ->
        schedule_processes(processes, queue, [ {number, result} | results ])
    end
  end
end
```

The public API for the scheduler is the run function. It receives the number of processes to spawn, the module and function to spawn, and a list of things to process. The scheduler is pleasantly ignorant of the actual task being performed.

Let's emphasize that last point. Our scheduler knows nothing about Fibonacci numbers. Exactly the same code will happily manage processes working on DNA sequencing or cracking passwords.

The run function spawns the correct number of processes and records their PIDs. It then calls the workhorse function, schedule_processes.

This function is basically a receive loop. If it gets a :ready message from a server, it sees if there is more work in the queue. If there is, it passes the next number to the calculator and then recurses with one fewer number in the queue.

If the work queue is empty when it receives a :ready message, it sends a shutdown to the server. If this is the last process, then we're done and it sorts the accumulated results. If it isn't the last process, it removes the process from the list of processes and recurses to handle another message.

Finally, if it gets an :answer message, it records the answer in the result accumulator and recurses to handle the next message.

We drive the scheduler with the following code:

```
spawn/fib.exs
to_process = [ 37, 37, 37, 37, 37, 37 ]

Enum.each 1..10, fn num_processes ->
  {time, result} = :timer.tc(
    Scheduler, :run,
    [num_processes, FibSolver, :fib, to_process]
  )

  if num_processes == 1 do
    IO.puts inspect result
    IO.puts "\n #   time (s)"
  end
  :io.format "~2B      ~.2f~n", [num_processes, time/1000000.0]
end
```

The to_process list contains the numbers we'll be passing to our fib servers. In our case, we give it the same number, 37, six times. The intent here is to load each of our processors.

We run the code a total of 10 times, varying the number of spawned processes from 1 to 10. We use :timer.tc to determine the elapsed time of each iteration, reporting the result in seconds. The first time around the loop, we also display the numbers we calculated.

```
$ elixir fib.exs
[{37, 24157817}, {37, 24157817}, {37, 24157817},
 {37, 24157817}, {37, 24157817}, {37, 24157817}]

 #    time (s)
 1     6.55
 2     3.28
 3     3.35
 4     3.17
 5     3.45
 6     3.15
 7     3.17
 8     3.18
 9     3.31
10     3.25
```

On my four-core system, we see a dramatic reduction in elapsed time when we increase the concurrency from one to two, small decreases until we hit four processes, then fairly flat performance after that. The Activity Monitor showed a consistent 380% CPU use once the concurrency got above 4. (If you want to see similar results on systems with more cores, you'll need to increase the number of entries in the to_process list.)

Your Turn

➤ *Exercise: WorkingWithMultipleProcesses-8*
Run the Fibonacci code on your machine. Do you get comparable timings? If your machine has multiple cores and/or processors, do you see improvements in the timing as we increase the application's concurrency?

➤ *Exercise: WorkingWithMultipleProcesses-9*
Take this scheduler code and update it to let you run a function that finds the number of times the word "cat" appears in each file in a given directory. Run one server process per file. The function File.ls! returns the names of files in a directory, and File.read! reads the contents of a file as a binary. Can you write it as a more generalized scheduler?

Run your code on a directory with a reasonable number of files (maybe around 100) so you can experiment with the effects of concurrency.

Agents—A Teaser

Our Fibonacci code is seriously inefficient. To calculate fib(5), we calculate this:

```
fib(5)
=  fib(4)                                          + fib(3)
=  fib(3)                    + fib(2)              + fib(2)         + fib(1)
=  fib(2)          + fib(1) + fib(1) + fib(0) + fib(1) + fib(0) + fib(1)
=  fib(1) + fib(0) + fib(1) + fib(1) + fib(0) + fib(1) + fib(0) + fib(1)
```

Look at all that duplication. If only we could cache the intermediate values.

As you know, Elixir modules are basically buckets of functions—they cannot hold state. But processes can hold state. And Elixir comes with a library module called Agent that makes it easy to wrap a process containing state in a nice module interface. Don't worry about the details of the code that follows—we cover agents and tasks on page 255. For now, just see how processes are among the tools we use to add persistence to Elixir code. (This code comes from a mailing-list post by José Valim, written in response to some really ugly code I wrote.)

```
spawn/fib_agent.exs
defmodule FibAgent do
  def start_link do
    Agent.start_link(fn -> %{ 0 => 0, 1 => 1 } end)
  end

  def fib(pid, n) when n >= 0 do
    Agent.get_and_update(pid, &do_fib(&1, n))
  end

  defp do_fib(cache, n) do
    case cache[n] do
      nil ->
        { n_1, cache } = do_fib(cache, n-1)
        result         = n_1 + cache[n-2]
        { result, Map.put(cache, n, result) }

      cached_value ->
        { cached_value , cache }
    end
  end

end

{:ok, agent} = FibAgent.start_link()
IO.puts FibAgent.fib(agent, 2000)
```

Let's run it:

```
$ elixir fib_agent.exs
42246963333923048787067256023414827825798528402506810980102801373143085843701
30707224123599639141511088446087538909603607640194711643596029271983312598737
32625355580260699158591522949245390499872225679531698287448247299226390183371
67780606070116154978867198798583114688708762645973690867228840236544222952433
47964480139515349562972087652656069529806499841977448720155612802665404554171
717881930324025204312082516817125
```

If we'd tried to caluluate fib(2000) using the noncached version, the sun would grow to engulf the Earth while we were waiting for it to finish.

Thinking in Processes

If you first started programming with procedural languages and then moved to an object-oriented style, you'll have experienced a period of dislocation as you tried to get your head to think in terms of objects.

The same will be happening now as you start to think of your work in terms of processes. Just about every decent Elixir program will have many, many processes, and by and large they'll be just as easy to create and manage as the objects were in object-oriented programming. But learning to think that way takes awhile. Stick with it.

So far we've been running our processes in the same VM. But if we're planning on taking over the world, we need to be able to scale. And that means running on more than one machine.

The abstraction for this is the *node*, and that's the subject of the next chapter.

## CHAPTER 15

Nodes—The Key to Distributing Services

There's nothing mysterious about a *node*. It is simply a running Erlang VM. Throughout this book we've been running our code on a node.

The Erlang VM, called *Beam*, is more than a simple interpreter. It's like its own little operating system running on top of your host operating system. It handles its own events, process scheduling, memory, naming services, and interprocess communication. In addition to all that, a node can connect to other nodes—in the same computer, across a LAN, or across the Internet—and provide many of the same services across these connections that it provides to the processes it hosts locally.

Naming Nodes

So far we haven't needed to give our node a name—we've had only one. If we ask Elixir what the current node is called, it'll give us a made-up name:

```
iex> Node.self
:nonode@nohost
```

We can set the name of a node when we start it. With iex, use either the --name or --sname option. The former sets a fully qualified name:

```
$ iex --name wibble@light-boy.local
iex(wibble@light-boy.local)> Node.self
:"wibble@light-boy.local"
```

The latter sets a short name.

The name that's returned is an atom—it's in quotes because it contains characters not allowed in a literal atom.

```
$ iex --sname wobble
iex(wobble@light-boy)> Node.self
:"wobble@light-boy"
```

Note that in both cases the iex prompt contains the node's name along with my machine's name (light-boy).

Now I want to show you what happens when we have two nodes running. The easiest way to do this is to open two terminal windows and run a node in each. To represent these windows in the book, I'll show them stacked vertically.

Let's run a node called node_one in the top window and node_two in the bottom one. We'll then use the Elixir Node module's list function to display a list of known nodes, then connect from one to the other.

Window #1

```
$ iex --sname node_one
iex(node_one@light-boy)>
```

Window #2

```
$ iex --sname node_two
iex(node_two@light-boy)> Node.list
[]
iex(node_two@light-boy)> Node.connect :"node_one@light-boy"
true
iex(node_two@light-boy)> Node.list
[:"node_one@light-boy"]
```

Initially, node_two doesn't know about any other nodes. But after we connect to node_one (notice that we pass an atom containing that node's name), the list shows the other node. And if we go back to node one, it will now know about node two.

```
iex(node_one@light-boy)> Node.list
[:"node_two@light-boy"]
```

Now that we have two nodes, we can try running some code. On node one, let's create an anonymous function that outputs the current node name.

```
iex(node_one@light-boy)> func = fn -> IO.inspect Node.self end
#Function<erl_eval.20.82930912>
```

We can run this with the spawn function.

```
iex(node_one@light-boy)> spawn(func)
#PID<0.59.0>
node_one@light-boy
```

But spawn also lets us specify a node name. The process will be spawned on that node.

```
iex(node_one@light-boy)> Node.spawn(:"node_one@light-boy", func)
#PID<0.57.0>
node_one@light-boy
iex(node_one@light-boy)> Node.spawn(:"node_two@light-boy", func)
#PID<7393.48.0>
node_two@light-boy
```

We're running on node one. When we tell spawn to run on node_one@light-boy, we see two lines of output. The first is the PID spawn returns, and the second line is the value of Node.self that the function writes.

The second spawn is where it gets interesting. We pass it the name of node two and the same function we used the first time. Again we get two lines of output. The first is the PID and the second is the node name. Notice the PID's contents. The first field in a PID is the node number. When running on a local node, it's zero. But here we're running on a remote node, so that field has a positive value (7393). Then look at the function's output. It reports that it is running on node two. I think that's pretty cool.

You may have been expecting the output from the second spawn to appear in the lower window. After all, the code runs on node two. But it was created on node one, so it inherits its process hierarchy from node one. Part of that hierarchy is something called the *group leader*, which (among other things) determines where IO.puts sends its output. So in a way, what we're seeing is doubly impressive. We start on node one, run a process on node two, and when the process outputs something, it appears back on node one.

Your Turn

➤ *Exercise: Nodes-1*

Set up two terminal windows, and go to a different directory in each. Then start up a named node in each. In one window, write a function that lists the contents of the current directory.

```
fun = fn -> IO.puts(Enum.join(File.ls!, ",")) end
```

Run it twice, once on each node.

Nodes, Cookies, and Security

Although this is cool, it might also ring some alarm bells. If you can run arbitrary code on any node, then anyone with a publicly accessible node has just handed over his machine to any random hacker.

But that's not the case. Before a node will let another connect, it checks that the remote node has permission. It does that by comparing that node's *cookie* with its own cookie. A cookie is just an arbitrary string (ideally fairly long and very random). As an administrator of a distributed Elixir system, you need to create a cookie and then make sure all nodes use it.

If you are running the iex or elixir commands, you can pass in the cookie using the --cookie option.

```
$ iex --sname one --cookie chocolate-chip
iex(one@light-boy)> Node.get_cookie
:"chocolate-chip"
```

If we repeat our two-node experiment and explicitly set the cookie names to be different, what happens?

Window #1

```
$ iex --sname node_one --cookie cookie-one
iex(node_one@light-boy)> Node.connect :"node_two@light-boy"
false
```

Window #2

```
$ iex --sname node_two --cookie cookie-two
iex(node_two@light-boy)>
=ERROR REPORT==== 27-Apr-2013::21:27:43 ===
** Connection attempt from disallowed node 'node_one@light-boy' **
```

The node that attempts to connect receives false, indicating the connection was not made. And the node that it tried to connect to logs an error describing the attempt.

But why does it succeed when we don't specify a cookie? When Erlang starts, it looks for an .erlang.cookie file in your home directory. If that file doesn't exist, Erlang creates it and stores a random string in it. It uses that string as the cookie for any node the user starts. That way, all nodes you start on a particular machine are automatically given access to each other.

Be careful when connecting nodes over a public network—the cookie is transmitted in plain text.

Naming Your Processes

Although a PID is displayed as three numbers, it contains just two fields; the first number is the node ID and the next two numbers are the low and high bits of the process ID. When you run a process on your current node, its node ID will always be zero. However, when you export a PID to another node, the node ID is set to the number of the node on which the process lives.

That works well once a system is up and running and everything is knitted together. If you want to register a callback process on one node and an event-generating process on another, just give the callback PID to the generator.

But how can the callback find the generator in the first place? One way is for the generator to register its PID, giving it a name. The callback on the other node can look up the generator by name, using the PID that comes back to send messages to it.

Here's an example. Let's write a simple server that sends a notification about every 2 seconds. To receive the notification, a client has to register with the server. And we'll arrange things so that clients on different nodes can register.

While we're at it, we'll do a little packaging so that to start the server you run Ticker.start, and to start the client you run Client.start. We'll also add an API Ticker.register to register a client with the server.

Here's the server code:

```
nodes/ticker.ex
defmodule Ticker do

  @interval 2000    # 2 seconds
  @name     :ticker

  def start do
    pid = spawn(__MODULE__, :generator, [[]])
    :global.register_name(@name, pid)
  end

  def register(client_pid) do
    send :global.whereis_name(@name), { :register, client_pid }
  end

  def generator(clients) do
    receive do
      { :register, pid } ->
        IO.puts "registering #{inspect pid}"
        generator([pid|clients])
    after
      @interval ->
        IO.puts "tick"
        Enum.each clients, fn client ->
          send client, { :tick }
        end
        generator(clients)
    end
  end
end
```

We define a start function that spawns the server process. It then uses :global.register_name to register the PID of this server under the name :ticker.

Clients who want to register to receive ticks call the register function. This function sends a message to the Ticker server, asking it to add those clients to its list. Clients could have done this directly by sending the :register message to the server process. Instead, we give them an interface function that hides the registration details. This helps decouple the client from the server and gives us more flexibility to change things in the future.

Before we look at the actual tick process, let's stop to consider the start and register functions. These are not part of the tick process—they are simply chunks of code in the Ticker module. This means they can be called directly wherever we have the module loaded—no message passing required. This is a common pattern; we have a module that is responsible both for spawning a process and for providing the external interface to that process.

Back to the code. The last function, generator, is the spawned process. It waits for two events. When it gets a tuple containing :register and a PID, it adds the PID to the list of clients and recurses. Alternatively, it may time out after 2 seconds, in which case it sends a {:tick} message to all registered clients.

(This code has no error handling and no means of terminating the process. I just wanted to illustrate passing PIDs and messages between nodes.)

The client code is simple:

nodes/ticker.ex
```
defmodule Client do

  def start do
    pid = spawn(__MODULE__, :receiver, [])
    Ticker.register(pid)
  end

  def receiver do
    receive do
      { :tick } ->
        IO.puts "tock in client"
        receiver
    end
  end
end
```

It spawns a receiver to handle the incoming ticks, and passes the receiver's PID to the server as an argument to the register function. Again, it's worth noting that this function call is local—it runs on the same node as the client.

However, inside the Ticker.register function, it locates the node containing the server and sends it a message. As our client's PID is sent to the server, it becomes an external PID, pointing back to the client's node.

The spawned client process simply loops, writing a cheery message to the console whenever it receives a tick message.

Let's run it. We'll start up our two nodes. We'll call Ticker.start on node one. Then we'll call Client.start on both node one and node two.

Window #1

```
nodes % iex --sname one
iex(one@light-boy)> c("ticker.ex")
[Client,Ticker]
iex(one@light-boy)> Node.connect :"two@light-boy"
true
iex(one@light-boy)> Ticker.start
:yes
tick
tick
iex(one@light-boy)> Client.start
registering #PID<0.59.0>
{:register,#PID<0.59.0>}
tick
tock in client
tick
tock in client
tick
tock in client
tick
tock in client
  :   :   :
```

Window #2

```
nodes % iex --sname two
iex(two@light-boy)> c("ticker.ex")
[Client,Ticker]
iex(two@light-boy)> Client.start
{:register,#PID<0.53.0>}
tock in client
tock in client
tock in client
  :   :   :
```

To stop this, you'll need to exit iex on both nodes.

When to Name Processes

When you name something, you are recording some global state. And as we all know, global state can be troublesome. What if two processes try to register the same name, for example?

The runtime has some tricks to help us. In particular, we can list the names our application will register in the app's mix.exs file. (We'll cover how when we look at packaging an application on page 238.) However, the general rule is to register your process names when your application starts.

Your Turn

> *Exercise: Nodes-2*
> When I introduced the interval server, I said it sent a tick "about every 2 seconds." But in the receive loop, it has an explicit timeout of 2,000 ms. Why did I say "about" when it looks as if the time should be pretty accurate?

> *Exercise: Nodes-3*
> Alter the code so that successive ticks are sent to each registered client (so the first goes to the first client, the second to the next client, and so on). Once the last client receives a tick, the process starts back at the first. The solution should deal with new clients being added at any time.

I/O, PIDs, and Nodes

Input and output in the Erlang VM are performed using I/O servers. These are simply Erlang processes that implement a low-level message interface. You never have to deal with this interface directly (which is a good thing, as it is complex). Instead, you use the various Elixir and Erlang I/O libraries and let them do the heavy lifting.

In Elixir you identify an open file or device by the PID of its I/O server. And these PIDs behave just like all other PIDs—you can, for example, send them between nodes.

If you look at the implementation of Elixir's IO.puts function, you'll see

```
def puts(device \\ group_leader(), item) do
    erl_dev = map_dev(device)
    :io.put_chars erl_dev, [to_iodata(item), ?\n]
end
```

(To see the source of an Elixir library module, view the online documentation at http://elixir-lang.org/docs/, navigate to the function in question, and click the *Source* link.)

The default device it uses is returned by the function :erlang.group_leader. (The group_leader function is imported from the :erlang module at the top of the IO module.) This will be the PID of an I/O server.

So, bring up two terminal windows and start a different named node in each. Connect to node one from node two, and register the PID returned by group_leader under a global name (we use :two).

Window #1
```
$ iex --sname one
iex(one@light-boy) >
```

Window #2
```
$ iex --sname two
iex(two@light-boy) > Node.connect(:"one@light-boy")
true
iex(two@light-boy) > :global.register_name(:two, :erlang.group_leader)
:yes
```

Note that once we've registered the PID, we can access it from the other node. And once we've done that, we can pass it to IO.puts; the output appears in the other terminal window.

Window #1
```
iex(one@light-boy) > two = :global.whereis_name :two
#PID<7419.30.0>
iex(one@light-boy) > IO.puts(two, "Hello")
:ok
iex(one@light-boy) > IO.puts(two, "World!")
:ok
```

Window #2
```
Hello
World
iex(two@light-boy) >
```

Your Turn

➤ *Exercise: Nodes-4*

The ticker process in this chapter is a central server that sends events to registered clients. Reimplement this as a ring of clients. A client sends a tick to the next client in the ring. After 2 seconds, *that* client sends a tick to *its* next client.

When thinking about how to add clients to the ring, remember to deal with the case where a client's receive loop times out just as you're adding a new process. What does this say about who has to be responsible for updating the links?

Nodes Are the Basis of Distribution

We've seen how we can create and interlink a number of Erlang virtual machines, potentially communicating across a network. This is important, both to allow your application to scale and to increase reliability. Running all your code on one machine is like having all your eggs in one basket. Unless you're writing a mobile omelet app, this is probably not a good idea.

It's easy to write concurrent applications with Elixir. But writing code that follows the happy path is a lot easier than writing bullet-proof, scalable, and hot-swappable world-beating apps. For that, you're going to need some help.

In the worlds of Elixir and Erlang, that help is called OTP, and it is the subject of the next few chapters.

## CHAPTER 16

OTP: Servers

If you've been following Elixir or Erlang, you've probably come across OTP. It is often hyped as the answer to all high-availability distributed-application woes. It isn't, but it certainly solves many problems that you'd otherwise need to solve yourself, including application discovery, failure detection and management, hot code swapping, and server structure.

First, the obligatory one-paragraph history. OTP stands for the *Open Telecom Platform*, but the full name is largely of historical interest and everyone just says *OTP*. It was initially used to build telephone exchanges and switches. But these devices have the same characteristics we want from any large online application, so OTP is now a general-purpose tool for developing and managing large systems.

OTP is actually a bundle that includes Erlang, a database (wonderfully called *Mnesia*), and an innumerable number of libraries. It also defines a structure for your applications. But, as with all large, complex frameworks, there is a lot to learn. In this book we'll focus on the essentials and I'll point you toward other information sources.

We've been using OTP all along—mix, the Elixir compiler, and even our issue tracker followed OTP conventions. But that use was implicit. Now we'll make it explicit and start writing servers using OTP.

Some OTP Definitions

OTP defines systems in terms of hierarchies of *applications*. An application consists of one or more processes. These processes follow one of a small number of OTP conventions, called *behaviors* (or *behaviours*). There is a behavior used for general-purpose servers, one for implementing event handlers, and one for finite-state machines. Each implementation of one of these behaviors will run in its own process (and may have additional associated processes). In this chapter we'll be implementing the *server* behavior, called *GenServer*.

A special behavior, called *supervisor*, monitors the health of these processes and implements strategies for restarting them if needed.

We'll look at these components from the bottom up—this chapter will look at servers, the next will explore supervisors, and finally we'll implement applications.

An OTP Server

When we wrote our Fibonacci server in the previous chapter, on page 192, we had to do all the message handling ourselves. It wasn't difficult, but it was tedious. Our scheduler also had to keep track of three pieces of state information: the queue of numbers to process, the results generated so far, and the list of active PIDs.

Most servers have a similar set of needs, so OTP provides libraries that do all the low-level work for us.

When we write an OTP server, we write a module containing one or more callback functions with standard names. OTP will invoke the appropriate callback to handle a particular situation. For example, when someone sends a request to our server, OTP will call our handle_call function, passing in the request, the caller, and the current server state. Our function responds by returning a tuple containing an action to take, the return value for the request, and an updated state.

State and the Single Server

Way back when we summed the elements in a list, on page 74, we came across the idea of an accumulator, a value that was passed as a parameter when a looping function calls itself recursively.

```
lists/sum.exs
defmodule MyList do
  def sum([], total),              do: total
  def sum([ head | tail ], total), do: sum(tail, head+total)
end
```

The parameter total maintains the state while the function trundles down the list.

In our Fibonacci code, we maintained a lot of state in the schedule_processes function. In fact, all three of its parameters were used for state information.

Now think about servers. They use recursion to loop, handling one request on each call. So they can also pass state to themselves as a parameter in this recursive call. And that's one of the things OTP manages for us. Our handler functions get passed the current state (as their last parameter), and they return (among other things) a potentially updated state. Whatever state a function returns is the state that will be passed to the next request handler.

Our First OTP Server

Let's write what is possibly the simplest OTP server. You pass it a number when you start it up, and that becomes the current state of the server. When you call it with a :next_number request, it returns that current state to the caller, and at the same time increments the state, ready for the next call. Basically, each time you call it you get an updated sequence number.

Create a New Project Using Mix

Start by creating a new mix project in your work directory. We'll call it sequence.

```
$ mix new sequence
* creating README.md
* creating .gitignore
* creating mix.exs
* creating lib
* creating lib/sequence.ex
* creating lib/sequence
* creating test
* creating test/test_helper.exs
* creating test/sequence_test.exs
```

Create the Basic Sequence Server

Now we'll create Sequence.Server, our server module. Add the file server.ex to the sequence/ directory under lib.

```
otp-server/1/sequence/lib/sequence/server.ex
Line 1  defmodule Sequence.Server do
     2    use GenServer
     3
     4    def handle_call(:next_number, _from, current_number) do
     5      { :reply, current_number, current_number+1 }
     6    end
     7  end
```

The first thing to note is line 2. The use line effectively adds the OTP *GenServer* behavior to our module. This is what lets it handle all the callbacks. It also means we don't have to define every callback in our module—the behavior defines defaults for them all.

When a client calls our server, GenServer invokes the handle_call function that follows. It receives

- the information the client passed to the call as its first parameter,
- the PID of the client as the second parameter,
- and the server state as the third parameter.

Our implementation is simple: we return a tuple to OTP.

```
{ :reply, current_number, current_number+1 }
```

The reply element tells OTP to reply to the client, passing back the value that is the second element. Finally, the tuple's third element defines the new state. This will be passed as the last parameter to handle_call the next time it is invoked.

Fire Up Our Server Manually

We can play with our server in iex. Open it in the project's main directory, remembering the -S mix option.

```
$ iex -S mix
iex> { :ok, pid } = GenServer.start_link(Sequence.Server, 100)
{:ok,#PID<0.71.0>}
iex> GenServer.call(pid, :next_number)
100
iex> GenServer.call(pid, :next_number)
101
iex> GenServer.call(pid, :next_number)
102
```

We're using two functions from the Elixir GenServer module. The start_link function behaves like the spawn_link function we used in the previous chapter. It asks GenServer to start a new process and link to us (so we'll get notifications if it fails). We pass in the module to run as a server: the initial state (100 in this case). We could also pass GenServer options as a third parameter, but the defaults work fine here.

We get back a status (:ok) and the server's PID. The call function takes this PID and calls the handle_call function in the server. The call's second parameter is passed as the first argument to handle_call.

In our case, the only value we need to pass is the identity of the action we want to perform, :next_number. If you look at the definition of handle_call in the server, you'll see that its first parameter is :next_number. When Elixir invokes the function, it pattern-matches the argument in the call with this first parameter in the function. A server can support multiple actions by implementing multiple handle_call functions with different first parameters.

If you want to pass more than one thing in the call to a server, pass a tuple. For example, our server might need a function to reset the count to a given value. We could define the handler as

```
def handle_call({:set_number, new_number}, _from, _current_number) do
  { :reply, new_number, new_number }
end
```

and call it with

```
iex> GenServer.call(pid, {:set_number, 999})
999
```

Similarly, a handler can return multiple values by packaging them into a tuple or list.

```
def handle_call({:factors, number}, _, _) do
  { :reply, { :factors_of, number, factors(number)}, [] }
end
```

Your Turn

➤ *Exercise: OTP-Servers-1*

You're going to start creating a server that implements a stack. The call that initializes your stack will pass in a list of the initial stack contents.

For now, implement only the pop interface. It's acceptable for your server to crash if someone tries to pop from an empty stack.

For example, if initialized with [5,"cat",9], successive calls to pop will return 5, "cat", and 9.

One-Way Calls

The call function calls a server and waits for a reply. But sometimes you won't want to wait because there is no reply coming back. In those circumstances, use the GenServer cast function. (Think of it as casting your request into the sea of servers.)

Just like call is passed to handle_call in the server, cast is sent to handle_cast. Because there's no response possible, the handle_cast function takes only two parameters: the call argument and the current state. And because it doesn't want to send a reply, it will return the tuple {:noreply, new_state}.

Let's modify our sequence server to support an :increment_number function. We'll treat this as a cast, so it simply sets the new state and returns.

```
otp-server/1/sequence/lib/sequence/server.ex
defmodule Sequence.Server do
  use GenServer

  def handle_call(:next_number, _from, current_number) do
    { :reply, current_number, current_number+1 }
  end

➤  def handle_cast({:increment_number, delta}, current_number) do
➤    { :noreply, current_number + delta}
➤  end
end
```

Notice that the cast handler takes a tuple as its first parameter. The first element is :increment_number, and is used by pattern matching to select the handlers to run. The second element of the tuple is the delta to add to our state. The function simply returns a tuple, where the state is the previous state plus this number.

To call this from our iex session, we first have to recompile our source. The r command takes a module name and recompiles the file containing that module.

```
iex> r Sequence.Server
.../sequence/lib/sequence/server.ex:2: redefining module Sequence.Server
{Sequence.Server,[Sequence.Server]}
```

Even though we've recompiled the code, the old version is still running. The VM doesn't hot-swap code until you explicitly access it by module name. So, to try our new functionality we'll create a new server. When it starts, it will pick up the latest version of the code.

```
iex> { :ok, pid } = GenServer.start_link(Sequence.Server, 100)
{:ok,#PID<0.60.0>}
iex> GenServer.call(pid, :next_number)
100
iex> GenServer.call(pid, :next_number)
101
iex> GenServer.cast(pid, {:increment_number, 200})
:ok
iex> GenServer.call(pid, :next_number)
302
```

Tracing a Server's Execution

The third parameter to start_link is a set of options. A useful one during development is the debug trace, which logs message activity to the console.

We enable tracing using the debug option:

```
iex> {:ok,pid} = GenServer.start_link(Sequence.Server, 100, [debug: [:trace]])
{:ok,#PID<0.68.0>}
iex> GenServer.call(pid, :next_number)
*DBG* <0.68.0> got call next_number from <0.25.0>
*DBG* <0.68.0> sent 100 to <0.25.0>, new state 101
100
iex> GenServer.call(pid, :next_number)
*DBG* <0.68.0> got call next_number from <0.25.0>
*DBG* <0.68.0> sent 101 to <0.25.0>, new state 102
101
```

See how it traces the incoming call and the response we send back. A nice touch is that it also shows the next state.

We can also include :statistics in the debug list to ask a server to keep some basic statistics:

```
iex> {:ok,pid} = GenServer.start_link(Sequence.Server, 100,
...>                                 [debug: [:statistics]])
{:ok,#PID<0.69.0>}
iex> GenServer.call(pid, :next_number)
100
iex> GenServer.call(pid, :next_number)
101
iex> :sys.statistics pid, :get
{:ok,[start_time: {{2013,4,26},{18,17,16}}, current_time: {{2013,4,26},{18,17,28}},
     reductions: 50, messages_in: 2, messages_out: 0]}
```

Most of the fields should be fairly obvious. Timestamps are given as {{y,m,d},{h,m,s}} tuples. And the reductions value is a measure of the amount of work the server does. It is used in process scheduling as a way of making sure all processes get a fair share of the available CPU.

The Erlang sys module is your interface to the world of *system messages*. These are sent in the background between processes—they're a bit like the backchatter in a multiplayer video game. While two players are engaged in an attack (their real work), they can also be sending each other background messages: "Where are you?", "Stop moving", and so on.

The list associated with the debug parameter you give to GenServer is simply the names of functions to call in the sys module. If you say [debug: [:trace, :statistics]], then those functions will be called in sys, passing in the server's PID. Look at the documentation for sys to see what's available.[1]

---

1.   http://www.erlang.org/documentation/doc-5.8.3/lib/stdlib-1.17.3/doc/html/sys.html

This also means you can turn things on and off *after* you have started a server. For example, you can enable tracing on an existing server using the following:

```
iex> :sys.trace pid, true
:ok
iex> GenServer.call(pid, :next_number)
*DBG* <0.69.0> got call next_number from <0.25.0>
*DBG* <0.69.0> sent 105 to <0.25.0>, new state 106
105
iex> :sys.trace pid, false
:ok
iex> GenServer.call(pid, :next_number)
106
```

get_status is another useful sys function:

```
iex> :sys.get_status pid
{:status,#PID<0.57.0>,{:module,:gen_server},[["$ancestors": [#PID<0.25.0>],
"$initial_call":
{Sequence.Server,:init,1}],:running,#PID<0.25.0>,[],
[header: 'Status for generic server <0.57.0>',
data: [{'Status',:running},{'Parent',#PID<0.25.0>}},{'Logged events',[]}],
data: [{'State',102}]]]}
```

This is the default formatting of the status message GenServer provides. You have the option to change the 'State' part to return a more application-specific message by defining format_status. This receives an option describing why the function was called, as well as a list containing the server's process dictionary and the current state. (Note that in the code that follows, the string *State* in the response is in single quotes.)

otp-server/1/sequence/lib/sequence/server.ex
```
def format_status(_reason, [ _pdict, state ]) do
  [data: [{'State', "My current state is '#{inspect state}', and I'm happy"}]]
end
```

If we ask for the status in iex, we get the new message (after restarting the server):

```
iex> :sys.get_status pid
{:status,#PID<0.61.0>,{:module,:gen_server},[["$ancestors": [#PID<0.25.0>],
"$initial_call": {Sequence.Server,:init,1}],:running,#PID<0.25.0>,
[trace: true],[header: 'Status for generic server <0.61.0>',
{'Parent',#PID<0.25.0>}},{'Logged events',[]}],
data: [{'State',"My current state is '103', and I'm happy"}]]]}
```

Digging Even Deeper

As you might expect from a platform that has been running demanding and critical applications for 20 years, Erlang (and by extension Elixir) has some great server monitoring tools.

One of the easiest to use is already baked in. Inside IEx, run

```
iex> :observer.start()
```

Use this to get basic system information:

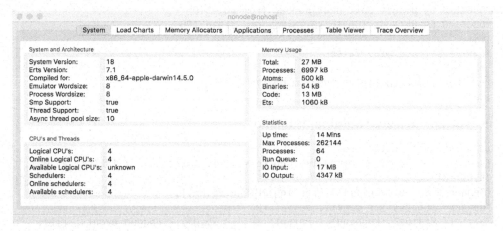

Dynamic charts of load:

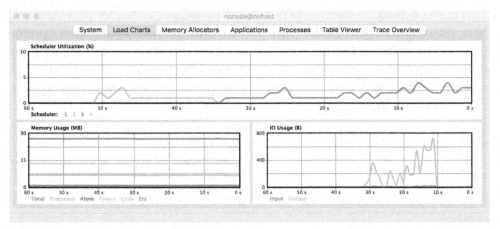

Running processes:

Table Name	Table Id	Objects	Size (kB)	Owner Pid	Owner Name
Elixir.IEx.Config		1	2	<0.43.0>	
elixir_config		11	3	<0.36.0>	
elixir_modules		0	2	<0.39.0>	elixir_code_server

nonode@nohost

And running applications:

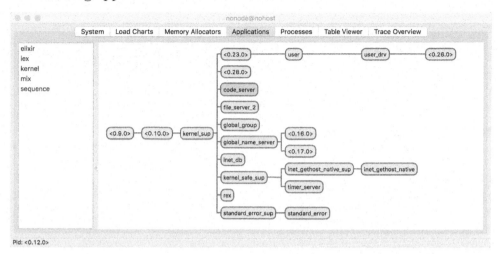

Memory allocation:

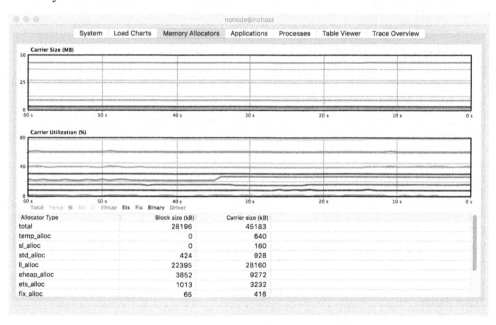

Information and contents of Erlang ETS tables:

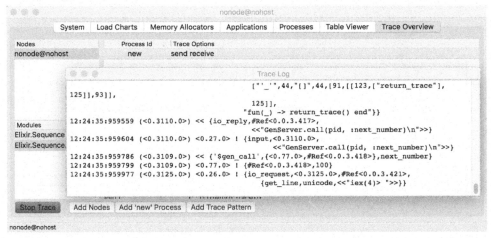

And tracing of function calls, messages, and events:

For application-level monitoring, you might want to look at Elixometer[2] from Pinterest.

Your Turn

➤ *Exercise: OTP-Servers-2*

Extend your stack server with a push interface that adds a single value to the top of the stack. This will be implemented as a cast.

Experiment in iex with pushing and popping values.

---

2.   https://github.com/pinterest/elixometer

GenServer Callbacks

GenServer is an OTP protocol. OTP works by assuming that your module defines a number of callback functions (six, in the case of a GenServer). If you were writing a GenServer in Erlang, your code would have to contain implementations of all six.

When you add the line use GenServer to a module, Elixir creates default implementations of these six callback functions. All we have to do is override the ones where we add our own application-specific behaviour. Our examples so far have used the two callbacks handle_call and handle_cast. Here's a full list:

init(start_arguments)

Called by GenServer when starting a new server. The parameter is the second argument passed to start_link. Should return {:ok, state} on success, or {:stop, reason} if the server could not be started.

You can specify an optional timeout using {:ok, state, timeout}, in which case GenServer sends the process a :timeout message whenever no message is received in a span of *timeout* ms. (The message is passed to the handle_info function.)

The default GenServer implementation sets the server state to the argument you pass.

handle_call(request, from, state)

Invoked when a client uses GenServer.call(pid, request). The from parameter is a tuple containing the PID of the client and a unique tag. The state parameter is the server state.

On success returns {:reply, result, new_state}. The list that follows this one, on page 222, shows other valid responses.

The default implementation stops the server with a :bad_call error, so you'll need to implement handle_call for every call request type your server implements.

handle_cast(request, state)

Called in response to GenServer.cast(pid, request).

A successful response is {:noreply, new_state}. Can also return {:stop, reason, new_state}.

The default implementation stops the server with a :bad_cast error.

handle_info(info, state)

Called to handle incoming messages that are not call or cast requests. For example, timeout messages are handled here. So are termination messages from any linked processes. In addition, messages sent to the PID using send (so they bypass GenServer) will be routed to this function.

terminate(reason, state)

Called when the server is about to be terminated. However, as we'll discuss in the next chapter, once we add supervision to our servers, we don't have to worry about this.

code_change(from_version, state, extra)

OTP lets us replace a running server without stopping the system. However, the new version of the server may represent its state differently from the old version. The code_change callback is invoked to change from the old state format to the new.

format_status(reason, [pdict, state])

Used to customize the state display of the server. The conventional response is [data: [{'State', state_info}]].

The call and cast handlers return standardized responses. Some of these responses can contain an optional :hibernate or timeout parameter. If hibernate is returned, the server state is removed from memory but is recovered on the next request. This saves memory at the expense of some CPU. The timeout option can be the atom :infinite (which is the default) or a number. If the latter, a :timeout message is sent if the server is idle for the specified number of milliseconds.

The first two responses are common between call and cast.

{ :noreply, new_state [, :hibernate | timeout] }

{ *:stop, reason, new_state* }

Signal that the server is to terminate.

Only handle_call can use the last two.

{ *:reply, response, new_state [, :hibernate | timeout]* }

Send response to the client.

{ *:stop, reason, reply, new_state* }

Send the response and signal that the server is to terminate.

Naming a Process

The idea of referencing processes by their PID gets old quickly. Fortunately, there are a number of alternatives.

The simplest is local naming. We assign a name that is unique for all OTP processes on our server, and then we use that name instead of the PID whenever we reference it. To create a locally named process, we use the name: option when we start the server:

```
iex> { :ok, pid } = GenServer.start_link(Sequence.Server, 100, name: :seq)
{:ok,#PID<0.58.0>}
iex> GenServer.call(:seq, :next_number)
100
iex> GenServer.call(:seq, :next_number)
101
iex> :sys.get_status :seq
{:status, #PID<0.69.0>, {:module, :gen_server},
 [["$ancestors": [#PID<0.58.0>],
   "$initial_call": {Sequence.Server, :init, 1}],
  :running, #PID<0.58.0>, [],
  [header: 'Status for generic server seq',
   data: [{'Status', :running},
          {'Parent', #PID<0.58.0>},
          {'Logged events', []}],
   data: [{'State', "My current state is '102', and I'm happy"}]]]}
```

Tidying Up the Interface

As we left it, our server works but is ugly to use. Our callers have to make explicit GenServer calls, and they have to know the registered name for our server process. We can do better. Let's wrap this interface in a set of three functions in our server module: start_link, next_number, and increment_number. The first of these calls the GenServer start_link method. As we'll cover in a couple of chapters when we look at supervisors, the name start_link is a convention. start_link must return the correct status values to OTP; as our code simply delegates to the GenServer module, this is taken care of.

Following the definition of start_link, the next two functions are the external API to issue call and cast requests to the running server process.

We'll also use the name of the module as our server's registered local name (hence the name: _MODULE_ when we start it, and the _MODULE_ parameter when we use call or cast).

```
otp-server/2/sequence/lib/sequence/server.ex
defmodule Sequence.Server do
  use GenServer

  #####
  # External API

➤ def start_link(current_number) do
    GenServer.start_link(__MODULE__, current_number, name: __MODULE__)
  end

➤ def next_number do
    GenServer.call __MODULE__, :next_number
  end

➤ def increment_number(delta) do
    GenServer.cast __MODULE__, {:increment_number, delta}
  end

  #####
  # GenServer implementation

  def handle_call(:next_number, _from, current_number) do
    { :reply, current_number, current_number+1 }
  end

  def handle_cast({:increment_number, delta}, current_number) do
    { :noreply, current_number + delta}
  end

  def format_status(_reason, [ _pdict, state ]) do
    [data: [{'State', "My current state is '#{inspect state}', and I'm happy"}]]
  end
end
```

When we run this code in iex, it's a lot cleaner:

```
$ iex -S mix
iex> Sequence.Server.start_link 123
{:ok,#PID<0.57.0>}
iex> Sequence.Server.next_number
123
iex> Sequence.Server.next_number
124
iex> Sequence.Server.increment_number 100
:ok
iex> Sequence.Server.next_number
225
```

This is the pattern you should use in your servers.

Your Turn

➤ *Exercise: OTP-Servers-3*

Give your stack server process a name, and make sure it is accessible by that name in iex.

➤ *Exercise: OTP-Servers-4*

Add the API to your stack module (the functions that wrap the GenServer calls).

➤ *Exercise: OTP-Servers-5*

Implement the terminate callback in your stack handler. Use IO.puts to report the arguments it receives.

Try various ways of terminating your server. For example, popping an empty stack will raise an exception. You might add code that calls System.halt(n) if the push handler receives a number less than 10. (This will let you generate different return codes.) Use your imagination to try different scenarios.

An OTP GenServer is just a regular Elixir process in which the message handling has been abstracted out. The GenServer behavior defines a message loop internally and maintains a state variable. That message loop then calls out to various functions that we define in our server module: handle_call, handle_cast, and so on.

We also saw that GenServer provides fairly detailed tracing of the messages received and responses sent by our server modules.

Finally, we wrapped our message-based API in module functions, which gives our users a cleaner interface and decouples them from our implementation.

But we still have an issue if our server crashes. We'll deal with this in the next chapter, when we look at supervisors.

## CHAPTER 17

OTP: Supervisors

I've said it a few times now: the *Elixir way* says not to worry much about code that crashes; instead, make sure the overall application keeps running.

This might sound contradictory, but really it is not.

Think of a typical application. If an unhandled error causes an exception to be raised, the application stops. Nothing else gets done until it is restarted. If it's a server handling multiple requests, they all might be lost.

The issue here is that one error takes the whole application down.

But imagine that instead your application consists of hundreds or thousands of processes, each handling just a small part of a request. If one of those crashes, everything else carries on. You might lose the work it's doing, but you can design your applications to minimize even that risk. And when that process gets restarted, you're back running at 100%.

In the Elixir and OTP worlds, *supervisors* perform all of this process monitoring and restarting.

Supervisors and Workers

An Elixir supervisor has just one purpose—it manages one or more worker processes. (As we'll discuss later, it can also manage other supervisors.)

At its simplest, a supervisor is a process that uses the OTP supervisor behavior. It is given a list of processes to monitor and is told what to do if a process dies, and how to prevent restart loops (when a process is restarted, dies, gets restarted, dies, and so on).

To do this, the supervisor uses the Erlang VM's process-linking and -monitoring facilities. We talked about these when we covered spawn on page 187.

You can write supervisors as separate modules, but the Elixir style is to include them inline. The easiest way to get started is to create your project with the --sup flag. Let's do this for our sequence server.

```
$ mix new --sup sequence
* creating README.md
* creating .gitignore
* creating mix.exs
* creating config
* creating config/config.exs
* creating lib
* creating lib/sequence.ex
* creating test
* creating test/test_helper.exs
* creating test/sequence_test.exs
```

Nothing looks different, but open lib/sequence.ex.

```
defmodule Sequence do
  use Application

  def start(_type, _args) do
    import Supervisor.Spec, warn: false

    children = [
      # Define workers and child supervisors to be supervised
      # worker(Sequence.Worker, [arg1, arg2, arg3])
    ]

    opts = [strategy: :one_for_one, name: Sequence.Supervisor]
    Supervisor.start_link(children, opts)
  end
end
```

Our start function now creates a supervisor for our application. All we need to do is tell it what we want supervised. Create a lib/sequence directory and copy the Sequence.Server module from the last chapter into it. Then uncomment the worker call in the children list to reference it.

```
otp-supervisor/1/sequence/lib/sequence.ex
def start(_type, _args) do
  import Supervisor.Spec, warn: false

  children = [
    worker(Sequence.Server, [123])
  ]

  opts = [strategy: :one_for_one, name: Sequence.Supervisor]
  {:ok, _pid} = Supervisor.start_link(children, opts)
end
```

Let's look at the sequence of events.

- When our application starts, the start function is called.

- It creates a list of child servers. It uses the worker function to create a specification of each one. In our case, we want to start Sequence.Server and pass it the parameter 123.

- We call Supervisor.start_link, passing it the list of child specifications and a set of options. This creates a supervisor process.

- Now our supervisor process calls the start_link function for each of its managed children. In our case, this is the function in Sequence.Server. This code is unchanged—it calls GenServer.start_link to create a GenServer process.

Now we're up and running. Let's try it:

```
$ iex -S mix
Compiled lib/sequence.ex
Compiled lib/sequence/server.ex
Generated sequence app
iex> Sequence.Server.increment_number 3
:ok
iex> Sequence.Server.next_number
126
```

So far, so good. But the key thing with a supervisor is that it is supposed to manage our worker process. If it dies, for example, we want it to be restarted. Let's try that. If we pass increment_number something that isn't a number, the process should die trying to add it to the current number.

```
iex(3)> Sequence.Server.increment_number "cat"
:ok
iex(4)> 14:22:06.269 [error] GenServer Sequence.Server terminating
Last message: {:"$gen_cast", {:increment_number, "cat"}}
State: [data: [{'State', "My current state is '127', and I'm happy"}]]
** (exit) an exception was raised:
    ** (ArithmeticError) bad argument in arithmetic expression
        (sequence) lib/sequence/server.ex:27: Sequence.Server.handle_cast/2
        (stdlib) gen_server.erl:599: :gen_server.handle_msg/5
        (stdlib) proc_lib.erl:239: :proc_lib.init_p_do_apply/3
iex(4)> Sequence.Server.next_number
123
iex(5)> Sequence.Server.next_number
124
```

We get a wonderful error report that shows us the exception, along with a stack trace from the process. We can also see the message we sent that triggered the problem.

But when we then ask our server for a number, it responds as if nothing had happened. The supervisor restarted our process for us.

This is excellent, but there's a problem. The supervisor restarted our sequence process with the initial parameters we passed in, and the numbers started again from 123. A reincarnated process has no memory of its past lives, and no state is retained across a crash.

Your Turn

➤ *Exercise: OTP-Supervisors-1*

Add a supervisor to your stack application. Use iex to make sure it starts the server correctly. Use the server normally, and then crash it (try popping from an empty stack). Did it restart? What were the stack contents after the restart?

Managing Process State Across Restarts

Some servers are effectively stateless. If we had a server that calculated the factors of numbers or responded to network requests with the current time, we could simply restart it and let it run.

But our server is not stateless—it needs to remember the current number so it can generate an increasing sequence.

All of the approaches to this involve storing the state outside of the process. Let's choose a simple option—we'll write a separate worker process that can store and retrieve a value. We'll call it our *stash*. The sequence server can store its current number in the stash whenever it terminates, and then we can recover the number when we restart.

At this point, we have to think about lifetimes. Our sequence server should be fairly robust, but we've already found one thing that crashes it. So in actuarial terms, it isn't the fittest process in the scheduler queue. But our stash process must be more robust—it must outlive the sequence server, at the very least.

We have to do two things to make this happen. First, we make it as simple as possible. The fewer moving parts in a chunk of code, the less likely it is to go wrong.

Second, we have to supervise it separately. In fact, we'll create a supervision tree. It'll look like the following diagram.

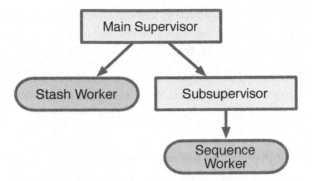

Here we have a top-level supervisor that is responsible for the health of two things: the stash worker and a second supervisor. That second supervisor then manages the worker that generates the sequence.

Our sequence generator needs to know the PID of the stash in order to retrieve and store the sequence value. We *could* register the stash process under a name (just as we did with the sequence worker itself), but as this is purely a local affair, we can pass it the PID directly. However, to do that we need to get the stash worker spawned first. This leads to a slightly different design for the top-level supervisor. We'll move the code that starts the top-level supervisor out of sequence.ex and into a separate module. Then we'll initialize it with no children and add the stash and the subsupervisor manually. Once we start the stash worker, we'll have its PID, and we can then pass it on to the subsupervisor (which in turn will pass it to the sequence worker). Our overall supervisor looks like this:

```
otp-supervisor/2/sequence/lib/sequence/supervisor.ex
Line 1  defmodule Sequence.Supervisor do
   -      use Supervisor
   -      def start_link(initial_number) do
   -        result = {:ok, sup } = Supervisor.start_link(__MODULE__, [initial_number])
   5        start_workers(sup, initial_number)
   -        result
   -      end
   -      def start_workers(sup, initial_number) do
   -        # Start the stash worker
  10        {:ok, stash} =
   -           Supervisor.start_child(sup, worker(Sequence.Stash, [initial_number]))
   -        # and then the subsupervisor for the actual sequence server
   -        Supervisor.start_child(sup, supervisor(Sequence.SubSupervisor, [stash]))
   -      end
  15      def init(_) do
   -        supervise [], strategy: :one_for_one
   -      end
   -    end
```

On line 4 we start up the supervisor. This automatically invokes the init call-back. This in turn calls supervise, but passes in an empty list. The supervisor is now running but has no children.

At this point, OTP returns control to our start_link function, which then calls the start_workers function. This starts the stash worker, passing it the initial number. We get back a status of (:ok) and a PID. We then pass the PID to the subsupervisor.

This subsupervisor is basically the same as our very first supervisor—it simply spawns the sequence worker. But instead of passing in a current number, it passes in the stash's PID.

otp-supervisor/2/sequence/lib/sequence/subsupervisor.ex
```elixir
defmodule Sequence.SubSupervisor do
  use Supervisor

  def start_link(stash_pid) do
    {:ok, _pid} = Supervisor.start_link(__MODULE__, stash_pid)
  end
  def init(stash_pid) do
    child_processes = [ worker(Sequence.Server, [stash_pid]) ]
    supervise child_processes, strategy: :one_for_one
  end
end
```

The sequence worker has two changes. First, when it is initialized it must get the current number from the stash. Second, when it terminates it stores the then-current number back in the stash. To make these changes, we'll override two more GenServer callbacks: init and terminate.

otp-supervisor/2/sequence/lib/sequence/server.ex
```elixir
defmodule Sequence.Server do
  use GenServer

  #####
  # External API

  def start_link(stash_pid) do
    {:ok, _pid} = GenServer.start_link(__MODULE__, stash_pid, name: __MODULE__)
  end
  def next_number do
    GenServer.call __MODULE__, :next_number
  end
  def increment_number(delta) do
    GenServer.cast __MODULE__, {:increment_number, delta}
  end
```

```
  #####
  # GenServer implementation

  def init(stash_pid) do
    current_number = Sequence.Stash.get_value stash_pid
    { :ok, {current_number, stash_pid} }
  end
  def handle_call(:next_number, _from, {current_number, stash_pid}) do
    { :reply, current_number, {current_number+1, stash_pid} }
  end
  def handle_cast({:increment_number, delta}, {current_number, stash_pid}) do
    { :noreply, {current_number + delta, stash_pid}}
  end
  def terminate(_reason, {current_number, stash_pid}) do
    Sequence.Stash.save_value stash_pid, current_number
  end
end
```

The stash itself is trivial:

otp-supervisor/2/sequence/lib/sequence/stash.ex

```
defmodule Sequence.Stash do
  use GenServer

  #####
  # External API

  def start_link(current_number) do
    {:ok,_pid} = GenServer.start_link( __MODULE__, current_number)
  end

  def save_value(pid, value) do
    GenServer.cast pid, {:save_value, value}
  end

  def get_value(pid) do
    GenServer.call pid, :get_value
  end

  #####
  # GenServer implementation

  def handle_call(:get_value, _from, current_value) do
    { :reply, current_value, current_value }
  end

  def handle_cast({:save_value, value}, _current_value) do
    { :noreply, value}
  end
end
```

And finally, our top-level module has to start the top-level supervisor:

```
otp-supervisor/2/sequence/lib/sequence.ex
defmodule Sequence do
  use Application

  def start(_type, _args) do
➤    {:ok, _pid} = Sequence.Supervisor.start_link(123)
  end
end
```

Let's work through what is going on here.

- We start the top-level supervisor, passing it an initial value for the counter. It starts up the stash worker, giving it this number. It then starts the subsupervisor, passing it the stash's PID.

- The subsupervisor in turn starts the sequence worker. This goes to the stash, gets the current value, and uses that value and the stash PID as its state. The next_number and increment_number functions are unchanged (except they receive the more complex state).

- If the sequence worker terminates for any reason, GenServer calls its terminate function. It stores its current value in the stash before dying.

- The subsupervisor will notice that a child has died. It will restart the child, passing in the stash PID, and the newly incarnated worker will pick up the current value that was stored when the previous instance died.

At least that's the theory. Let's try it:

```
$ iex -S mix
Compiled lib/sequence.ex
Compiled lib/sequence/server.ex
Compiled lib/sequence/stash.ex
Compiled lib/sequence/subsupervisor.ex
Compiled lib/sequence/supervisor.ex
Generated sequence app
iex> Sequence.Server.next_number
123
iex> Sequence.Server.next_number
124
iex> Sequence.Server.increment_number 100
:ok
iex> Sequence.Server.next_number
225
iex> Sequence.Server.increment_number "cause it to crash"
:ok
iex>
14:35:07.337 [error] GenServer Sequence.Server terminating
```

```
Last message: {:"$gen_cast", {:increment_number, "cause it to crash"}}
State: {226, #PID<0.70.0>}
** (exit) an exception was raised:
    ** (ArithmeticError) bad argument in arithmetic expression
        (sequence) lib/sequence/server.ex:32: Sequence.Server.handle_cast/2
        (stdlib) gen_server.erl:599: :gen_server.handle_msg/5
        (stdlib) proc_lib.erl:239: :proc_lib.init_p_do_apply/3
iex> Sequence.Server.next_number
226
iex> Sequence.Server.next_number
227
```

Even though we crashed our sequence worker, it got restarted and the state was preserved. Now we begin to see how careful supervision is critical if we want to write reliable applications.

Supervisors Are the Heart of Reliability

Think about our previous example; it was both trivial and profound. It was trivial because there are many ways of achieving some kind of fault tolerance with a library that returns successive numbers. But it was profound because it is a concrete representation of the idea of building rings of confidence in our code. The outer ring, where our code interacts with the world, should be as reliable as we can make it. But within that ring there are other, nested rings. And in those rings, things can be less than perfect. The trick is to ensure that the code in each ring knows how to deal with failures of the code in the next ring down.

And that's where supervisors come into play. In this chapter we've seen only a small fraction of supervisors' capabilities. They have different strategies for dealing with the termination of a child, different ways of terminating children, and different ways of restarting them. There's plenty of information online about using OTP supervisors.

But the real power of supervisors is that they exist. The fact that you use them to manage your workers means you are forced to think about reliability and state as you design your application. And that discipline leads to applications with very high availability—in *Programming Erlang (2nd edition)* *[Arm13]*, Joe Armstrong says OTP has been used to build systems with 99.9999999% reliability. That's nine nines. And that ain't bad.

There's one more level in our lightning tour of OTP—the application. And that's the next chapter's topic.

Your Turn

➤ *Exercise: OTP-Supervisors-2*

Rework your stack server to use a supervision tree with a separate stash process to hold the state. Verify that it works and that when you crash the server the state is retained across a restart.

## CHAPTER 18

OTP: Applications

So far in our quick tour of Elixir and OTP we've looked at server processes and the supervisors that monitor them. There's one more stage in our journey—the application.

This Is Not Your Father's Application

Because OTP comes from the Erlang world, it uses Erlang names for things. And unfortunately, some of these names are not terribly descriptive. The name *application* is one of these. When most of us talk about applications, we think of a program we run to do something—maybe on our computer or phone, or via a web browser. An application is a self-contained whole.

But in the OTP world, that's not the case. Instead, an application is a bundle of code that comes with a descriptor. That descriptor tells the runtime what dependencies the code has, what global names it registers, and so on. In fact, an OTP application is more like a dynamic link library or a shared object than a conventional application.

It might help to see the word *application* and in your head but pronounce it *component* or *service*.

For example, back when we were fetching GitHub issues using the HTTPoison library, what we actually installed was an independent application containing HTTPoison. Although it looked like we were just using a library, mix automatically loaded the HTTPoison application. When we then started it, HTTPoison in turn started a couple of other applications that it needed (SSL and Hackney), which in turn kicked off their own supervisors and workers. And all of this was transparent to us.

I've said that applications are components; but there are some applications that are at the top of the tree and are meant to be run directly.

In this chapter we'll look at both types of application component (see what I did there?). In reality they're virtually the same, so let's cover the common ground first.

The Application Specification File

You probably noticed that every now and then mix will talk about a file called *name*.app, where *name* is your application's name.

This file is called an *application specification* and is used to define your application to the runtime environment. Mix creates this file automatically from the information in mix.exs combined with information it gleans from compiling your application.

When you run your application this file is consulted to get things loaded.

Your application does not need to use all the OTP functionality—this file will always be created and referred to. However, once you start using OTP supervision trees, stuff you add to mix.exs will get copied into the .app file.

Turning Our Sequence Program into an OTP Application

So, here's the good news. The application in the previous chapter is already a full-blown OTP application. When mix created the initial project tree, it added a supervisor (which we then modified) and enough information to our mix.exs file to get the application started. In particular, it filled in the application function:

```
def application do
  [mod: { Sequence, [] }]
end
```

This says that the top-level module of our application is called Sequence. OTP assumes this module will implement a start function, and it will pass that function an empty list as a parameter.

In our previous version of the start function, we ignored the arguments and instead hard-wired the call to start_link to pass 123 to our application. Let's change that to take the value from mix.exs instead. First, change mix.exs to pass an initial value (we'll use 456):

```
def application do
  [mod: { Sequence, 456 }]
end
```

Then change the sequence.ex code to use this passed-in value:

```
otp-app/sequence/lib/sequence.ex
defmodule Sequence do
  use Application

  def start(_type, initial_number) do
    Sequence.Supervisor.start_link(initial_number)
  end
end
```

We can check that this works:

```
$ iex -S mix
Compiled lib/sequence.ex
Compiled lib/sequence/subsupervisor.ex
Compiled lib/sequence/stash.ex
Compiled lib/sequence/server.ex
Compiled lib/sequence/supervisor.ex
Generated sequence app

iex> Sequence.Server.next_number
456
```

Let's look at the application function again.

The mod: option tells OTP the module that is the main entry point for our app. If our app is a conventional runnable application, then it will need to start somewhere, so we'd write our kickoff function here. But even pure library applications may need to be initialized. (For example, a logging library may start a background logger process or connect to a central logging server.)

For the sequence app, we tell OTP that the Sequence module is the main entry point. OTP will call this module's start function when it starts the application. The second element of the tuple is the parameter to pass to this function. In our case, it's the initial number for the sequence.

There's a second option we'll want to add to this.

The registered: option lists the names that our application will register. We can use this to ensure each name is unique across all loaded applications in a node or cluster. In our case, the sequence server registers itself under the name Sequence.Server, so we'll update the configuration to read as follows:

```
otp-app/sequence/mix.exs
# Configuration for the OTP application
def application do
  [
    mod: { Sequence, 456 },
    registered: [ Sequence.Server ]
  ]
end
```

Now that we've done the configuring in mix, we run mix compile, which both compiles the app and updates the sequence.app application specification file with information from mix.exs. (The same thing happens if we run mix using iex -S mix.)

```
$ mix compile
Compiled lib/sequence.ex
Compiled lib/sequence/server.ex
Compiled lib/sequence/stash.ex
Compiled lib/sequence/subsupervisor.ex
Compiled lib/sequence/supervisor.ex
Generated sequence app
```

Mix tells us it has created a sequence.app file, but where is it? You'll find it tucked away in _build/dev/lib/sequence/ebin. Although a little obscure, the directory structure under _build is compatible with Erlang's OTP way of doing things. This makes life easier when you release your code. You'll notice that the path has dev in it—this keeps things you're doing in development separate from other build products.

Let's look at the sequence.app that was generated.

otp-app/sequence/_build/dev/lib/sequence/ebin/sequence.app
```
{application,sequence,
            [{description,"sequence"},
             {mod,{'Elixir.Sequence',[]}},
             {registered,[sequence]},
             {env,[{initial_value,456}]},
             {vsn,"0.0.1"},
             {modules,['Elixir.Sequence','Elixir.Sequence.Server',
                       'Elixir.Sequence.Stash',
                       'Elixir.Sequence.SubSupervisor',
                       'Elixir.Sequence.Supervisor']},
             {applications,[kernel,stdlib,elixir]}]}.
```

This file contains an Erlang tuple that defines the app. Some of the information comes from the project and application section of mix.exs. Mix also automatically added a list of the names of all the compiled modules in our app (the .beam files) and a list of the apps our app depends on (kernel, stdlib, and elixir). That's pretty smart.

More on Application Parameters

In the previous example, we passed the integer 456 to the application as an initial parameter. Although valid(ish), we really should have passed in a keyword list instead. That's because Elixir provides a function, Application.get_env, to retrieve these values from anywhere in our code. So we probably should have set up mix.exs with

```
def application do
  [
    mod:         { Sequence, [] },
    env:         [initial_number: 456],
    registered:  [ Sequence.Server ]
  ]
end
```

and then accessed the value using get_env. We call this with the application name and the name of the environment parameter to fetch:

```
defmodule Sequence do
  use Application

  def start(_type, _args) do
    Sequence.Supervisor.start_link(Application.get_env(:sequence, :initial_number))
  end

end
```

Your call.

Supervision Is the Basis of Reliability

Let's briefly recap. In that last example, we ran our OTP sequence application using mix. Looking at just our code, we see that two supervisor processes and two worker processes got started. These were knitted together so our system continued to run with no loss of state even if the worker that we talked to crashed. And any other Erlang process on this node (including iex itself) can talk to our sequence application and enjoy its stream of freshly minted integers.

You probably noticed that the start function takes two parameters. The second corresponds to the value we specified in the mod: option in the mix.exs file (in our case, the counter's initial value). The first parameter specifies the status of the restart, which we're not going to get into, because...

Your Turn

> *Exercise: OTP-Applications-1*
  Turn your stack server into an OTP application.

> *Exercise: OTP-Applications-2*
  So far, we haven't written any tests for the application. Is there anything you can test? See what you can do.

Releasing Your Code

One way Erlang achieves nine-nines application availability is by having a rock-solid release management system. Elixir takes this system and makes it easy to use.

Before we get too far, let's talk terminology.

A *release* is a bundle that contains a particular version of your application, its dependencies, its configuration, and any metadata it requires to get running and stay running. A *deployment* is a way of getting a release into an environment where it can be used.

A *hot upgrade* is a kind of deployment that allows the release of a currently running application to be changed while that application continues to run—the upgrade happens in place with no user detectable disruption.

In this section we'll talk about releases and hot upgrades. We won't dig too deeply into deployment.

EXRM—the Elixir Release Manager

exrm is an Elixir package that makes most release tasks easy. It is built on top of the Erlang relx package, which in turn uses some special features of the Erlang virtual machine.

Imagine you were managing the deployment of hundreds of thousands of lines of code into running telephone switches, while maintaining all the ongoing connections, providing a full audit trail, and maintaining contractual uptime guarantees. This is clearly complex. Very complex. And this is the task the Erlang folks faced, so they created tools that help.

relx and exrm are layers of abstraction on top of this complexity. Normally they manage to hide it, but sometimes the lower levels leak out and you get to see how the sausage is made.

This book isn't going to get that deep. Instead, I just want to give you a feel for the process.

Before we Start

In Elixir, we version both the application code and the data it operates on. The two are independent—we might go for a dozen code releases without changing any data structures.

The code version is stored in the project dictionary in mix.exs. But how do we version the data. Come to think of it, where do we even define the data?

In an OTP application, all state is maintained by servers, and each server's state is independent. So it makes sense to version the app data within each server module. Perhaps a server initially holds its state in a 2 element tuple. That could be version 0. Later, it is changed to hold state in a three element tuple. That could be version 1.

We'll see the significance of this later. For now, let's just set the version of the state data in our server. We use the @vsn (version) directive:

```
otp-app/sequence_v0/lib/sequence/server.ex
defmodule Sequence.Server do
  use GenServer

  @vsn "0"
```

Now let's generate a release.

Your First Release

First, we have to add exrm as a project dependency. Open up the sequence project's mix.exs file and update the deps function.

```
otp-app/sequence_v0/mix.exs
defp deps do
  [
    {:exrm, "~> 1.0.0-rc7"}
  ]
end
```

Install it:

```
$ mix do deps.get, deps.compile
```

exrm makes sensible choices for the various configuration options, so for a basic app like this we're now ready to create of first release.

```
$ mix release
Compiled lib/sequence.ex
  .   .   .
Compiled lib/sequence/supervisor.ex
Generated sequence app
Consolidated String.Chars
  .   .   .
Building release with MIX_ENV=dev.
==> The release for sequence-0.0.1 is ready!
==> You can boot a console running your release with
        `$ rel/sequence/bin/sequence console`
```

exrm got the application name and version number from your mix.exs file, and packaged your app into the rel/ directory:

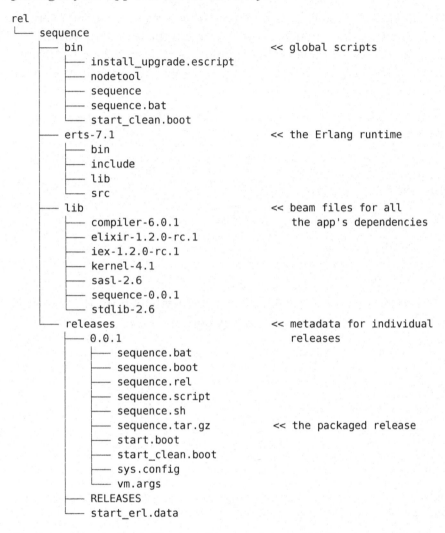

```
rel
└── sequence
    ├── bin                                    << global scripts
    │   ├── install_upgrade.escript
    │   ├── nodetool
    │   ├── sequence
    │   ├── sequence.bat
    │   └── start_clean.boot
    ├── erts-7.1                               << the Erlang runtime
    │   ├── bin
    │   ├── include
    │   ├── lib
    │   └── src
    ├── lib                                    << beam files for all
    │   ├── compiler-6.0.1                        the app's dependencies
    │   ├── elixir-1.2.0-rc.1
    │   ├── iex-1.2.0-rc.1
    │   ├── kernel-4.1
    │   ├── sasl-2.6
    │   ├── sequence-0.0.1
    │   └── stdlib-2.6
    └── releases                               << metadata for individual
        ├── 0.0.1                                 releases
        │   ├── sequence.bat
        │   ├── sequence.boot
        │   ├── sequence.rel
        │   ├── sequence.script
        │   ├── sequence.sh
        │   ├── sequence.tar.gz                << the packaged release
        │   ├── start.boot
        │   ├── start_clean.boot
        │   ├── sys.config
        │   └── vm.args
        ├── RELEASES
        └── start_erl.data
```

The most important file is rel/sequence/releases/0.0.1/sequence.tar.gz. It contains everything needed to run this release. This is the file we deploy to our servers.

A Toy Deployment Environment

I don't want to slow things down by having you provision a server in the cloud, so I'm going to deploy to my local machine. However, to make it a little more realistic, I'll pretend this machine is remote, and use ssh to do all the deploying. I'll also be creating directories and copying files manually. In practice, you'd want to automate all of this with something like Capistrano or Ansible.

We'll store the releases in a deploy directory. I'll put this inside my home directory—feel free to put it anywhere (writable) you want.

```
$ ssh localhost mkdir ~/deploy
```

Deploy and Run the App

Now we need to set up the initial release and its directory structure. Copy the sequence.tar.gz file into the deploy directory, and then extract its contents.

```
$ scp rel/sequence/releases/0.0.1/sequence.tar.gz localhost:deploy
$ ssh localhost tar -x -f ~/deploy/sequence.tar.gz -C ~/deploy
```

The app is now ready to run. The scripts in deploy/bin control it. These in turn delegate to scripts in the current release directory (all on the server).

Let's start an iex console. (The ssh -t option lets us control the remote iex with ^C and ^G).

```
$ ssh -t localhost ~/deploy/bin/sequence console
Using /Users/dave/deploy/releases/0.0.1/sequence.sh
Interactive Elixir (1.2.0-rc.1) - press Ctrl+C to exit (type h() ENTER for help)

iex(sequence@127.0.0.1)2> Sequence.Server.next_number
456
iex(sequence@127.0.0.1)3> Sequence.Server.next_number
457
```

(Leave this session running—we'll use it to demonstrate hot code reloading).

A Second Release

Our marketing team ran a focus group. It seems our customers want the next_number function to return a message like "the next number is 458". Let's oblige.

First, we'll change server.ex:

otp-app/sequence_v1/lib/sequence/server.ex
```
def next_number do
  with number = GenServer.call(__MODULE__, :next_number),
  do: "The next number is #{number}"
end
```

Then we'll bump the application's version number in mix.exs.

otp-app/sequence_v1/mix.exs
```
  def project do
    [ app:     :sequence,
      version: "0.0.2",
      deps:    deps ]
  end
```

```
# Configuration for the OTP application
def application do
  [
    mod:        { Sequence, 456 },
    registered: [ Sequence.Server ]
  ]
end

defp deps do
  [ exrm: "~> 1.0.0-rc7" ]
end
end
```

(We don't have to change the @VSN value—the representation of the server's state is not affected by this change.)

After exhaustive testing, we decide we're ready to create a new release:

```
$ mix release
Building release with MIX_ENV=dev.
This is an upgrade, verifying appups exist for updated dependencies..
==> All dependencies have appups ready for release!
==> Generated .appup for sequence 0.0.1 -> 0.0.2
===> relup successfully created!
==> The release for sequence-0.0.2 is ready!
```

exrm worked out we're transitioning from 0.0.1 to 0.0.2 and created a release that will do that.

The deployment of the first release of an app is special, as it has to create an environment for that app. Now that's in place, this release (and all subsequent releases) will be slightly different. We have to create release directory on the server and copy the tarball into it. The directory will be under deploy/releases, and will be named the same as the release's version number.

```
$ ssh localhost mkdir deploy/releases/0.0.2
$ scp rel/sequence/releases/0.0.2/sequence.tar.gz localhost:deploy/releases/0.0.2
```

Now let's upgrade the running code.

```
$ ~/deploy/bin/sequence upgrade 0.0.2
Using /Users/dave/deploy/releases/0.0.1/sequence.sh
Release 0.0.2 not found, attempting to unpack releases/0.0.2/sequence.tar.gz
Unpacked successfully: "0.0.2"
Generating vm.args/sys.config for upgrade...
sys.config ready!
vm.args ready!
Release 0.0.2 is already unpacked, now installing.
Installed Release: 0.0.2
Made release permanent: "0.0.2"
```

Head back over to the terminal session that's talking to the app. Don't restart it—just make another request.

```
iex(sequence@127.0.0.1)4> Sequence.Server.next_number
"The next number is 458"
iex(sequence@127.0.0.1)5> Sequence.Server.next_number
"The next number is 459"
```

Erlang can actually run two versions of a module at the same time. Currently executing code will continue to use the old version until that code explicitly cites the name of the module that has changed. At that point, and for that particular process, execution will swap to the new version.

This is a critical part of hot loading of code. We want to let code that is currently running continue without interruption, but the new release may not be compatible with it. So Erlang lets it run on the old release. But the next request will reference the module explicitly, and the new code will be loaded.

In our case, when we say Sequence.Server.next_number, the reference to Sequence.Server triggers the reload, so the 0.0.2 release handles the next request.

What if our new release was a disaster? That's not a problem—we can always downgrade to a previous version.

```
$ ssh localhost ~/deploy/bin/sequence downgrade 0.0.1
```

```
Warning: "/Users/dave/deploy/releases/0.0.1/relup" missing (optional)
```

```
iex(sequence@127.0.0.1)6> Sequence.Server.next_number
460
iex(sequence@127.0.0.1)7> Sequence.Server.next_number
461
```

Cool. Let's go back to the current version before continuing.

```
$ ssh localhost ~/deploy/bin/sequence upgrade 0.0.2
```

Migrating Server State

Our boss calls. We're about to go for a second round of funding on our wildly successfully sequence-server business, but customers have noticed a bug. We implemented increment_number to add a delta to the current number—a one-time change. But apparently it was instead supposed to set the difference between successive numbers we served.

Let's try the existing code in our already-running console:

```
iex(sequence@127.0.0.1)8> Sequence.Server.next_number
462
iex(sequence@127.0.0.1)9> Sequence.Server.increment_number 10
```

```
:ok
iex(sequence@127.0.0.1)10> Sequence.Server.next_number
472
iex(sequence@127.0.0.1)10> Sequence.Server.next_number
473
```

Yup, we're applying the delta only once.

Well, that's an easy change to the code. We simply have to keep one extra thing in the state—a delta value. Here's the updated server code:

otp-app/sequence_v2/lib/sequence/server.ex

```elixir
defmodule Sequence.Server do
  use GenServer
  require Logger

  defmodule State do
    defstruct current_number: 0, stash_pid: nil, delta: 1
  end

  @vsn "1"

  #####
  # External API

  def start_link(stash_pid) do
    GenServer.start_link(__MODULE__, stash_pid, name: __MODULE__)
  end

  def next_number do
    with GenServer.call(__MODULE__, :next_number),
    do: "The next number is #{number}"
  end

  def increment_number(delta) do
    GenServer.cast __MODULE__, {:increment_number, delta}
  end

  #####
  # GenServer implementation

  def init(stash_pid) do
    current_number = Sequence.Stash.get_value stash_pid
    {
      :ok,
      %State{current_number: current_number, stash_pid: stash_pid}
    }
  end

  def handle_call(:next_number, _from, state) do
    {
```

```
        :reply,
         state.current_number,
          %{ state | current_number: state.current_number + state.delta  }
      }
    end

    def handle_cast({:increment_number, delta}, state) do
      {
        :noreply,
         %{ state | current_number: state.current_number + delta, delta: delta }
      }
    end

    def terminate(_reason, state) do
      Sequence.Stash.save_value state.stash_pid, state.current_number
    end
end
```

The big change is that we made the state a struct rather than a tuple and added the delta value. We updated the increment handler to change the value of delta, and the next number handler now adds in the delta each time.

The format of the state changed, so we updated the version number to 1.

If we simply stop the old server and start the new one, we'll lose the state stored in the old one. But we can't just copy the state across—the old server had a single integer and the new one has a struct.

Fortunately, OTP has a callback for this. In the new server, implement the code_change function.

otp-app/sequence_v2/lib/sequence/server.ex
```
def code_change("0", old_state = { current_number, stash_pid }, _extra) do
  new_state = %State{current_number: current_number,
                     stash_pid: stash_pid,
                     delta: 1
                     }
  Logger.info "Changing code from 0 to 1"
  Logger.info inspect(old_state)
  Logger.info inspect(new_state)
  { :ok, new_state }
end
```

The callback takes three arguments—the old version number, the old state, and an additional parameter we don't use. The callback's job is to return {:ok, new_state}. In our case, the new state is a struct containing the stash PID and the old current number, along with the new delta value, initialized to 1. We'll use the logger to report on what we did, so we need to add it to the applications list in mix.exs and require it at the top of our server). While we're in mix.exs, we'll bump the version number. This is shown on the next page.

```
otp-app/sequence_v2/mix.exs
defmodule Sequence.Mixfile do
  use Mix.Project

  def project do
    [ app:      :sequence,
➤    version: "0.0.3",
      deps:    deps ]
  end

  def application do
    [
      mod:          { Sequence, 456 },
      registered:   [ Sequence.Server ],
➤    applications: [ :logger ]
    ]
  end

  defp deps do
    [ exrm: "~> 1.0.0-rc7" ]
  end
end
```

Time to create the new release:

```
$ mix release
Building release with MIX_ENV=dev.
This is an upgrade, verifying appups exist for updated dependencies..
==> All dependencies have appups ready for release!
==> Generated .appup for sequence 0.0.2 -> 0.0.3
===> relup successfully created!
==> The release for sequence-0.0.3 is ready!
```

Copy it into the deployment location:

```
$ ssh localhost mkdir ~/deploy/releases/0.0.3/
$ scp rel/sequence/releases/0.0.3/sequence.tar.gz localhost:deploy/releases/0.0.3/
```

Cross your fingers, and upgrade the app:

```
$ ssh localhost ~/deploy/bin/sequence upgrade 0.0.3
Using /Users/dave/deploy/releases/0.0.2/sequence.sh
Release 0.0.3 not found, attempting to unpack releases/0.0.3/sequence.tar.gz
Unpacked successfully: "0.0.3"
Generating vm.args/sys.config for upgrade...
sys.config ready!
vm.args ready!
Release 0.0.3 is already unpacked, now installing.
Installed Release: 0.0.3
Made release permanent: "0.0.3"
```

But the real magic happened over in the console window:

```
16:09:07.890 [info]  Changing code from 0 to 1
16:09:07.893 [info]  {474, #PID<0.49.0>}
16:09:07.899 [info]  %Sequence.Server.State{current_number: 474,
                                  delta: 1, stash_pid:  #PID<0.49.0>}
```

That's the logging that we added to our code_change function. We seem to have migrated the server's state into our new structure. Let's try it out:

```
iex(sequence@127.0.0.1)10> Sequence.Server.next_number
"The next number is 474"
iex(sequence@127.0.0.1)11> Sequence.Server.increment_number 10
:ok
iex(sequence@127.0.0.1)13> Sequence.Server.next_number
"The next number is 485"
iex(sequence@127.0.0.1)14> Sequence.Server.next_number
"The next number is 495"
```

That's the new behavio(u)r, running with our new state structure. We updated the code twice, and migrated data once, all while the application continued to run. There was no service disruption, and no loss of data.

Plutarch records the story of a ship called Theseus. Over the course of many years most of the ship's structure was replaced, piece by piece. While this was happening, the ship was in continuous use. Plutarch raises the question "is the renovated Theseus the same as the original?"

Using Elixir release management, our applications can work the same way the Theseus did, running continuously but being updated all the time.

Is the latest application the same as the original? Who cares, as long as it's still running?

OTP Is Big—Unbelievably Big

This book barely scratches OTP's surface. But (I hope) it does introduce the major concepts and give you an idea of what's possible.

More advanced uses of OTP may include release management (including hot code-swapping), handling of distributed failover, automated scaling, and so on. But if you have an application that needs such things, you likely will already have or will soon need dedicated operations experts who know the low-level details of making OTP apps perform the way you need them to.

There is never anything simple about scaling out to the kind of size and sophistication that is possible with OTP. But now you know you can start small and get there.

However, there are ways of writing *some* OTP servers more simply, and that's the subject of the next chapter.

Your Turn

➤ *Exercise: OTP-Applications-3*

Our boss notices that after we applied our version-0-to-version-1 code change, the delta indeed works as specified. However, she also notices that if the server crashes, the delta is forgotten—only the current number is retained. Create a new release that stashes both values.

## CHAPTER 19

Tasks and Agents

This part of the book is about processes and process distribution. So far we've covered two extremes. In the first chapters we looked at the spawn primitive, along with message sending and receiving and multinode operations. We then looked at OTP, the 800-pound gorilla of process architecture.

Sometimes, though, we want something in the middle. We want to be able to run simple processes, either for background processing or for maintaining state. But we don't want to be bothered with the low-level details of spawn, send, and receive, and we really don't need the extra control that writing our own GenServer gives us.

Enter tasks and agents, two simple-to-use Elixir abstractions. These use OTP's features but insulate us from these details.

Tasks

An Elixir task is a function that runs in the background.

```
tasks/tasks1.exs
defmodule Fib do
  def of(0), do: 0
  def of(1), do: 1
  def of(n), do: Fib.of(n-1) + Fib.of(n-2)
end


IO.puts "Start the task"
worker = Task.async(fn -> Fib.of(20) end)
IO.puts "Do something else"
# ...
IO.puts "Wait for the task"
result = Task.await(worker)

IO.puts "The result is #{result}"
```

The call to Task.async creates a separate process that runs the given function. The return value of async is a task descriptor (actually a PID and a ref) that we'll use to identify the task later.

Once the task is running, the code continues with other work. When it wants to get the function's value, it calls Task.await, passing in the task descriptor. This call waits for our background task to finish and returns its value.

When we run this, we see

```
$ elixir tasks1.exs
Start the task
Do something else
Wait for the task
The result is 6765
```

We can also pass Task.async the name of a module and function, along with any arguments:

tasks/tasks2.exs
```
worker = Task.async(Fib, :of, [20])
result = Task.await(worker)
IO.puts "The result is #{result}"
```

Tasks and Supervision

Tasks are implemented as OTP servers, which means we can add them to our application's supervision tree. We can do this in two ways.

First, we can link a task to a currently supervised process by calling start_link instead of async. This has less impact than you might think. If the function running in the task crashes and we use start_link, our process will be terminated immediately. If instead we use async, our process will be terminated only when we subsequently call await on the crashed task.

The second way to supervise tasks is to run them directly from a supervisor. This is pretty much the same as specifying any other worker:

```
import Supervisor.Spec

children = [
  worker(Task, [ fn -> do_something_extraordinary() end ])
]

supervise children, strategy: :one_for_one
```

Agents

An agent is a background process that maintains state. This state can be accessed at different places within a process or node, or across multiple nodes.

The initial state is set by a function we pass in when we start the agent.

We can interrogate the state using Agent.get, passing it the agent descriptor and a function. The agent runs the function on its current state and returns the result.

We can also use Agent.update to change the state held by an agent. As with the get operator, we pass in a function. Unlike with get, the function's result becomes the new state.

Here's a bare-bones example. We start an agent whose state is the integer 0. We then use the identity function, &(&1), to return that state. Calling Agent.update with &(&1+1) increments the state, as verified by a subsequent get.

```
iex> { :ok, count } = Agent.start(fn -> 0 end)
{:ok, #PID<0.69.0>}
iex> Agent.get(count, &(&1))
0
iex> Agent.update(count, &(&1+1))
:ok
iex> Agent.update(count, &(&1+1))
:ok
iex> Agent.get(count, &(&1))
2
```

In the previous example, the variable count holds the agent process's PID. We can also give agents a local or global name and access them using this name. In this case we exploit the fact that an uppercase bareword in Elixir is converted into an atom with the prefix Elixir., so when we say Sum it is actually the atom :Elixir.Sum.

```
iex> Agent.start(fn -> 1 end, name: Sum)
{:ok, #PID<0.78.0>}
iex> Agent.get(Sum, &(&1))
1
iex> Agent.update(Sum, &(&1+99))
:ok
iex> Agent.get(Sum, &(&1))
100
```

The following example shows a more typical use. The Frequency module maintains a list of word/frequency pairs in a hashdict. The dictionary itself is stored in an agent, which is named after the module.

This is all initialized with the start_link function, which, presumably, is invoked during application initialization.

```
tasks/agent_dict.exs
defmodule Frequency do

  def start_link do
    Agent.start_link(fn -> %{} end, name: __MODULE__)
  end

  def add_word(word) do
    Agent.update(__MODULE__,
                 fn map ->
                      Map.update(map, word, 1, &(&1+1))
                 end)
  end

  def count_for(word) do
    Agent.get(__MODULE__, fn map -> map[word] end)
  end

  def words do
    Agent.get(__MODULE__, fn map -> Map.keys(map) end)
  end

end
```

We can play with this code in iex.

```
iex> c "agent_dict.exs"
[Frequency]
iex> Frequency.start_link
{:ok, #PID<0.101.0>}
iex> Frequency.add_word "dave"
:ok
iex> Frequency.words
["dave"]
iex(41)> Frequency.add_word "was"
:ok
iex> Frequency.add_word "here"
:ok
iex> Frequency.add_word "he"
:ok
iex> Frequency.add_word "was"
:ok
iex> Frequency.words
["he", "dave", "was", "here"]
iex> Frequency.count_for("dave")
1
iex> Frequency.count_for("was")
2
```

In a way, you can look at our Frequency module as the implementation part of a gen_server—using agents has simply abstracted away all the housekeeping we had to do.

A Bigger Example

Let's rewrite our anagram code to use both tasks and an agent.

We'll load words in parallel from a number of separate dictionaries. A separate task handles each dictionary. We'll use an agent to store the resulting list of words and signatures.

tasks/anagrams.exs
```elixir
defmodule Dictionary do

  @name __MODULE__

  ##
  # External API

  def start_link,
  do: Agent.start_link(fn -> %{} end, name: @name)

  def add_words(words),
  do: Agent.update(@name, &do_add_words(&1, words))

  def anagrams_of(word),
  do: Agent.get(@name, &Map.get(&1, signature_of(word)))

  ##
  # Internal implementation

  defp do_add_words(map, words),
  do: Enum.reduce(words, map, &add_one_word(&1, &2))

  defp add_one_word(word, map),
  do: Map.update(map, signature_of(word), [word], &[word|&1])

  defp signature_of(word),
  do: word |> to_char_list |> Enum.sort |> to_string

end

defmodule WordlistLoader do
  def load_from_files(file_names) do
    file_names
    |> Stream.map(fn name -> Task.async(fn -> load_task(name) end) end)
    |> Enum.map(&Task.await/1)
  end
```

```elixir
  defp load_task(file_name) do
    File.stream!(file_name, [], :line)
    |> Enum.map(&String.strip/1)
    |> Dictionary.add_words
  end
end
```

Our four wordlist files contain the following:

list1	list2	list3	list4
angor	ester	palet	rogan
argon	estre	patel	ronga
caret	goran	pelta	steer
carte	grano	petal	stere
cater	groan	pleat	stree
crate	leapt	react	terse
creat	nagor	recta	tsere
creta	orang	reest	tepal

Let's run it:

```
$ iex anagrams.exs
iex> Dictionary.start_link
{:ok, #PID<0.66.0>}
iex> Enum.map(1..4, &"words/list#{&1}") |> WordlistLoader.load_from_files
[:ok, :ok, :ok, :ok]
iex> Dictionary.anagrams_of "organ"
["ronga", "rogan", "orang", "nagor", "groan", "grano", "goran",
 "argon", "angor"]
```

Making It Distributed

Because agents and tasks run as OTP servers, they can already be distributed. All we need to do is give our agent a globally accessible name. That's a one-line change:

```
@name {:global, __MODULE__}
```

Now we'll load our code into two separate nodes and connect them. (Remember that we have to specify names for the nodes so they can talk.)

Window #1

```
$ iex --sname one anagrams_dist.exs
iex(one@FasterAir)>
```

Window #2

```
$ iex --sname two anagrams_dist.exs
iex(two@FasterAir)> Node.connect :one@FasterAir
true
iex(two@FasterAir)> Node.list
[:one@FasterAir]
```

We'll start the dictionary agent in node one—this is where the actual dictionary will end up. We'll then load the dictionary using both nodes one and two:

Window #1

```
iex(one@FasterAir)> Dictionary.start_link
{:ok, #PID<0.68.0>}
iex(one@FasterAir)> WordlistLoader.load_from_files(~w{words/list1 words/list2})
[:ok, :ok]
```

Window #2

```
iex(two@FasterAir)> WordlistLoader.load_from_files(~w{words/list3 words/list4})
[:ok, :ok]
```

Finally, we'll query the agent from both nodes:

Window #1

```
iex(one@FasterAir)> Dictionary.anagrams_of "argon"
["ronga", "rogan", "orang", "nagor", "groan", "grano", "goran", "argon",
 "angor"]
```

Window #2

```
iex(two@FasterAir)> Dictionary.anagrams_of "crate"
["recta", "react", "creta", "creat", "crate", "cater", "carte",
"caret"]
```

Agents and Tasks, or GenServer?

When do you use agents and tasks, and when do you use a GenServer?

The answer is to use the simplest approach that works. Agents and tasks are great when you are dealing with very-specific background activities, whereas GenServers (as their name suggests) are more general.

You can eliminate the need to make a decision by wrapping your agents and tasks in modules, as we did in our anagram example. That way you can always switch from the agent or task implementation to the full-blown GenServer without affecting the rest of the code base.

It's time to move on, and look at some advanced Elixir.

Part III

More-Advanced Elixir

Among the joys of Elixir is that it laughs at the concept of "what you see is what you get." Instead, you can extend it in many different ways. This allows you to add layers of abstraction to your code, which makes your code easier to work with.

This part covers macros (which let you extend the language's syntax), protocols (which let you add behaviors to existing modules), and use (which lets you add capabilities to a module). We finish with a grab-bag chapter of miscellaneous Elixir tricks and tips.

## CHAPTER 20

Macros and Code Evaluation

Have you ever felt frustrated that a language didn't have just the right feature for some code you were writing? Or have you found yourself repeating chunks of code that weren't amenable to factoring into functions? Or have you just wished you could program closer to your problem domain?

If so, then you'll love this chapter.

But, before we get into the details, here's a warning: macros can easily make your code harder to understand, because you're essentially rewriting parts of the language. For that reason, never use a macro when you could use a function. Let's repeat that:

> Never use a macro when you can use a function.

In fact, you'll probably not write a macro in regular application code. But if you're writing a library and want to use some of the other metaprogramming techniques that we show in later chapters, you'll need to know how macros work.

Implementing an if Statement

Let's imagine Elixir didn't have an if statement—all it has is case. Although we're prepared to abandon our old friend the while loop, not having an if statement is just too much to bear, so we set about implementing one.

We'll want to call it using something like

```
myif «condition» do
  «evaluate if true»
else
  «evaluate if false»
end
```

We know that blocks in Elixir are converted into keyword parameters, so this is equivalent to

```
myif «condition»,
  do:    «evaluate if true»,
  else: «evaluate if false»
```

Here's a sample call:

```
My.myif 1==2, do: (IO.puts "1 == 2"), else: (IO.puts "1 != 2")
```

Let's try to implement myif as a function:

```
defmodule My do
  def myif(condition, clauses) do
    do_clause   = Keyword.get(clauses, :do, nil)
    else_clause = Keyword.get(clauses, :else, nil)

    case condition do
        val when val in [false, nil]
            -> else_clause
        _otherwise
            -> do_clause
    end
  end
end
```

When we run it, we're (mildly) surprised to get the following output:

```
iex> My.myif 1==2, do: (IO.puts "1 == 2"), else: (IO.puts "1 != 2")
1 == 2
1 != 2
:ok
```

When we call the myif function, Elixir has to evaluate all of its parameters before passing them in. So both the do: and else: clauses are evaluated, and we see their output. Because IO.puts returns :ok on success, what actually gets passed to myif is

```
myif 1==2, do: :ok, else: :ok
```

This is why the final return value is :ok.

Clearly we need a way of delaying the execution of these clauses. And this is where macros come in. But before we implement our myif macro, we need a little background.

Macros Inject Code

Let's pretend we're the Elixir compiler. We read a module's source top to bottom and generate a representation of the code we find. That representation is a nested Elixir tuple.

If we want to support macros, we need a way to tell the compiler that we'd like to manipulate a part of that tuple. We do that using defmacro, quote, and unquote.

In the same way that def defines a function, defmacro defines a macro. You'll see what that looks like shortly. However, the real magic starts not when we define a macro, but when we use one.

When we pass parameters to a macro, Elixir doesn't evaluate them. Instead, it passes them as tuples representing their code. We can examine this behavior using a simple macro definition that prints out its parameter.

```
macros/dumper.exs
defmodule My do
  defmacro macro(param) do
    IO.inspect param
  end
end

defmodule Test do
  require My

  # These values represent themselves
  My.macro :atom        #=> :atom
  My.macro 1            #=> 1
  My.macro 1.0          #=> 1.0
  My.macro [1,2,3]      #=> [1,2,3]
  My.macro "binaries"   #=> "binaries"
  My.macro { 1, 2 }     #=> {1,2}
  My.macro do: 1        #=> [do: 1]
  My.macro do           #=> [do: 1]
    1
  end

  # And these are represented by 3-element tuples

  My.macro { 1,2,3,4,5 }
  # => {:"{}",[line: 20],[1,2,3,4,5]}

  My.macro do: ( a = 1; a+a )
  # => [do:
  #      {:__block__,[],
  #        [{:=,[line: 22],[{:a,[line: 22],nil},1]},
```

```
#           {:+,[line: 22],[{:a,[line: 22],nil},{:a,[line: 22],nil}]}]}]
```

```
My.macro do
  1+2
else
  3+4
end
# =>   [do: {:+,[line: 24],[1,2]},
#        else: {:+,[line: 26],[3,4]}]

end
```

This shows us that atoms, numbers, lists (including keyword lists), binaries, and tuples with two elements are represented internally as themselves. All other Elixir code is represented by a three-element tuple. Right now, the internals of that representation aren't important.

Load Order

You may be wondering about the structure of the preceding code. We put the macro definition in one module, and the usage of that macro in another. And that second module included a require call.

Macros are expanded before a program executes, so the macro defined in one module must be available as Elixir is compiling another module that uses those macros. The require function tells Elixir to ensure the named module is compiled before the current one. In practice it is used to make the macros defined in one module available in another.

But the reason for the two modules is less clear. It has to do with the fact that Elixir first compiles source files and then runs them.

If we have one module per source file and we reference a module in file A from file B, Elixir will load the module from A, and everything just works. But if we have a module and the code that uses it in the same file, and the module is defined in the same scope in which we use it, Elixir will not know to load the module's code. We'll get this error:

```
** (CompileError)
   .../dumper.ex:7:
   module My is not loaded but was defined. This happens because you
   are trying to use a module in the same context it is defined. Try
   defining the module outside the context that requires it.
```

By placing the code that uses module My in a separate module, we force My to load.

The Quote Function

We've seen that when we pass parameters to a macro they are not evaluated. The language comes with a function, quote, that also forces code to remain in its unevaluated form. quote takes a block and returns the internal representation of that block. We can play with it in iex:

```
iex> quote do: :atom
:atom
iex> quote do: 1
1
iex> quote do: 1.0
1.0
iex> quote do: [1,2,3]
[1,2,3]
iex> quote do: "binaries"
"binaries"
iex> quote do: {1,2}
{1,2}
iex> quote do: [do: 1]
[do: 1]
iex> quote do: {1,2,3,4,5}
{:"{}",[],[1,2,3,4,5]}
iex> quote do: (a = 1; a + a)
{:__block__, [],
 [{:=, [], [{:a, [], Elixir}, 1]},
  {:+, [context: Elixir, import: Kernel],
   [{:a, [], Elixir}, {:a, [], Elixir}]}]}
iex> quote do: [ do: 1 + 2, else: 3 + 4]
[do: {:+, [context: Elixir, import: Kernel], [1, 2]},
 else: {:+, [context: Elixir, import: Kernel], [3, 4]}]
```

There's another way to think about quote. When we write "abc", we create a binary containing a string. The double quotes say "interpret what follows as a string of characters and return the appropriate representation."

quote is the same: it says "interpret the content of the block that follows as code, and return the internal representation."

Using the Representation As Code

When we extract the internal representation of some code (either via a macro parameter or using quote), we stop Elixir from adding it automatically to the tuples of code it is building during compilation—we've effectively created a free-standing island of code. How do we inject that code back into our program's internal representation?

There are two ways.

The first is our old friend the macro. Just like with a function, the value a macro returns is the last expression evaluated in that macro. That expression is expected to be a fragment of code in Elixir's internal representation. But Elixir does not return this representation to the code that invoked the macro. Instead it injects the code back into the internal representation of our program and returns to the caller the result of *executing* that code. But that execution takes place only if needed.

We can demonstrate this in two steps. First, here's a macro that simply returns its parameter (after printing it out). The code we give it when we invoke the macro is passed as an internal representation, and when the macro returns that code, that representation is injected back into the compile tree.

macros/eg.exs
```
defmodule My do
  defmacro macro(code) do
    IO.inspect code
    code
  end
end

defmodule Test do
  require My
  My.macro(IO.puts("hello"))
end
```

When we run this, we see

```
{{:.,[line: 11],[{:__aliases__,[line: 11],[:IO]},:puts]}, [line: 11],["hello"]}
hello
```

Now we'll change that file to return a different piece of code. We use quote to generate the internal form:

macros/eg1.exs
```
defmodule My do
  defmacro macro(code) do
    IO.inspect code
    quote do: IO.puts "Different code"
  end
end

defmodule Test do
  require My
```

```
  My.macro(IO.puts("hello"))
end
```

This generates

```
{{:.,[line: 11],[{:__aliases__,[line: 11],[:IO]},:puts]}, [line: 11],["hello"]}
Different code
```

Even though we passed IO.puts("hello") as a parameter, it was never executed. Instead, the code fragment we returned using quote was.

Before we can write our version of if, we need one more trick—the ability to substitute existing code into a quoted block. There are two ways of doing this: by using the unquote function and with bindings.

The Unquote Function

Let's get two things out of the way. First, we can use unquote only inside a quote block. Second, unquote is a silly name. It should really be something like inject_code_fragment.

Let's see why we need this. Here's a simple macro that tries to output the result of evaluating the code we pass it:

```
defmacro macro(code) do
  quote do
    IO.inspect(code)
  end
end
```

Unfortunately, when we run it, it reports an error:

```
** (CompileError).../eg2.ex:11: function code/0 undefined
```

Inside the quote block, Elixir is just parsing regular code, so the name code is inserted literally into the code fragment it returns. But we don't want that. We want Elixir to insert the evaluation of the code we pass in. And that's where we use unquote. It temporarily turns off quoting and simply injects a code fragment into the sequence of code being returned by quote.

```
defmodule My do
  defmacro macro(code) do
    quote do
      IO.inspect(unquote(code))
    end
  end
end
```

Inside the quote block, Elixir is busy parsing the code and generating its internal representation. But when it hits the unquote, it stops parsing and simply copies the code parameter into the generated code. After unquote, it goes back to regular parsing.

There's another way of thinking about this. Using unquote inside a quote is a way of deferring the execution of the unquoted code. It doesn't run when the quote block is parsed. Instead it runs when the code generated by the quote block is executed.

Or, we can think in terms of our quote-as-string-literal analogy. In this case, we can make a (slightly tenuous) case that unquote is a little like the interpolation we can do in strings. When we write "sum=#{1+2}", Elixir evaluates 1+2 and interpolates the result into the quoted string. When we write quote do: def unquote(name) do end, Elixir interpolates the contents of name into the code representation it is building as part of the list.

Expanding a List—unquote_splicing

Consider this code:

```
iex> Code.eval_quoted(quote do: [1,2,unquote([3,4])])
{[1,2,[3,4]],[]}
```

The list [3,4] is inserted, as a list, into the overall quoted list, resulting in [1,2,[3,4]].

If we instead wanted to insert just the elements of the list, we could use unquote_splicing.

```
iex> Code.eval_quoted(quote do: [1,2,unquote_splicing([3,4])])
{[1,2,3,4],[]}
```

Remembering that single-quoted strings are lists of characters, this means we can write

```
iex> Code.eval_quoted(quote do: [?a, ?= ,unquote_splicing('1234')])
{'a=1234',[]}
```

Back to Our myif Macro

We now have everything we need to implement an if macro.

```
macros/myif.ex
defmodule My do
  defmacro if(condition, clauses) do
    do_clause   = Keyword.get(clauses, :do, nil)
    else_clause = Keyword.get(clauses, :else, nil)
    quote do
      case unquote(condition) do
        val when val in [false, nil] -> unquote(else_clause)
        _                            -> unquote(do_clause)
```

```
      end
    end
  end
end


defmodule Test do
  require My
  My.if 1==2 do
    IO.puts "1 == 2"
  else
    IO.puts "1 != 2"
  end
end
```

It's worth studying this code.

The if macro receives a condition and a keyword list. The condition and any entries in the keyword list are passed as code fragments.

The macro extracts the do: and/or else: clauses from that list. It is then ready to generate the code for our if statement, so it opens a quote block. That block contains an Elixir case expression. This case expression has to evaluate the condition that is passed in, so it uses unquote to inject that condition's code as its parameter.

When Elixir executes this case statement, it evaluates the condition. At that point, case will match the first clause if the result is nil or false; otherwise it matches the second clause. When a clause matches (and only then), we want to execute the code that was passed in either the do: or else: values in the keyword list, so we use unquote again to inject that code into the case.

Your Turn

➤ *Exercise: MacrosAndCodeEvaluation-1*
Write a macro called myunless that implements the standard unless functionality. You're allowed to use the regular if expression in it.

➤ *Exercise: MacrosAndCodeEvaluation-2*
Write a macro called times_n that takes a single numeric argument. It should define a function called times_n in the caller's module that itself takes a single argument, and that multiplies that argument by n. So, calling times_n(3) should create a function called times_3, and calling times_3(4) should return 12. Here's an example of it in use:

```
defmodule Test do
  require Times
```

```
    Times.times_n(3)
    Times.times_n(4)
  end

  IO.puts Test.times_3(4)    #=> 12
  IO.puts Test.times_4(5)    #=> 20
```

Using Bindings to Inject Values

Remember that there are two ways of injecting values into quoted blocks. One is unquote. The other is to use a binding. However, the two have different uses and different semantics.

A binding is simply a keyword list of variable names and their values. When we pass a binding to quote the variables are set inside the body of that quote.

This is useful because macros are executed at compile time. This means they don't have access to values that are calculated at runtime.

Here's an example. The intent is to have a macro that defines a function that returns its own name:

```
defmacro mydef(name) do
  quote do
    def unquote(name)(), do: unquote(name)
  end
end
```

We try this out using something like mydef(:some_name). Sure enough, that defines a function that, when called, returns :some_name.

Buoyed by our success, we try something more ambitious:

macros/macro_no_binding.exs
```
defmodule My do
  defmacro mydef(name) do
    quote do
      def unquote(name)(), do: unquote(name)
    end
  end
end

defmodule Test do
  require My
  [ :fred, :bert ] |> Enum.each(&My.mydef(&1))
end

IO.puts Test.fred
```

And we're rewarded with this:

```
macro_no_binding.exs:12: invalid syntax in def _@1()
```

At the time the macro is called, the each loop hasn't yet executed, so we have no valid name to pass it. This is where bindings come in:

```
macros/macro_binding.exs
defmodule My do
  defmacro mydef(name) do
    quote bind_quoted: [name: name] do
      def unquote(name)(), do: unquote(name)
    end
  end
end

defmodule Test do
  require My
  [ :fred, :bert ] |> Enum.each(&My.mydef(&1))
end

IO.puts Test.fred    #=>   fred
```

Two things happen here. First, the binding makes the current value of name available inside the body of the quoted block. Second, the presence of the bind_quoted: option automatically defers the execution of the unquote calls in the body. This way, the methods are defined at runtime.

As its name implies, bind_quoted takes a quoted code fragment. Simple things such as tuples are the same as normal and quoted code, but for most values you probably want to quote them or use Macro.escape to ensure that your code fragment will be interpreted correctly.

Macros Are Hygienic

It is tempting to think of macros as some kind of textual substitution—a macro's body is expanded as text and then compiled at the point of call. But that's not the case. Consider this example:

```
macros/hygiene.ex
defmodule Scope do
  defmacro update_local(val) do
    local = "some value"
    result = quote do
      local = unquote(val)
      IO.puts "End of macro body, local = #{local}"
    end
    IO.puts "In macro definition, local = #{local}"
    result
  end
end
```

```
defmodule Test do
  require Scope

  local = 123
  Scope.update_local("cat")
  IO.puts "On return, local = #{local}"
end
```

Here's the result of running that code:

```
In macro definition, local = some value
End of macro body, local = cat
On return, local = 123
```

If the macro body was just substituted in at the point of call, both it and the module Test would share the same scope, and the macro would overwrite the variable local, so we'd see

```
In macro definition, local = some value
End of macro body, local = cat
On return, local = cat
```

But that isn't what happens. Instead the macro definition has both its own scope and a scope during execution of the quoted macro body. Both are distinct to the scope within the Test module. The upshot is that macros will not clobber each other's variables or the variables of modules and functions that use them.

The import and alias functions are also locally scoped. See the documentation for quote for a full description. This also describes how to turn off hygiene for variables and how to control the stack trace's format if things go wrong while executing a macro.

Other Ways to Run Code Fragments

We can use the function Code.eval_quoted to evaluate code fragments, such as those returned by quote.

```
iex> fragment = quote do: IO.puts("hello")
{{:.,[],[{:__aliases__,[alias: false],[:IO]},:puts]},[],["hello"]}
iex> Code.eval_quoted fragment
hello
{:ok,[]}
```

By default, the quoted fragment is hygienic, and so does not have access to variables outside its scope. Using var!(:name), we can disable this feature and allow a quoted block to access variables in the containing scope. In this case, we pass the binding to eval_quoted as a keyword list.

```
iex> fragment = quote do: IO.puts(var!(a))
{{:., [], [{:__aliases__, [alias: false], [:IO]}, :puts]}, [],
 [{:var!, [context: Elixir, import: Kernel], [{:a, [], Elixir}]}]}
iex> Code.eval_quoted fragment, [a: "cat"]
cat
{:ok,[a: "cat"]}
```

Code.string_to_quoted converts a string containing code to its quoted form, and
Macro.to_string converts a code fragment back into a string.

```
iex> fragment = Code.string_to_quoted("defmodule A do def b(c) do c+1 end end")
{:ok,{:defmodule,[line: 1],[{:__aliases__,[line: 1],[:A]},
[do: {:def,[line: 1],[{:b,[line: 1],[{:c,[line: 1],nil}]},
[do: {:+,[line: 1],[{:c,[line: 1],nil},1]}]]}]]}}
iex> Macro.to_string(fragment)
"{:ok, defmodule(A) do\n  def(b(c)) do\n    c + 1\n  end\nend}"
```

We can also evaluate a string directly using Code.eval_string.

```
iex> Code.eval_string("[a, a*b, c]", [a: 2, b: 3, c: 4])
{[2,6,4],[a: 2, b: 3, c: 4]}
```

Macros and Operators

(This is definitely dangerous ground.)

We can override the unary and binary operators in Elixir using macros. To
do so, we need to remove any existing definition first.

For example, the operator + (which adds two numbers) is defined in the Kernel
module. To remove the Kernel definition and substitute our own, we'd need to
do something like the following (which redefines addition to concatenate the
string representation of the left and right arguments).

macros/operators.ex

```
defmodule Operators do
  defmacro a + b do
    quote do
      to_string(unquote(a)) <> to_string(unquote(b))
    end
  end
end

defmodule Test do
  IO.puts(123 + 456)              #=> "579"
  import Kernel, except: [+: 2]
  import Operators
  IO.puts(123 + 456)              #=> "123456"
end

IO.puts(123 + 456)                #=> "579"
```

Note that the macro's definition is lexically scoped—the + operator is overridden from the point when we import the Operators module through the end of the module that imports it. We could also have done the import inside a single method, and the scoping would be just that method.

The Macro module has two functions that list the unary and binary operators:

```
iex> require Macro
nil
iex> Macro.binary_ops
[:===, :!==, :==, :!=, :<=, :>=, :&&, :||, :<>, :++, :--, :\\, :::, :<-, :..,
 :|>, :=~, :<, :>, :->, :+, :-, :*, :/, :=, :|, :., :and, :or, :when, :in,
 :~>>, :<<~, :~>, :<~, :<~>, :<|>, :<<<, :>>>, :|||, :&&&, :^^^, :~~~]
iex> Macro.unary_ops
[:!, :@, :^, :not, :+, :-, :~~~, :&]
```

Digging Deeper

The Code and Macro modules contain the functions that manipulate the internal representation of code.

Check the source of the Kernel module for a list of the majority of the operator macros, along with macros for things such as def, defmodule, alias, and so on. If we look at the source code, we'll see the calling sequence for these. However, many of the bodies will be absent, as the macros are defined within the Elixir source.

Digging Ridiculously Deep

Here's the internal representation of a simple expression:

```
iex(1)> quote do: 1 + 2
{:+, [context: Elixir, import: Kernel], [1, 2]}
```

It's just a three-element tuple. In this particular case, the first element is the function (or macro), the second is housekeeping metadata, and the third is the arguments.

We know we can evaluate this code fragment using eval_quoted, and we can save typing by leaving off the metadata:

```
iex> Code.eval_quoted {:+, [], [1,2]}
{3,[]}
```

And now we can start to see the promise (and danger) of a homoiconic language. Because code is just tuples and because we can manipulate those tuples, we rewrite the definitions of existing functions. We can create new code on the fly. And we can do it in a safe way because we can control the scope of both the changes and the access to variables.

Next we'll look at *protocols*, a way of adding functionality to built-in code and of integrating our code into other people's modules.

Your Turn

▶ *Exercise: MacrosAndCodeEvaluation-3*

The Elixir test framework, ExUnit, uses some clever code-quoting tricks. For example, if you assert

```
assert 5 < 4
```

You'll get the error "expected 5 to be less than 4."

The Elixir source code is on GitHub (at https://github.com/elixir-lang/elixir). The implementation of this is in the file elixir/lib/ex_unit/lib/ex_unit/assertions.ex. Spend some time reading this file, and work out how it implements this trick.

(Hard) Once you've done that, see if you can use the same technique to implement a function that takes an arbitrary arithmetic expression and returns a natural language version.

```
explain do: 2 + 3 * 4
#=> multiply 3 and 4, then add 2
```

## CHAPTER 21

Linking Modules: Behavio(u)rs and Use

When we wrote our OTP server, we wrote a module that started with code

```
defmodule Sequence.Server do
  use GenServer
  ...
```

In this chapter we'll explore what lines such as use GenServer actually do, and how we can write modules that extend the capabilities of other modules that use them.

Behaviours

An Elixir behaviour is nothing more than a list of functions. A module that declares that it implements a particular behaviour must implement all of the associated functions. If it doesn't, Elixir will generate a compilation warning. You can think of a behaviour definition as being like an abstract base class in some object-oriented languages.

A behaviour is therefore a little like an *interface* in Java. A module uses it to declare that it implements a particular interface. For example, an OTP GenServer should implement a standard set of callbacks (handle_call, handle_cast, and so on). By declaring that our module implements that behaviour, we let the compiler validate that we have actually supplied the necessary interface. This reduces the chance of an unexpected runtime error.

Defining Behaviours

We define a behaviour with defcallback definitions.

For example, the mix utility handles various source code control methods (SCM). Out of the box, it supports git and the local filesystem. However, the interface to the SCM is defined using a behaviour, allowing new version control systems to be added cleanly.

The behaviour is defined in the module Mix.Scm:

```
defmodule Mix.SCM do
  @moduledoc """
  This module provides helper functions and defines the behaviour
  required by any SCM used by Mix.
  """

  @type opts :: Keyword.t

  @doc """
  Returns a boolean if the dependency can be fetched or it is meant to
  be previously available in the filesystem.

  Local dependencies (i.e. non fetchable ones) are automatically
  recompiled every time the parent project is compiled.
  """
  @callback fetchable? :: boolean

  @doc """
  Returns a string representing the SCM. This is used when printing
  the dependency and not for inspection, so the amount of information
  should be concise and easy to spot.
  """
  @callback format(opts) :: String.t

  # and so on for 8 more callbacks
```

This module defines the interface that modules implementing the behaviour must support. It uses @callback to define the functions in the behaviour. But the syntax looks a little different. That's because we're using a minilanguage: Erlang type specifications. For example, the fetchable? function takes no parameters and returns a boolean. The format function takes a parameter of type opts (which is defined near the top of the code to be a keyword list) and returns a string. For more information on these type specifications, see Appendix 2, *Type Specifications and Type Checking*, on page 323.

In addition to the type specification, we can include module and function-level documentation with our behaviour definitions.

Declaring Behaviours

Having defined the behaviour, we can declare that another module implements it using the @behaviour attribute. Here's the start of the Git implementation for mix.

```elixir
defmodule Mix.SCM.Git do
  @behaviour Mix.SCM
  @moduledoc false

  def fetchable? do
    true
  end

  def format(opts) do
    opts[:git]
  end

  # . . .
end
```

The module defines each of the functions declared as callbacks in Mix.SCM. This module will compile cleanly. However, imagine we'd misspelled fetchable:

```elixir
defmodule Mix.SCM.Git do
  @behaviour Mix.SCM
  @moduledoc false

➤ def fetchible? do
    true
  end

  def format(opts) do
    opts[:git]
  end

  # . . .
end
```

When we compile the module, we'd get this error:

```
git.ex:1: warning: undefined behaviour function fetchable?/0
                (for behaviour Mix.SCM)
```

Behaviours give us a way of both documenting and enforcing the public functions that a module should implement.

Use and __using__

In one sense, use is a trivial function. You pass it a module along with an optional argument, and it invokes the function or macro __using__ in that module, passing it the argument.

Yet this simple interface gives you a powerful extension facility. For example, in our unit tests we write use ExUnit.Case and we get the test macro and assertion support. When we write an OTP server, we write use GenServer and we get both a behaviour that documents the gen_server callback and default implementations of those callbacks.

Typically, the _using_ callback will be implemented as a macro, as it will be used to invoke code in the original module.

Putting It Together—Tracing Method Calls

Let's work through a larger example. We want to write a module called Tracer. If we use Tracer in another module, entry and exit tracing will be added to any subsequently defined function. For example, given the following:

```
use/tracer.ex
defmodule Test do
  use Tracer
  def puts_sum_three(a,b,c),  do: IO.inspect(a+b+c)
  def add_list(list),         do: Enum.reduce(list, 0, &(&1+&2))
end

Test.puts_sum_three(1,2,3)
Test.add_list([5,6,7,8])
```

we'd get this output:

```
==> call     puts_sum_three(1, 2, 3)
6
<== returns 6
==> call     add_list([5,6,7,8])
<== returns 26
```

My approach to writing this kind of code is to start by exploring what we have to work with, and then to generalize. The goal is to metaprogram as little as possible.

It looks as if we have to override the def macro, which is defined in Kernel. So let's do that and see what gets passed to def when we define a method.

```
use/tracer1.ex
defmodule Tracer do
  defmacro def(definition, do: _content) do
    IO.inspect definition
    quote do: {}
  end
end

defmodule Test do
  import Kernel, except: [def: 2]
  import Tracer, only:   [def: 2]

  def puts_sum_three(a,b,c), do: IO.inspect(a+b+c)
```

```
    def add_list(list),          do: Enum.reduce(list, 0, &(&1+&2))
end

Test.puts_sum_three(1,2,3)
Test.add_list([5,6,7,8])
```

This outputs

```
{:puts_sum_three, [line: 15],
 [{:a, [line: 15], nil}, {:b, [line: 15], nil}, {:c, [line: 15], nil}]}
{:add_list, [line: 16], [{:list, [line: 16], nil}]}
tracer1.ex:12: unused import Kernel
** (UndefinedFunctionError) undefined function: Test.puts_sum_three/3
```

The definition part of each method is a three-element tuple. The first element is the name, the second is the line on which it is defined, and the third is a list of the parameters, where each parameter is itself a tuple.

We also get an error: puts_sum_three is undefined. That's not surprising—we intercepted the def that defined it, and we didn't create the function.

You may be wondering about the form of the macro definition: defmacro def(definition, do: _content).... The do: in the parameters is not special syntax: it's simply a pattern match on the block passed as the function body, which is a keyword list.

You may also be wondering whether we have affected the built-in Kernel.def macro. The answer is no. We've created another macro, also called def, which is defined in the scope of the Tracer module. In our Test module we tell Elixir not to import the Kernel version of def but instead to import the version from Tracer. Shortly, we'll make use of the fact that the original Kernel implementation is unaffected.

Let's see if we can define a real function given this information. That turns out to be surprisingly easy. We already have the two arguments passed to def. All we have to do is pass them on.

use/tracer2.ex

```
defmodule Tracer do
  defmacro def(definition, do: content) do
    quote do
      Kernel.def(unquote(definition)) do
        unquote(content)
      end
    end
  end
end

defmodule Test do
```

```elixir
  import Kernel, except: [def: 2]
  import Tracer, only:   [def: 2]

  def puts_sum_three(a,b,c), do: IO.inspect(a+b+c)
  def add_list(list),        do: Enum.reduce(list, 0, &(&1+&2))
end

Test.puts_sum_three(1,2,3)
Test.add_list([5,6,7,8])
```

When we run this, we see 6, the output from puts_sum_three.

Now it's time to add some tracing.

`use/tracer3.ex`
```elixir
defmodule Tracer do
  def dump_args(args) do
    args |> Enum.map(&inspect/1) |> Enum.join(", ")
  end


  def dump_defn(name, args) do
    "#{name}(#{dump_args(args)})"
  end

  defmacro def(definition={name,_,args}, do: content) do
    quote do
      Kernel.def(unquote(definition)) do
        IO.puts "==> call:    #{Tracer.dump_defn(unquote(name), unquote(args))}"
        result = unquote(content)
        IO.puts "<== result: #{result}"
        result
      end
    end
  end
end

defmodule Test do
  import Kernel, except: [def: 2]
  import Tracer, only:   [def: 2]

  def puts_sum_three(a,b,c), do: IO.inspect(a+b+c)
  def add_list(list),        do: Enum.reduce(list, 0, &(&1+&2))
end

Test.puts_sum_three(1,2,3)
Test.add_list([5,6,7,8])
```

Looking good:

```
==> call:    puts_sum_three(1, 2, 3)
6
```

```
<== result: 6
==> call:   add_list([5,6,7,8])
<== result: 26
```

Let's package our Tracer module so clients only have to add use Tracer to their own modules. We'll implement the _using_ callback. The tricky part here is differentiating between the two modules: Tracer and the module that uses it.

use/tracer4.ex

```elixir
defmodule Tracer do

  def dump_args(args) do
    args |> Enum.map(&inspect/1) |> Enum.join(", ")
  end

  def dump_defn(name, args) do
    "#{name}(#{dump_args(args)})"
  end

  defmacro def(definition={name,_,args}, do: content) do
    quote do
      Kernel.def(unquote(definition)) do
        IO.puts "==> call:    #{Tracer.dump_defn(unquote(name), unquote(args))}"
        result = unquote(content)
        IO.puts "<== result: #{result}"
        result
      end
    end
  end

  defmacro __using__(_opts) do
    quote do
      import Kernel, except: [def: 2]
      import unquote(__MODULE__), only: [def: 2]
    end
  end
end

defmodule Test do
  use Tracer
  def puts_sum_three(a,b,c), do: IO.inspect(a+b+c)
  def add_list(list),        do: Enum.reduce(list, 0, &(&1+&2))
end

Test.puts_sum_three(1,2,3)
Test.add_list([5,6,7,8])
```

Use use

Elixir behaviours are fantastic—they let you easily inject functionality into modules you write. And they're not just for library creators—use them in your own code to cut down on duplication and boilerplate.

Although behaviours let you add to modules that you are writing, you sometimes need to extend the functionality of modules written by others—code that you can't change. Fortunately, Elixir comes with *protocols*, the subject of the next chapter.

Your Turn

➤ *Exercise: LinkingModules-BehavioursAndUse-1*

In the body of the def macro, there's a quote block that defines the actual method. It contains

```
IO.puts "==> call:    #{Tracer.dump_dfn(unquote(name), unquote(args))}"
result = unquote(content)
IO.puts "<== result: #{result}"
```

Why does the first call to puts have to unquote the values in its interpolation but the second call does not?

➤ *Exercise: LinkingModules-BehavioursAndUse-2*

The built-in function IO.ANSI.format will insert ANSI escape sequences into a string. If you write the resulting strings to a terminal, you can add colors and bold, inverse, or underlined text.

```
iex(4)> IO.puts  IO.ANSI.format(["Hello, ", :inverse, :bright, "world!"], true)
Hello, world!
```

Explore the library. What is the return value of IO.ANSI.format, and why does it work when passed to IO.puts?

Use IO.ANSI.format to colorize our tracing's output.

➤ *Exercise: LinkingModules-BehavioursAndUse-3*

(Hard) Try adding a method definition with a guard clause to the Test module. You'll find that the tracing no longer works.

– Find out why.
– See if you can fix it.

## CHAPTER 22

Protocols—Polymorphic Functions

We have used the inspect function many times in this book. It returns a printable representation of any value as a binary (which is what we hard-core folks call strings).

But stop and think for a minute. Just how can Elixir, which doesn't have objects, know what to call to do the conversion to a binary? You can pass inspect anything, and Elixir somehow makes sense of it.

It *could* be done using guard clauses:

```
def inspect(value) when is_atom(value), do: ...
def inspect(value) when is_binary(value), do: ...
     :     :
```

But there's a better way.

Elixir has the concept of *protocols*. A protocol is a little like the behaviours we saw in the previous chapter in that it defines the functions that must be provided to achieve something. But a behaviour is internal to a module—the module implements the behaviour. Protocols are different—you can place a protocol's implementation completely outside the module. This means you can extend modules' functionality without having to add code to them—in fact, you can extend the functionality even if you don't have the modules' source code.

Defining a Protocol

Protocol definitions are very similar to basic module definitions. They can contain module- and function-level documentation (@moduledoc and @doc), and they will contain one or more function definitions. However, these functions will not have bodies—they are there simply to declare the interface that the protocol requires.

For example, here is the definition of the Inspect protocol:

```
defprotocol Inspect do
  def inspect(thing, opts)
end
```

Just like a module, the protocol defines one or more functions. But we implement the code separately.

Implementing a Protocol

The defimpl macro lets you give Elixir the implementation of a protocol for one or more types. The code that follows is the implementation of the Inspect protocol for PIDs and references.

```
defimpl Inspect, for: PID do
  def inspect(pid, _opts) do
    "#PID" <> IO.iodata_to_binary(pid_to_list(pid))
  end
end

defimpl Inspect, for: Reference do
  def inspect(ref, _opts) do
    '#Ref' ++ rest = :erlang.ref_to_list(ref)
    "#Reference" <> IO.iodata_to_binary(rest)
  end
end
```

Finally, the Kernel module implements inspect, which calls Inspect.inspect with its parameter. This means that when you call inspect(self), it becomes a call to Inspect.inspect(self). And because self is a PID, this in turn resolves to something like "#PID<0.25.0>".

Behind the scenes, defimpl puts the implementation for each protocol-and-type combination into a separate module. The protocol for Inspect for the PID type is in the module Inspect.PID. And because you can recompile modules, you can change the implementation of functions accessed via protocols.

```
iex> inspect self
"#PID<0.25.0>"
iex> defimpl Inspect, for: PID do
...>   def inspect(pid, _) do
...>     "#Process: " <> IO.iodata_to_binary(:erlang.pid_to_list(pid)) <> "!!"
...>   end
...> end
iex:3: redefining module Inspect.PID
{:module, Inspect.PID, <<70,79....
iex> inspect self
"#Process: <0.25.0>!!"
```

The Available Types

You can define implementations for one or more of the following types:

Any	Atom	BitString	Float	Function
Integer	List	Map	PID	Port
Record	Reference	Tuple		

The type BitString is used in place of Binary.

The type Any is a catchall, allowing you to match an implementation with any type. Just as with function definitions, you'll want to put the implementations for specific types before an implementation for Any.

You can list multiple types on a single defimpl. For example, the following protocol can be called to determine if a type is a collection:

```
protocols/is_collection.exs
defprotocol Collection do
  @fallback_to_any true
  def is_collection?(value)
end

defimpl Collection, for: [List, Tuple, BitString, Map] do
  def is_collection?(_), do: true
end

defimpl Collection, for: Any do
  def is_collection?(_), do: false
end

Enum.each [ 1, 1.0, [1,2], {1,2}, %{}, "cat" ], fn value ->
  IO.puts "#{inspect value}:  #{Collection.is_collection?(value)}"
end
```

We write defimpl stanzas for the collection types: List, Tuple, BitString, and Map. But what about the other types? To handle those, we use the special type Any in a second defimpl. If we use Any, though, we also have to add an annotation to the protocol definition. That's what the @fallback_to_any line does.

This produces

```
1:  false
1.0:  false
[1,2]:  true
{1,2}:  true
%{}:  true
"cat":  true
```

Your Turn

➤ *Exercise: Protocols-1*

A basic Caesar cypher consists of shifting the letters in a message by a fixed offset. For an offset of 1, for example, a will become b, b will become c, and z will become a. If the offset is 13, we have the ROT13 algorithm.

Lists and binaries can both be *stringlike*. Write a Caesar protocol that applies to both. It would include two functions: encrypt(string, shift) and rot13(string).

➤ *Exercise: Protocols-2*

Using a list of words in your language, write a program to look for words where the result of calling rot13(word) is also a word in the list. (For various English word lists, look at http://wordlist.sourceforge.net/. The SCOWL collection looks promising, as it already has words divided by size.)

Protocols and Structs

Elixir doesn't have classes, but (perhaps surprisingly) it does have user-defined types. It pulls off this magic using structs and a few conventions.

Let's play with a simple struct. Here's the definition:

```
protocols/basic.exs
defmodule Blob do
  defstruct content: nil
end
```

And here we use it in iex:

```
iex> c "basic.exs"
[Blob]
iex> b = %Blob{content: 123}
%Blob{content: 123}
iex> inspect b
"%Blob{content: 123}"
```

It looks for all the world as if we've created some new type, the blob. But that's only because Elixir is hiding something from us. By default, inspect recognizes structs. If we turn this off using the structs: false option, inspect reveals the true nature of our blob value:

```
iex> inspect b, structs: false
"%{__struct__: Blob, content: 123}"
```

A struct value is actually just a map with the key _struct_ referencing the struct's module (Blob in this case) and the remaining elements containing the keys and values for this instance. The inspect implementation for maps checks for this—if you ask it to inspect a map containing a key _struct_ that references a module, it displays it as a struct.

Many built-in types in Elixir are represented as structs internally. It's instructive to try creating values and inspecting them with structs: false.

Build-In Protocols

Elixir comes with the following protocols:

- Enumerable and Collectable
- Inspect
- List.Chars
- String.Chars

To play with these, we'll implement a trivial datatype that represents the col lection of 0s and 1s in an integer. The underlying representation is trivial:

```
protocols/bitmap.exs
defmodule Bitmap do
  defstruct value: 0

  @doc """
  A simple accessor for the 2^bit value in an integer

      iex> b = %Bitmap{value: 5}
      %Bitmap{value: 5}
      iex> Bitmap.fetch_bit(b,2)
      1
      iex> Bitmap.fetch_bit(b,1)
      0
      iex> Bitmap.fetch_bit(b,0)
      1
  """
  def fetch_bit(%Bitmap{value: value}, bit) do
    use Bitwise

    (value >>> bit) &&& 1
  end
end
```

The fetch_bit function uses the >>> and &&& functions in the built-in Bitwise library to extract a particular bit.

Built-in Protocols: Enumerable and Collectable

The Enumerable protocol is the basis of all the functions in the Enum module—any type implementing it can be used as a collection argument to Enum functions.

The protocol is defined in terms of three functions:

```
defprotocol Enumerable do
  def count(collection)
  def member?(collection, value)
  def reduce(collection, acc, fun)
end
```

count returns the number of elements in the collection, member? is truthy if the collection contains value, and reduce applies the given function to successive values in the collection and the accumulator; the value it reduces becomes the next accumulator. Perhaps surprisingly, all the Enum functions can be defined in terms of these three.

However, life isn't quite that simple. Maybe you're using Enum.find to find a value in a large collection. Once you've found it, you want to halt the iteration—continuing is pointless. Similarly, you may want to suspend an iteration and resume it sometime later. These two features become particularly important when we talk about streams, which let you enumerate a collection lazily.

Let's look at implementing the count part of the enumerable protocol. We return the number of bits required to represent the value.

protocols/bitmap_enumerable.exs
```
defimpl Enumerable,  for: Bitmap do
  import :math, only: [log: 1]
  def count(%Bitmap{value: value}) do
    { :ok, trunc(log(abs(value))/log(2)) + 1 }
  end
end
```

```
fifty = %Bitmap{value: 50}

IO.puts Enum.count fifty     # => 6
```

Our count method returns a tuple containing :ok and the actual count. If our collection was not countable (perhaps it represents data coming over a network connection), we would return {:error, __MODULE__}.

I've decided the member? function should return true if the number you pass it is greater than or equal to zero and less than the number of bits in our value. Again the implementation returns a tuple:

protocols/bitmap_enumerable.exs
```
  def member?(value, bit_number) do
    { :ok, 0 <= bit_number && bit_number < Enum.count(value) }
  end
```

```
IO.puts Enum.member? fifty, 4    # => true
IO.puts Enum.member? fifty, 6    # => false
```

However, the meaning of the :ok part is slightly different. You'll normally return {:ok, boolean} for all collections where you know the size, and {:error, __MODULE__} otherwise. In this way, it is like count. However, the reason you do it is different. If you return :ok it means you have a fast way of determining membership. If you return :error, you're saying you don't. In this case, the enumerable code will simply perform a linear search.

Finally, we get to reduce. First, remember the general form of the reduce function:

reduce(enumerable, accumulator, function)

Reduce takes each item in turn from enumerable, passing it and the current value of the accumulator to the function. The value the function returns becomes the accumulator's next value.

The reduce function we implement for the Enumerable protocol is the same. But it has some additional conventions associated with it. These conventions are used to manage the early halting and suspension when iterating over streams.

The first convention is that the accumulator value is passed as the second element of a tuple. The first element is a verb telling our reduce function what to do:

:cont   Continue processing.

:halt   Terminate processing.

:suspend   Temporarily suspend processing.

The second convention is that the value returned by reduce is another tuple. Again, the second element is the updated accumulator value. The first element passed back the state of the enumerator:

:done   This is the final value—we've reached the end of the enumerable.

:halted   We terminated the enumeration because we were passed :halt.

:suspended Response to a suspend.

The suspended case is special. Rather than return a new accumulator, we return a function that represents the current state of the enumeration. The library can call this function to kick off the enumeration again.

Once we implement this, our bitmap can participate in all the features of the Enum module:

protocols/bitmap_enumerable.exs

```
  def reduce(bitmap, {:cont, acc}, fun) do
    bit_count =  Enum.count(bitmap)
    _reduce({bitmap, bit_count}, { :cont, acc }, fun)
  end

  defp _reduce({_bitmap, -1}, { :cont, acc }, _fun), do: { :done, acc }

  defp _reduce({bitmap, bit_number}, { :cont, acc }, fun) do
    with bit = Bitmap.fetch_bit(bitmap, bit_number),
    do:  _reduce({bitmap, bit_number-1}, fun.(bit, acc), fun)
  end

  defp _reduce({_bitmap, _bit_number}, { :halt, acc }, _fun), do: { :halted, acc }

  defp _reduce({bitmap, bit_number}, { :suspend, acc }, fun),
  do: { :suspended, acc, &_reduce({bitmap, bit_number}, &1, fun), fun }

IO.inspect Enum.reverse fifty       # => [0, 1, 0, 0, 1, 1, 0]
IO.inspect Enum.join fifty, ":"     # => "0:1:1:0:0:1:0"
```

Because our bitmap is enumerable, we can use into to copy the individual bits into a list:

```
iex> fifty = %Bitmap{value: 50}
%Bitmap{value: 50}
iex> fifty |> Enum.into []
[0, 1, 1, 0, 0, 1, 0]
```

However, if we try putting the values from a list into a bitmap, we get an error:

```
iex> Enum.into [0,1,1,0,0,1,0], %Bitmap{value: 0}
** (Protocol.UndefinedError) protocol Collectable not implemented for %Bitmap{value: 0}
```

To fix this, our bitmap needs an implementation of the Collectable protocol.

Collectable

The target of Enum.into must implement the Collectable protocol. This defines a single function, somewhat confusingly also called into. This function returns a two-element tuple. The first element is the initial value of the target collection. The second is a function to be called to add each item to the collection. (If this reminds you of the second and third parameters passed to Enum.reduce, that's because in a way into is the opposite of reduce.

Let's look at the code first:

protocols/bitmap_collectable.exs

```
defimpl Collectable,   for: Bitmap do
  use Bitwise
```

```
    def into(%Bitmap{value: target}) do
      {target, fn
        acc, {:cont, next_bit} -> (acc <<< 1) ||| next_bit
        acc,  :done            -> %Bitmap{value: acc}
        _, :halt               -> :ok
      end}
    end
  end
end
```

We can call it in iex:

```
iex> Enum.into [1,1,0,0,1,0], %Bitmap{value: 0}
%Bitmap{value: 50}
```

It works like this:

- Enum.into calls the into function for Bitmap, passing it the target value (%Bitmap{value: 0} in this case.

- Bitmap.into returns a tuple. The first element is the value, extracted from the bitmap structure. This acts as the initial value for an accumulator. The second element of the tuple is a function.

- Enum.into then calls this function, passing it the accumulator and a command. If the command is :done, the iteration over collection being injected into the bitmap has finished, so we return a new bitmap using the accumulator as a value. If the command is :halt, the iteration has terminated early, and nothing needs to be done.

- The real work is done when the function is passed the {:cont, next_val} command. Here is where the Collectable adds the next value to the accumulator. In our case, we shift the accumulator up and OR the new value in.

Remember the Big Picture

If you think all this enumerable/collectable stuff is complicated—well, you're correct. It is. In part that's because these conventions allow all enumerable values to be used both eagerly and lazily. And when you're dealing with big (or even infinite) collections, this is a big deal.

Built-in Protocols: Inspect

This is the protocol that is used to inspect a value. The rule is simple—if you can return a representation that is a valid Elixir literal, do so. Otherwise, prefix the representation with #Typename.

We *could* just delegate the inspect function to the Elixir default. For our value 50, this would be %Bitmap{value: 50}. But let's override it. We need to implement the inspect function. It takes a value and some options. The listing's on the next page.

```
protocols/bitmap_inspect.exs
defmodule Bitmap do
  defstruct value: 0

  defimpl Inspect do
    def inspect(%Bitmap{value: value}, _opts) do
      "%Bitmap{#{value}=#{as_binary(value)}}"
    end
    defp as_binary(value) do
      to_string(:io_lib.format("~.2B", [value]))
    end
  end
end

fifty = %Bitmap{value: 50}

IO.inspect fifty                    # => %Bitmap{50=0110010}
IO.inspect fifty, structs: false    # => %{__struct__: Bitmap, value: 50}
```

There's a wrinkle here. If you pass structs: true to IO.inspect (or Kernel.inspect), it never calls our inspect function. Instead, it formats it as a tuple.

The formatting of our bitmap leaves a little to be desired for large numbers:

```
iex> %Bitmap{value: 12345678901234567890}
%Bitmap{12345678901234567890=010101011010101001010100110001100111 0
10110001111100001010110100010}
```

The output was all on one line, and was wrapped by the console. To fix this, we use a feature called *algebra documents*. An algebra document is a tree structure that represents some data you'd like to pretty-print.[1] Your job is to create the structure based on the data you want to inspect, and Elixir will then find a nice way to display it.

In our case, I'd like the bitmap values to display on a single line if they fit, and I'd like them to break intelligently onto multiple lines if not.

We do this by having our inspect function return an algebra document rather than a string. In that document, we indicate places where breaks are allowed (but not required) and we show how the nesting works:

```
protocols/bitmap_algebra.exs
defmodule Bitmap do
  defstruct value: 0

  defimpl Inspect, for: Bitmap do
    import Inspect.Algebra
    def inspect(%Bitmap{value: value}, _opts) do
```

---

1. http://citeseerx.ist.psu.edu/viewdoc/summary?doi=10.1.1.34.2200

```
      concat([
        nest(
         concat([
           "%Bitmap{",
           break(""),
           nest(concat([to_string(value),
                         "=",
                         break(""),
                         as_binary(value)]),
                2),
         ]), 2),
        break(""),
        "}"])
   end
   defp as_binary(value) do
     to_string(:io_lib.format("~.2B", [value]))
   end
  end
end


big_bitmap = %Bitmap{value: 12345678901234567890}

IO.inspect big_bitmap
IO.inspect big_bitmap, structs: false
```

We get this output:

```
iex> %Bitmap{value: 12345}
%Bitmap{12345=011000000111001}
iex> %Bitmap{value: 123456789123456789}
%Bitmap{
  123456789123456789=
    0110110110100110110100101110101100110100000101111100010101
}
```

For more information, see the documentation for Inspect.Algebra.

Built-in Protocols: List.Chars and String.Chars

The List.Chars protocol is used by the Kernel to_char_list function to convert a value into a list of characters (think *single quoted string*).

The String.Chars protocol is used to convert a value to a string (binary, or *double quoted string*). This is the protocol used for string interpolation:

The protocols are implemented identically, except List.Chars requires that you write a to_char_list function, and String.Chars requires you write to_string.

Here's a String.Chars implementation for our Bitmap. It simply chunks the bits in groups of three, putting an underscore between each.

```
protocols/bitmap_string.exs
defimpl String.Chars, for: Bitmap do
  def to_string(bitmap) do
    import Enum
    bitmap
    |> reverse
    |> chunk(3)
    |> map(fn three_bits -> three_bits |> reverse |> join end)
    |> reverse
    |> join("_")
  end
end
```

Let's try it:

```
iex> "Fifty in bits is: #{fifty}"
"Fifty in bits is: 110_010"
```

Protocols Are Polymorphism

When you want to write a function that behaves differently depending on the type of its arguments, you're looking at a polymorphic function. Elixir protocols give you a tidy and controlled way to implement this. Whether you're integrating your types into the existing Elixir library or creating a new library with a flexible interface, protocols let you package the behaviour in a well-documented and disciplined way.

And with that, we're almost done. But when you write about a language, there are always little details that don't seem to fit anywhere. That's why the next chapter is full of odds and ends.

Your Turn

➤ *Exercise: Protocols-3*

Collections that implement the Enumerable protocol define count, member?, and reduce functions. The Enum module uses these to implement methods such as each, filter, and map.

Implement your own versions of each, filter, and map in terms of reduce.

➤ *Exercise: Protocols-4*

In many cases, inspect will return a valid Elixir literal for the value being inspected. Update the inspect function for structs so that it returns valid Elixir code to construct a new struct equal to the value being inspected.

## CHAPTER 23

More Cool Stuff

Elixir is packed with features that make coding a joy. This chapter contains a smattering of them.

Writing Your Own Sigils

You know by now that you can create strings and regular-expression literals using sigils:

```
string = ~s{now is the time}
regex  = ~r{..h..}
```

Have you ever wished you could extend these sigils to add your own specific literal types? You can.

When you write a sigil such as ~s{...}, Elixir converts it into a call to the function sigil_s. It passes the function two values. The first is the string between the delimiters. The second is a list containing any lowercase letters that immediately follow the closing delimiter. (This second parameter is used to pick up any options you pass to a regex literal, such as ~r/cat/if.)

Here's the implementation of a sigil ~l that takes a multiline string and returns a list containing each line as a separate string. We know that ~l... is converted into a call to sigil_l, so we just write a simple function in the LineSigil module.

```
odds/line_sigil.exs
defmodule LineSigil do
  @doc """
  Implement the `~l` sigil, which takes a string containing
  multiple lines and returns a list of those lines.

  ## Example usage

      iex> import LineSigil
      nil
```

```
    iex> ~l"""
    ...> one
    ...> two
    ...> three
    ...> """
    ["one","two","three"]
  """
  def sigil_l(lines, _opts) do
    lines |> String.rstrip |> String.split("\n")
  end
end
```

We can play with this in a separate module:

`odds/line_sigil.exs`
```
defmodule Example do
  import LineSigil

  def lines do
    ~l"""
    line 1
    line 2
    and another line in #{__MODULE__}
    """
  end
end
```

```
IO.inspect Example.lines
```

This produces ["line 1","line 2","and another line in Elixir.Example"].

Because we import the sigil_l function inside the example module, the ~l sigil is lexically scoped to this module. Note also that Elixir performs interpolation before passing the string to our method. That's because we used a lowercase l. If our sigil were ~L{...} and the function were renamed sigil_L, no interpolation would be performed.

The predefined sigil functions are sigil_C, sigil_c, sigil_R, sigil_r, sigil_S, sigil_s, sigil_W, and sigil_w. If you want to override one of these, you'll need to explicitly import the Kernel module and use an except clause to exclude it.

In this example, we used the heredoc syntax ("""). This passes our function a multiline string with leading spaces removed. Sigil options are not supported with heredocs, so we'll switch to a regular literal syntax to play with them.

Picking Up the Options

Let's write a sigil that enables us to specify color constants. If we say ~c{red}, we'll get 0xff0000, the RGB representation. We'll also support the option h to return an HSB value, so ~c{red}h will be {0,100,100}.

Here's the code:

```
odds/color.exs
defmodule ColorSigil do

  @color_map [
    rgb: [ red: 0xff0000, green: 0x00ff00, blue: 0x0000ff, # ...
         ],
    hsb: [ red: {0,100,100}, green: {120,100,100}, blue: {240,100,100}
         ]
  ]


  def sigil_c(color_name, []),  do: _c(color_name, :rgb)
  def sigil_c(color_name, 'r'), do: _c(color_name, :rgb)
  def sigil_c(color_name, 'h'), do: _c(color_name, :hsb)

  defp _c(color_name, color_space) do
    @color_map[color_space][String.to_atom(color_name)]
  end

  defmacro __using__(_opts) do
    quote do
      import Kernel, except: [sigil_c: 2]
      import unquote(__MODULE__), only: [sigil_c: 2]
    end
  end
end

defmodule Example do
  use ColorSigil

  def rgb, do: IO.inspect ~c{red}
  def hsb, do: IO.inspect ~c{red}h
end

Example.rgb   #=> 16711680  (== 0xff0000)
Example.hsb   #=> {0,100,100}
```

The three clauses for the sigil_c function let us select the colorspace to use based on the option passed. As the single-quoted string 'r' is actually represented by the list [?r], we can use the string literal to pattern match the options parameter.

Because I'm overriding a built-in sigil, I decided to implement a _using_ macro that automatically removes the Kernel version and adds our own (but only in the lexical scope that calls use on our module).

The fact that we can write our own sigils is liberating. But misuse could lead to some pretty impenetrable code.

Your Turn

➤ *Exercise: MoreCoolStuff-1*

Write a sigil ~v that parses multiple lines of comma-separated data, returning a list where each element is a row of data and each row is a list of values. Don't worry about quoting—just assume each field is separated by a comma.

```
csv = ~v"""
1,2,3
cat,dog
"""
```

would generate [["1","2","3"], ["cat","dog"]].

➤ *Exercise: MoreCoolStuff-2*

The function Float.parse converts leading characters of a string to a float, returning either a tuple containing the value and the rest of the string, or the atom :error.

Update your CSV sigil so that numbers are automatically converted.

```
csv = ~v"""
1,2,3.14
cat,dog
"""
```

should generate [[1.0,2.0,3.14], ["cat","dog"]].

➤ *Exercise: MoreCoolStuff-3*

(Hard) Sometimes the first line of a CSV file is a list of the column names. Update your code to support this, and return the values in each row as a keyword list, using the column names as the keys.

```
csv = ~v"""
Item,Qty,Price
Teddy bear,4,34.95
Milk,1,2.99
Battery,6,8.00
"""
```

would generate

```
[
  [Item: "Teddy bear", Qty: 4, Price: 34.95],
  [Item: "Milk", Qty: 1, Price: 2.99],
  [Item: "Battery", Qty: 6, Price: 8.00]
]
```

Multi-app Umbrella Projects

It is unfortunate that Erlang chose to call self-contained bundles of code *apps*. In many ways, they are closer to being shared libraries. And as your projects grow, you may find yourself wanting to split your code into multiple libraries, or apps. Fortunately, mix makes this painless.

To illustrate the process, we'll create a simple Elixir evaluator. Given a set of input lines, it will return the result of evaluating each. This will be one app.

To test it, we'll need to pass in lists of lines. We've already written a trivial ~l sigil that creates lists of lines for us, so we'll make that sigil code into a separate application.

Elixir calls these multi-app projects *umbrella projects*.

Create an Umbrella Project

We use mix new to create an umbrella project, passing it the --umbrella option.

```
$ mix new --umbrella eval
* creating README.md
* creating mix.exs
* creating apps
```

Compared to a normal mix project, the umbrella is pretty lightweight—just a mix file and an apps directory.

Create the Subprojects

Subprojects are stored in the apps directory. There's nothing special about them—they are simply regular projects created using mix new. Let's create our two projects now:

```
$ cd eval/apps
$ mix new line_sigil
* creating README.md
  ... and so on
$ mix new evaluator
* creating README.md
  ... and so on
* creating test/evaluator_test.exs
```

At this point we can try out our umbrella project. Go back to the overall project directory and try mix compile.

```
$ cd ..
$ mix compile
==> evaluator
```

```
Compiled lib/evaluator.ex
Generated evaluator app
==> line_sigil
Compiled lib/line_sigil.ex
Generated line_sigil app
```

Now we have an umbrella project containing two regular projects. Because there's nothing special about the subprojects, you can use all the regular mix commands in them. At the top level, though, you can build all the subprojects as a unit.

Making the Subproject Decision

The fact that subprojects are just regular mix projects means you don't have to worry about whether to start a new project using an umbrella. Simply start as a simple project. If you later discover the need for an umbrella project, create it and move your existing simple project into the apps directory.

The LineSigil Project

This project is trivial—just copy the LineSigil module from the previous section into apps/line_sigil/lib/line_sigil.ex. Verify it builds by running mix compile—in either the top-level directory or the line_sigil directory.

The Evaluator Project

The evaluator takes a list of strings containing Elixir expressions and evaluates them. It returns a list containing the expressions intermixed with the value of each. For example, given

```
a = 3
b = 4
a + b
```

Our code will return

```
code>  a = 3
value> 3
code>  b = 4
value> 4
code>  a + b
value> 7
```

We'll use Code.eval_string to execute the Elixir expressions. To have the values of variables pass from one expression to the next, we'll also need to explicitly maintain the current binding.

Here's the code:

odds/eval/apps/evaluator/lib/evaluator.ex
```elixir
defmodule Evaluator do

  def eval(list_of_expressions) do
    { result, _final_binding } =
        Enum.reduce(list_of_expressions,
                      {_result = [], _binding = binding()},
                      &evaluate_with_binding/2)
    Enum.reverse result
  end

  defp evaluate_with_binding(expression, { result, binding }) do
    { next_result, new_binding } = Code.eval_string(expression, binding)
    { [ "value> #{next_result}", "code>  #{expression}" | result ], new_binding }
  end
end
```

Linking the Subprojects

Now we need to test our evaluator. It makes sense to use our ~l sigil to create lists of expressions, so let's write our tests that way.

odds/eval/apps/evaluator/test/evaluator_test.exs
```elixir
defmodule EvaluatorTest do
  use ExUnit.Case

  import LineSigil

  test "evaluates a basic expression" do
    input = ~l"""
    1 + 2
    """

    output = ~l"""
    code>  1 + 2
    value> 3
    """

    run_test input, output
  end

  test "variables are propagated" do
    input = ~l"""
    a = 123
    a + 1
    """
    output = ~l"""
    code>  a = 123
    value> 123
    code>  a + 1
    value> 124
```

```
      """

      run_test input, output
    end

    defp run_test(lines, output) do
      assert output == Evaluator.eval(lines)
    end
end
```

But if we simply run this, Elixir won't be able to find the LineSigil module. To remedy that we need to add it as a dependency of our project. But we want that dependency only in the test environment, so our mix.exs gets a little more complicated.

odds/eval/apps/evaluator/mix.exs
```
defmodule Evaluator.Mixfile do
  use Mix.Project

  def project do
    [
      app:              :evaluator,
      version:          "0.0.1",
      build_path:       "../../_build",
      config_path:      "../../config/config.exs",
      deps_path:        "../../deps",
      lockfile:         "../../mix.lock",
      elixir:           "~> 1.2",
      build_embedded:   Mix.env == :prod,
      start_permanent:  Mix.env == :prod,
      deps:             deps
    ]
  end

  def application do
    [
      applications: [:logger]
    ]
  end

  defp deps do
    []
  end
end
```

Now we can run tests from the top-level directory.

```
$ mix test
...

Finished in 0.06 seconds (0.06s on load, 0.00s on tests)
```

```
3 tests, 0 failures
```

```
Finished in 0.00 seconds
0 tests, 0 failures
```

The first stanza of test output is for the evaluator tests, and the second is for line_sigil, which currently is test-free.

But Wait! There's More!

We've reached the end of our Elixir exploration.

This book was never intended to be exhaustive. Instead, it is intended to hit the highlights, and to give you enough information to start coding apps in Elixir yourself.

That means there's a lot more to learn, both about the language and about how to write great apps in it.

And I think that's fun. Enjoy!

Exceptions: raise and try, catch and throw

Elixir (like Erlang) takes the view that errors should normally be fatal to the processes in which they occur. A typical Elixir application's design involves many processes, which means the effects of an error will be localized. A supervisor will detect the failing process, and the restart will be handled at that level.

For that reason, you won't find much exception-handling code in Elixir programs. Exceptions are raised, but you rarely catch them.

Use exceptions for things that are exceptional—things that should never happen.

Exceptions do exist. This appendix is an overview of how to generate them and how to catch them when they occur.

Raising an Exception

You can raise an exception using the raise function. At its simplest, you pass it a string and it generates an exception of type RuntimeError.

```
iex> raise "Giving up"
** (RuntimeError) Giving up
    erl_eval.erl:572: :erl_eval.do_apply/6
```

You can also pass the type of the exception, along with other optional fields. All exceptions implement at least the message field.

```
iex> raise RuntimeError
** (RuntimeError) runtime error
    erl_eval.erl:572: :erl_eval.do_apply/6
iex> raise RuntimeError, message: "override message"
** (RuntimeError) override message
    erl_eval.erl:572: :erl_eval.do_apply/6
```

You can intercept exceptions using the try function. It takes a block of code to execute, and optional rescue, catch, and after clauses.

The rescue and catch clauses look a bit like the body of a case function—they take patterns and code to execute if the pattern matches. The subject of the pattern is the exception that was raised.

Here's an example of exception handling in action. We define a module that has a public function, start. It calls a different helper function depending on the value of its parameter. With 0, it runs smoothly. With 1, 2, or 3, it causes the VM to raise an error, which we catch and report.

exceptions/exception.ex

```elixir
defmodule Boom do

  def start(n) do
    try do
      raise_error(n)
    rescue
      [ FunctionClauseError, RuntimeError ] ->
        IO.puts "no function match or runtime error"
      error in [ArithmeticError]  ->
        IO.inspect error
        IO.puts "Uh-oh! Arithmetic error"
        reraise "too late, we're doomed", System.stacktrace
      other_errors ->
        IO.puts "Disaster! #{inspect other_errors}"
    after
        IO.puts "DONE!"
    end
  end

  defp raise_error(0) do
    IO.puts "No error"
  end

  defp raise_error(val = 1) do
    IO.puts "About to divide by zero"
    1 / (val-1)
  end

  defp raise_error(2) do
    IO.puts "About to call a function that doesn't exist"
    raise_error(99)
  end

  defp raise_error(3) do
    IO.puts "About to try creating a directory with no permission"
    File.mkdir!("/not_allowed")
  end
```

end

We define three different exception patterns. The first matches one of the two exceptions, FunctionClauseError or RuntimeError. The second matches an ArithmeticError and stores the exception value in the variable error. And the last clause catches *any* exception into the variable other_error.

We also include an after clause. This will always run at the end of the try function, regardless of whether an exception was raised.

Finally, look at the handling of ArithmeticError. As well as reporting the error, we call reraise. This raises the current exception, but lets us add a message. We also pass in the stack trace (which is actually the stack trace at the point the original exception was raised). Let's see all this in iex:

```
iex c("exception.ex")
[Boom]
iex> Boom.start 1
About to divide by zero
%ArithmeticError{}
Uh-oh! Arithmetic error
DONE!
** (RuntimeError) too late, we're doomed
    exception.ex:26: Boom.raise_error/1
    exception.ex:5: Boom.start/1

iex> Boom.start 2
About to call a function that doesn't exist
no function match or runtime error
DONE!
:ok

iex> Boom.start 3
About to try creating a directory with no permission
Disaster! %File.Error{action: "make directory", path: "/not_allowed",
                       reason: :eacces}
DONE!
:ok
```

catch, exit, and throw

Elixir code (and the underlying Erlang libraries) can raise a second kind of error. These are generated when a process calls error, exit, or throw. All three take a parameter, which is available to the catch handler.

Here's an example:

exceptions/catch.ex
```
defmodule Catch do
```

```elixir
def start(n) do
  try do
    incite(n)
  catch
    :exit, code    -> "Exited with code #{inspect code}"
    :throw, value  -> "throw called with #{inspect value}"
    what, value    -> "Caught #{inspect what} with #{inspect value}"
  end
end


defp incite(1) do
  exit(:something_bad_happened)
end

defp incite(2) do
  throw {:animal, "wombat"}
end

defp incite(3) do
  :erlang.error "Oh no!"
end
end
```

Calling the start function with 1, 2, or 3 will cause an exit, a throw, or an error to be thrown. Just to illustrate wildcard pattern matching, we handle the last case by matching any type into the variable what.

```
iex> c("catch.ex")
[Catch]
iex> Catch.start 1
"Exited with code :something_bad_happened"
iex> Catch.start 2
"throw called with {:animal,\"wombat\"}"
iex> Catch.start 3
"Caught :error with \"Oh no!\""
```

Defining Your Own Exceptions

Exceptions in Elixir are basically records. You can define your own exceptions by creating a module. Inside it, use defexception to define the various fields in the exception, along with their default values. Because you're creating a module, you can also add functions—often these are used to format the exception's fields into meaningful messages.

Say we're writing a library to talk to a Microsoft Kinect controller. It might want to raise an exception on various kinds of communication error. Some of these are permanent, but others are likely to be transient and can be retried.

We'll define our exception with its (required) message field and an additional can_retry field. We'll also add a function that formats these two fields into a nice message.

```
exceptions/defexception.ex
defmodule KinectProtocolError do

  defexception message: "Kinect protocol error",
              can_retry: false

  def full_message(me) do
    "Kinect failed: #{me.message}, retriable: #{me.can_retry}"
  end

end
```

Users of our library could write code like this:

```
exceptions/defexception.ex
try do
  talk_to_kinect
rescue
  error in [KinectProtocolError] ->
    IO.puts KinectProtocolError.full_message(error)
    if error.can_retry, do: schedule_retry
end
```

If an exception gets raised, the code handles it and possibly retries:

```
Kinect failed: usb unplugged, retriable: true
Retrying in 10 seconds
```

Now Ignore This Appendix

The Elixir source code for the mix utility contains no exception handlers. The Elixir compiler itself contains a total of five (but it is doing some pretty funky things).

If you find yourself defining new exceptions, ask if you should be isolating the code in a separate process instead. After all, if it can go wrong, wouldn't you want to isolate it?

Type Specifications and Type Checking

When we looked at defcallback, on page 283, we saw that we defined callbacks in terms of their parameter types and return value. For example, we might write

```
defcallback parse(uri_info :: URI.Info.t) :: URI.Info.t
defcallback default_port() :: integer
```

The terms URI.Info.t and integer are examples of type specifications. And, as José Valim pointed out to me, the cool thing is that they are implemented (by Yurii Rashkovskii) directly in the Elixir language itself—no special parsing is involved. This is a fantastic illustration of the power of Elixir metaprogramming.

In this appendix we'll discuss how to specify types in Elixir. But before we do, there's another question to address: *Why bother?*

When Specifications Are Used

Elixir type specifications come from Erlang. It is very common to see Erlang code where every exported (public) function is preceded by a -spec line. This is metadata that gives type information. The following code comes from the Elixir parser (which is [currently] written in Erlang). It says the return_error function takes two parameters, an integer and any type, and never returns.

```
-spec return_error(integer(), any()) -> no_return().
return_error(Line, Message) ->
      throw({error, {Line, ?MODULE, Message}}).
```

One of the reasons the Erlang folks do this is to document their code. You can read it inline while reading the source, and you can also read it in the pages created by their documentation tool.

The other reason is that they have tools such as *dialyzer* that perform static analysis of Erlang code and report on some kinds of type mismatches.[1]

These same benefits can apply to Elixir code. We have the @spec module attribute for documenting a function's type specification; in iex we have the s helper for displaying specifications and the t helper for showing user-defined types. You can also run Erlang tools such as dialyzer on compiled Elixir .beam files.

However, type specifications are not currently in wide use in the Elixir world. Whether you use them is a matter of personal taste.

Specifying a Type

A type is simply a subset of all possible values in a language. For example, the type integer means all the possible integer values, but excludes lists, binaries, PIDs, and so on.

The basic types in Elixir are any, atom, char_list (a single-quoted string), float, fun, integer, map, none, pid, port, reference, and tuple.

The type any (and its alias, _) is the set of all values, and none is the empty set.

A literal atom or integer is the set containing just that value.

The value nil can be represented as [] or nil.

Collection Types

A list is represented as [*type*], where *type* is any of the basic or combined types. This notation does not signify a list of one element—it simply says that elements of the list will be of the given type. If you want to specify a nonempty list, use [*type*, ...]. As a convenience, the type list is an alias for [any].

Binaries are represented using this syntax:

<< >>
   An empty binary (size 0)

<< _ :: *size* >>
   A sequence of *size* bits. This is called a *bitstring*.

<< _ :: *size* * *unit_size* >>
   A sequence of *size* units, where each unit is *unit_size* bits long.

---

1. http://www.erlang.org/doc/man/dialyzer.html

In the last two instances, *size* can be specified as _, in which case the binary has an arbitrary number of bits/units.

The predefined type bitstring is equivalent to <<_::_>>, an arbitrarily sized sequence of bits. Similarly, binary is defined as <<_::_*8>>, an arbitrary sequence of 8-bit bytes.

Tuples are represented as { *type, type,...* }, or using the type tuple, so both {atom,integer} and tuple(atom,integer) represent a tuple whose first element is an atom and whose second element is an integer.

Combining Types

The range operator (..) can be used with literal integers to create a type representing that range. The three built-in types non_neg_integer, pos_integer, and neg_integer represent integers that are greater than or equal to, greater than, or less than zero, respectively.

The union operator (|) indicates that the acceptable values are the unions of its arguments.

Parentheses may be used to group terms in a type specification.

Types and Structures

As structures are basically maps, you could just use the map type for them, but doing so throws away a lot of useful information. Instead, I recommend that you define a specific type for each struct:

```
defmodule LineItem do
  defstruct sku: "", quantity: 1
  @type t :: %LineItem{sku: String.t, quantity: integer}
end
```

You can then reference this type as LineItem.t.

Anonymous Functions

Anonymous functions are specified using (*head -> return_type*).

The *head* specifies the arity and possibly the types of the function parameters. It can be ..., meaning an arbitrary number of arbitrarily typed arguments, or a list of types, in which case the number of types is the function's arity.

```
(... -> integer)                # Arbitrary parameters; returns an integer
(list(integer) -> integer)      # Takes a list of integers and returns an integer
(() -> String.t)                # Takes no parameters and returns an Elixir string
(integer, atom -> list(atom))   # Takes an integer and an atom and returns
                                # a list of atoms
```

You can put parentheses around the head if you find it more clear:

```
( atom, float -> list )
( (atom, float) -> list )
(list(integer) -> integer)
((list(integer)) -> integer)
```

Handling Truthy Values

The type as_boolean(T) says that the actual value matched will be of type T, but the function that uses the value will treat it as a *truthy* value (anything other than nil or false is considered true). Thus the specification for the Elixir function Enum.count is

```
@spec count(t, (element -> as_boolean(term))) :: non_neg_integer
```

Some Examples

integer | float
> Any number (Elixir has an alias for this).

[{atom, any}]
list(atom, any)
> A list of key/value pairs. The two forms are the same.

non_neg_integer | {:error, String.t}
> An integer greater than or equal to zero, or a tuple containing the atom :error and a string.

(integer, atom -> { :pair, atom, integer })
> An anonymous function that takes an integer and an atom and returns a tuple containing the atom :pair, an atom, and an integer.

*<< _ :: _ * 4 >>*
> A sequence of 4-bit nibbles.

Defining New Types

The attribute @type can be used to define new types.

```
@type type_name :: type_specification
```

Elixir uses this to predefine some built-in types and aliases.

```
@type term      :: any
@type binary    :: <<_::_*8>>
@type bitstring :: <<_::_*1>>
@type boolean   :: false | true
@type byte      :: 0..255
@type char      :: 0..0x10ffff
```

```
@type list       :: [ any ]
@type list(t)    :: [ t ]
@type number     :: integer | float
@type module     :: atom
@type mfa        :: {module, atom, byte}
@type node       :: atom
@type timeout    :: :infinity | non_neg_integer
@type no_return :: none
```

As the list entries show, you can parameterize the types in a new definition. Simply use one or more identifiers as parameters on the left side, and use these identifiers where you'd otherwise use type names on the left. Then when you use the newly defined type, pass in actual types for each of these parameters:

```
@type variant(type_name, type) = { :variant, type_name, type)
```

```
@spec create_string_tuple(:string, String.t) :: variant(:string, String.t)
```

As well as @type, Elixir has the @typep and @opaque module attributes. They have the same syntax as @type, and do basically the same thing. The difference is in the visibility of the result.

@typep defines a type that is local to the module that contains it—the type is private. @opaque defines a type whose name may be known outside the module but whose definition is not.

Specs for Functions and Callbacks

The @spec specifies a function's parameter count, types, and return-value type. It can appear anywhere in a module that defines the function, but by convention it sits immediately before the function definition, following any function documentation.

We've already seen the syntax:

@spec *function_name(param1_type, ...)* :: *return_type*

Let's see some examples. These come from the built-in Dict module.

```
Line 1  @type key    :: any
     2  @type value :: any
     3  @type keys   :: [ key ]
     4  @type t      :: tuple | list    # `t` is the type of the collection
     5
     6  @spec values(t) :: [value]
     7  @spec size(t) :: non_neg_integer
     8  @spec has_key?(t, key) :: boolean
     9  @spec update(t, key, value, (value -> value)) :: t
```

Line 6

> values takes a collection (tuple or list) and returns a list of values (any).

Line 7

> size takes a collection and returns an integer (>= 0).

Line 8

> has_key? takes a collection and a key, and returns true or false.

Line 9

> update takes a collection, a key, a value, and a function that maps a value
> to a value. It returns a (new) collection.

For functions with multiple heads (or those that have default values), you
can specify multiple @spec attributes. Here's an example from the Enum module:

```
@spec at(t, index) :: element | nil
@spec at(t, index, default) :: element | default

def at(collection, n, default \\ nil) when n >= 0 do
  ...
end
```

The Enum module also has many examples of the use of as_boolean:

```
@spec filter(t, (element -> as_boolean(term))) :: list
def filter(collection, fun) when is_list(collection) do
  ...
end
```

This says filter takes something enumerable and a function. That function
maps an element to a term (which is an alias for any), and the filter function
treats that value as being truthy. filter returns a list.

For more information on Elixir support for type specifications, look at the
documentation for the Kernel.Typespec module.[2]

Using Dialyzer

Dialyzer analyzes code that runs on the Erlang VM, looking for potential
errors. To use it with Elixir, we have to compile our source into .beam files and
make sure that the debug_info compiler option is set (which it is when running
mix in the default, development mode). Let's see how to do that by creating
a trivial project with two source files.

---

2.   http://elixir-lang.org/docs/stable/elixir/Kernel.Typespec.html

```
$ mix new simple
...
$ cd simple
```

Inside the project, let's create a simple function. Being lazy, I haven't implemented the body yet.

```
defmodule Simple do
  @type atom_list :: list(atom)
  @spec count_atoms(atom_list)  :: non_neg_integer
  def count_atoms(list) do
    # ...
  end
end
```

Let's run dialyzer on our code. Because it works from .beam files, we have to remember to compile before we run dialyzer.

```
$ mix compile
.../simple/lib/simple.ex:4: variable list is unused
Compiled lib/simple.ex
Generated simple app
$ dialyzer _build/dev/lib/simple/ebin
  Checking whether the PLT /Users/dave/.dialyzer_plt is up-to-date...
dialyzer: Could not find the PLT: /Users/dave/.dialyzer_plt
Use the options:
   --build_plt   to build a new PLT; or
   --add_to_plt  to add to an existing PLT

For example, use a command like the following:
   dialyzer --build_plt --apps erts kernel stdlib mnesia
Note that building a PLT such as the above may take 20 mins or so

If you later need information about other applications, say crypto,
you can extend the PLT by the command:
   dialyzer --add_to_plt --apps crypto
For applications that are not in Erlang/OTP use an absolute file name.
```

Oops. This looks serious, but it's not. Dialyzer needs the specifications for all the runtime libraries you're using. It stores them in a cache, which it calls a *persistent lookup table*, or *plt*. For now we'll initialize this with the basic Erlang runtime (erts), and the basic Elixir runtime. You can always add more apps to it later.

To do this, you first have to *find* your Elixir libraries. Fire up iex, and run:

```
iex> :code.lib_dir(:elixir)
/users/dave/Play/elixir/lib/elixir
```

The path on my system is a little unusual, as I build locally. But take whatever path it shows you, and add /ebin to it—that's what we'll give to dialyzer. (This will take several minutes.)

```
$ dialyzer --build_plt --apps erts /Users/dave/Play/elixir/lib/elixir/ebin
  Compiling some key modules to native code... done in 0m29.87s
  Creating PLT /Users/dave/.dialyzer_plt ...
Unknown functions:
  'Elixir.Collectable.Atom':'__impl__'/1
  'Elixir.Collectable.Float':'__impl__'/1
      :       :
```

You can safely ignore the warnings about unknown functions and types.

Now let's rerun our project analysis.

```
$ dialyzer _build/dev/lib/simple/ebin
  Checking whether the PLT /Users/dave/.dialyzer_plt is up-to-date... yes
  Proceeding with analysis...
simple.ex:1: Invalid type specification for function
'Elixir.Simple':count_atoms/1. The success typing is (_) -> 'nil'
 done in 0m0.29s
done (warnings were emitted)
```

It's complaining that the typespec for count_atoms doesn't agree with the implementation. The *success typing* (think of this as the *actual type*)[3] returns nil, but the spec says it is an integer. Dialyzer has caught our stubbed-out body. Let's fix that:

```
defmodule Simple do
  @type atom_list :: list(atom)
  @spec count_atoms(atom_list)  :: non_neg_integer
  def count_atoms(list) do
    length list
  end
end
```

Compile and dialyze:

```
$ mix compile
Compiled lib/simple.ex
Generated simple app
$ dialyzer _build/dev/lib/simple/ebin
  Checking whether the PLT /Users/dave/.dialyzer_plt is up-to-date... yes
  Proceeding with analysis... done in 0m0.29s
done (passed successfully)
```

Let's add a second module that calls our count_atoms function:

---

3. http://www.it.uu.se/research/group/hipe/papers/succ_types.pdf

```
typespecs/simple/lib/simple/client.ex
defmodule Client do
  @spec other_function() :: non_neg_integer
  def other_function do
    Simple.count_atoms [1, 2, 3]
  end
end
```

Compile and dialyze:

```
$ mix compile
Compiled lib/client.ex
Compiled lib/simple.ex
Generated simple app
$ dialyzer _build/dev/lib/simple/ebin
  Checking whether the PLT /Users/dave/.dialyzer_plt is up-to-date... yes
  Proceeding with analysis...
client.ex:4: Function other_function/0 has no local return
client.ex:5: The call 'Elixir.Simple':count_atoms([1 | 2 | 3,...])
breaks the contract (atom_list()) -> non_neg_integer()
 done in 0m0.29s
```

That's pretty cool. Dialyzer noticed that we called count_atoms with a list of integers, and it is specified to receive a list of atoms. It also decided this would raise an error, so the function would never return (that's the *no local return* warning). Let's fix that.

```
defmodule Client do
  @spec other_function() :: non_neg_integer
  def other_function do
    Simple.count_atoms [:a, :b, :c]
  end
end
```

```
$ mix compile
Compiled lib/client.ex
Compiled lib/simple.ex
Generated simple app
$ dialyzer _build/dev/lib/simple/ebin
  Checking whether the PLT /Users/dave/.dialyzer_plt is up-to-date... yes
  Proceeding with analysis... done in 0m0.27s
done (passed successfully)
```

And so it goes...

Dialyzer and Type Inference

In this appendix, we've shown dialyzer working with type specs that we added to our functions. But it also does a credible job with unannotated code. This is because dialyzer knows the types of the built-in functions (remember when we ran it with --build_plt?) and can infer (some of) your function types from this. Here's a simple example:

```elixir
defmodule NoSpecs do
  def length_plus_n(list, n) do
    length(list) + n
  end
  def call_it do
    length_plus_n(2, 1)
  end
end
```

Compile this, and run dialyzer on the .beam file:

```
$ dialyzer _build/dev/lib/simple/ebin/Elixir.NoSpecs.beam
  Checking whether the PLT /Users/dave/.dialyzer_plt is up-to-date... yes
  Proceeding with analysis...
no_specs.ex:7: Function call_it/0 has no local return
no_specs.ex:8: The call 'Elixir.NoSpecs':length_plus_n(2,1) will never
return since it differs in the 1st argument from the success typing
arguments: ([any()],number())
 done in 0m0.28s
done (warnings were emitted)
```

Here it noticed that the length_plus_n function called length on its first parameter, and length requires a list as an argument. This means length_plus_n also needs a list argument, and so it complains.

What happens if we change the call to length_plus_n([:a, :b], :c)?

```elixir
defmodule NoSpecs do
  def length_plus_n(list, n) do
    length(list) + n
  end
  def call_it do
    length_plus_n([:a, :b], :c)
  end
end
```

```
$ dialyzer _build/dev/lib/simple/ebin/Elixir.NoSpecs.beam
  Checking whether the PLT /Users/dave/.dialyzer_plt is up-to-date... yes
  Proceeding with analysis...
no_specs.ex:7: Function call_it/0 has no local return
no_specs.ex:8: The call 'Elixir.NoSpecs':length_plus_n(['a', 'b'],'c')
will never return since it differs in the 2nd argument from the
success typing arguments: ([any()],number())
 done in 0m0.29s
done (warnings were emitted)
```

This is even cooler. It knows that + (which is implemented as a function) takes two numeric arguments. When we pass an atom as the second parameter, dialyzer recognizes that this makes no sense, and complains. But look at the error. It isn't complaining about the addition. Instead, it has assigned a default typespec to our function, based on its analysis of what we call inside that function.

This is *success typing*. Dialyzer attempts to infer the most permissive types that are compatible with the code—it assumes the code is correct until it finds a contradiction. This makes it a powerful tool, as it can make assumptions as it runs.

Does that mean you don't need @spec attributes? That's your call. Try it with and without. Often, adding a @spec will further constrain a function's type signature. We saw this with our count_of_atoms function, where the spec made it explicit that we expected a list of atoms as an argument.

Ultimately, dialyzer is a tool, not a test of your coding chops. Use it as such, but don't waste time adding specs to get a gold star.

Bibliography

[Arm13]   Joe Armstrong. *Programming Erlang (2nd edition).* The Pragmatic Bookshelf,
           Raleigh, NC, and Dallas, TX, 2nd, 2013.

Index

Swig Some More Elixir

Explore Elixir metaprogramming, and develop incredible high-performance Elixir server-side applications.

Metaprogramming Elixir

Write code that writes code with Elixir macros. Macros make metaprogramming possible and define the language itself. In this book, you'll learn how to use macros to extend the language with fast, maintainable code and share functionality in ways you never thought possible. You'll discover how to extend Elixir with your own first-class features, optimize performance, and create domain-specific languages.

Chris McCord
(128 pages) ISBN: 9781680500417. $17
https://pragprog.com/book/cmelixir

Programming Phoenix

Don't accept the compromise between fast and beautiful: you can have it all. Phoenix creator Chris McCord, Elixir creator José Valim, and award-winning author Bruce Tate walk you through building an application that's fast and reliable. At every step, you'll learn from the Phoenix creators not just what to do, but why. Packed with insider insights, this definitive guide will be your constant companion in your journey from Phoenix novice to expert, as you build the next generation of web applications.

Chris McCord, Bruce Tate, and José Valim
(230 pages) ISBN: 9781680501452. $34
https://pragprog.com/book/phoenix

Erlang and More

Get up to speed on the robust, battle-tested, industrial-strength environment of Erlang, and rediscover the joy and fascinating weirdness of pure mathematics.

Programming Erlang (2nd edition)

A multi-user game, web site, cloud application, or networked database can have thousands of users all interacting at the same time. You need a powerful, industrial-strength tool to handle the really hard problems inherent in parallel, concurrent environments. You need Erlang. In this second edition of the best-selling *Programming Erlang*, you'll learn how to write parallel programs that scale effortlessly on multicore systems.

Joe Armstrong
(548 pages) ISBN: 9781937785536. $42
https://pragprog.com/book/jaerlang2

Good Math

Mathematics is beautiful—and it can be fun and exciting as well as practical. *Good Math* is your guide to some of the most intriguing topics from two thousand years of mathematics: from Egyptian fractions to Turing machines; from the real meaning of numbers to proof trees, group symmetry, and mechanical computation. If you've ever wondered what lay beyond the proofs you struggled to complete in high school geometry, or what limits the capabilities of the computer on your desk, this is the book for you.

Mark C. Chu-Carroll
(282 pages) ISBN: 9781937785338. $34
https://pragprog.com/book/mcmath

Seven in Seven

From Web Frameworks to Concurrency Models, see what the rest of the world is doing with this introduction to seven different approaches.

Seven Web Frameworks in Seven Weeks

Whether you need a new tool or just inspiration, *Seven Web Frameworks in Seven Weeks* explores modern options, giving you a taste of each with ideas that will help you create better apps. You'll see frameworks that leverage modern programming languages, employ unique architectures, live client-side instead of server-side, or embrace type systems. You'll see everything from familiar Ruby and JavaScript to the more exotic Erlang, Haskell, and Clojure.

Jack Moffitt, Fred Daoud
(302 pages) ISBN: 9781937785635. $38
https://pragprog.com/book/7web

Seven Concurrency Models in Seven Weeks

Your software needs to leverage multiple cores, handle thousands of users and terabytes of data, and continue working in the face of both hardware and software failure. Concurrency and parallelism are the keys, and *Seven Concurrency Models in Seven Weeks* equips you for this new world. See how emerging technologies such as actors and functional programming address issues with traditional threads and locks development. Learn how to exploit the parallelism in your computer's GPU and leverage clusters of machines with MapReduce and Stream Processing. And do it all with the confidence that comes from using tools that help you write crystal clear, high-quality code.

Paul Butcher
(296 pages) ISBN: 9781937785659. $38
https://pragprog.com/book/pb7con

The Pragmatic Bookshelf

The Pragmatic Bookshelf features books written by developers for developers. The titles continue the well-known Pragmatic Programmer style and continue to garner awards and rave reviews. As development gets more and more difficult, the Pragmatic Programmers will be there with more titles and products to help you stay on top of your game.

Visit Us Online

This Book's Home Page
https://pragprog.com/book/elixir12
Source code from this book, errata, and other resources. Come give us feedback, too!

Register for Updates
https://pragprog.com/updates
Be notified when updates and new books become available.

Join the Community
https://pragprog.com/community
Read our weblogs, join our online discussions, participate in our mailing list, interact with our wiki, and benefit from the experience of other Pragmatic Programmers.

New and Noteworthy
https://pragprog.com/news
Check out the latest pragmatic developments, new titles and other offerings.

Save on the eBook

Save on the eBook versions of this title. Owning the paper version of this book entitles you to purchase the electronic versions at a terrific discount.

PDFs are great for carrying around on your laptop—they are hyperlinked, have color, and are fully searchable. Most titles are also available for the iPhone and iPod touch, Amazon Kindle, and other popular e-book readers.

Buy now at *https://pragprog.com/coupon*

Contact Us

Online Orders:	*https://pragprog.com/catalog*
Customer Service:	*support@pragprog.com*
International Rights:	*translations@pragprog.com*
Academic Use:	*academic@pragprog.com*
Write for Us:	*http://write-for-us.pragprog.com*
Or Call:	+1 800-699-7764

CPSIA information can be obtained at www.ICGtesting.com
Printed in the USA
BVOW09s1001250216

438050BV00001B/1/P